PORTSMOUTH FOOTBALL CLUB
THE OFFICIAL YEARBOOK 2006/07

Editorial
Helen Wood, Adam Reed

Writers
Johnny Moore, Eleanor Frost

Sidan Press Team
Simon Rosen, Julian Hill-Wood, Marc Fiszman, Mark Peters, Karim Biria, Rob Cubbon,
Anette Lundebye, Marina Kravchenko, Gareth Peters, Janet Calcott, Trevor Scimes, John Fitzroy,
Jenny Middlemarch, Anders Rasmussen, Lim Wai-Lee, Emma Turner, Charles Grove, Tim Ryman

Photography
Action Images

Sidan Press, 63-64 Margaret St, London W1W 8SW
Tel: 020 7580 0200
Email: info@sidanpress.com

sidanpress.com

Club Directory

Owner Alexandre Gaydamak

Chairman Milan Mandaric

Vice Chairman David Chissick

Board of Directors
Alexandre Gaydamak, David Chissick, Mark Johnson, Milan Mandaric, Peter Storrie

Chief Executive Officer Peter Storrie

Chief Financial Officer Mark Johnson

Club Secretary Paul Weld

Marketing Director Paul Bell

Communications Director and Press Officer
Helen Wood

Team Manager Harry Redknapp

Assistant Tony Adams

Technical Director Abraham Grant

Coach Joe Jordan

Head of Scouting Ian Broomfield

Goalkeeping Coach David Coles

Reserve Team Coach Paul Groves

Exercise Physiologist John Dalzell

Club Doctor Dr. Nigel Sellars

Physiotherapist Gary Sadler MCSP SRP

Physiotherapist
Ian Catchpole BSc(Hons)MSc MCSP SRP

Rehab/Masseur Chris Neville

Masseur Colin Clement

Kit Manager Kevin McCormack

Head of Youth Development Mark Kelly

Youth Team Coach Shaun Brookes

Head Coach – Centre of Excellence
Paul Hardyman

Youth Recruitment Officer Dave Hurst

Youth Development and Recruitment
Steve Martin

Community Development Manager
Rosie Francis

Pompey in the Community Manager
TBC

Sponsorship & Advertising Manager
Alan Kimber

Retail Buyer Andy Hall

Conference & Banqueting Manager
Iain Robertson

Conference & Banqueting Sales Manager
Tracie Barnes

Contacts

Club Switchboard (for general enquiries)
Tel: 023 9273 1204
Email: info@pompeyfc.co.uk

Tickets and Memberships
Tel: 0871 230 1898
Fax: 0871 230 1899
Email: tickets@pompeyfc.co.uk
Disabled Supporters Contact: Alison McNeil

Merchandise
Email: pompeyshop@pompeyfc.co.uk
Mail Order Hotline: 023 9220 1479

Portsmouth Football Club
Fratton Park
Frogmore Road
Portsmouth
Hampshire
PO4 8RA

Contents

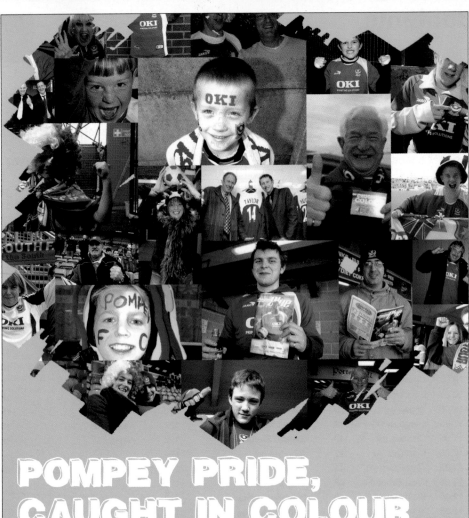

POMPEY PRIDE, CAUGHT IN COLOUR

Look out for the OKI Hot Shots Team at every Fratton Park match and you too could be "Caught in Colour!" and win one of many fabulous prizes. Check out the web site below for full details. Play up Pompey!

askoki.co.uk/Portsmouth

Chairman's Message

Milan Mandaric

There have been some dramatic seasons during my time at the club, but this last one probably beats them all. With the luxury of looking back in pleasure and contentment on how things concluded, I am now totally convinced that the only way is onwards and upwards for Pompey from this juncture.

In the final analysis the end justified the means. When you enter the Christmas period, as we did, without a home win and very few away either, the next decision you make has to be spot on. In my view there was only one man to dig us out of the hole that had materialised and I know through the mountain of mail I received on the subject that the majority of fans felt the same. So Harry Redknapp returned and off we went.

Of course there was also another important arrival. In January, not long after Harry's appointment, I introduced my respected partner Alexandre Gaydamak whose arrival was also perfectly timed and lifted a burden from my shoulders. Since the first day I came to this club I had always said I would seek partners when the time was right. Here is a man who can eventually take this club forward in the way I always envisaged with its best interests at heart. I cannot stress how important this addition was. Therefore 2005/06 will truly go down as a season when the tempo of this football club was raised along with its profile and where, in our survival, we came out at the other end immensely stronger.

When in years to come fans look back on this season they will remember it as one of the great ones. It is funny how differently we can look at things with hindsight. Up to the middle of March it was on course to be remembered as a thoroughly miserable one. Then that late Pedro Mendes strike against Manchester City lit the fuse and we never looked back. It was almost worth enduring the wretched part of the season in order to experience the magnificent turn around. How often is it the way that to find true pleasure you have to first endure despair?

The last three months or so totally transformed our season to make history and through this club publication you can now re-live the lows and highs at the turn of a page: From a pretty mundane beginning, a slightly more sustainable middle, through to a quite dramatic finish. They tell me the best of novels follow this format, so ours should be amongst the best sellers.

Of course no season could be commented upon without making reference to our twelfth man. From the very first match you backed us to the hilt, never lost faith in the plot, and stayed faithful through to the fruitful conclusion. In fact you helped write the script because our supporters are as much part of the ending and success story as anyone: A family that we can count on, not only during the good times, but the bad as well. The fans were the reason we all remained so strong throughout and ultimately obtained our objective.

As for the future, quite simply the sky is now the limit.

Owner's Message

Alexandre Gaydamak

As you know, I arrived at this club in January when Pompey's status in the Premier League was far from certain. Milan had the heart and the foresight to welcome me into the club and for that I am sincerely grateful.

I could sense the potential and was willing to invest in players at a time when Harry told me reinforcement was needed. I went through the very same emotions that you, the fans, did from January through to May and it was not easy. How sweet was that April day at Wigan when Harry and the squad proved just what they were capable of.

I would like to take this opportunity to thank you all for your fantastic support. It was in fact one of the first things to impress me when I came to Portsmouth and subsequent experiences left me in no doubt whatsoever that you are by far the best fans in the Premier League.

This book chronicles another year in the history of this fine club. Now it is time to look to the future. We have the foundations to be one of the UK's top football clubs.

My vision is to build up properly off and on the pitch and see us regularly competing for a place in the top 6-10 in the Premier League. We, owners, directors, managers and staff alike are committed to working towards our goals and we have worked hard to create and put in place the business plan to support this vision.

We are committed to transforming Pompey into a first class football club, with state of the art facilities to match. We are dedicated to building a team of professionals behind the scenes who can lead this club forward while with a strong emphasis on excellence, professionalism, and undivided commitment.

Be our business or Premiership ranking better or worse, there is one thing which will always remain my top priority and that is to never lose sight of the importance of the Portsmouth community which provides the life and soul of Pompey and is the heart and soul of the club.

I will always be committed to give and contribute to this wonderful community and hope to do enough to match the achievements and expectations of the people of Portsmouth and Pompey fans everywhere.

I hope to meet with many of you in the near future and to get a little closer to the people who are central to Pompey's future glory. Together we will savour the success you all so very well deserve.

See you on the 19th August for what I promise will be an exciting, successful season and the dawn of a new Pompey era.

Manager's Message
Harry Redknapp

When I came back to Fratton Park in December, in a lot of ways it felt like I had never been away. On that dark, winter afternoon I had a vision of delivering Premier League survival to this club and being able to celebrate it in front of what I knew would be deliriously happy fans. Some doubtless thought it unlikely, but most visions can be.

Without knowing all the facts it may be viewed as pessimistic setting your sights on survival before Christmas. Those in football know if anything, this was in fact optimism at its highest. There we were on ten points with almost half the season gone, still waiting for a win at home and a series of tough fixtures on the horizon. Some said I was mad, but for me there was absolutely no hesitation. This was a mission I wanted to take.

I knew the club intimately, I knew the fans and Milan Mandaric. I experienced my highest achievements in management at Fratton Park and had some marvellous memories that nobody could ever take away. Though some say you never go back, I felt there was unfinished business for me to attend to. I was deeply sorry at the way my last stint at Pompey had ended and it should have never happened in that way. Here was a unique, sent from heaven chance to put it right.

Of course I knew there were some who were waiting for me to fail because of where I went on leaving Pompey. Having said that, amongst the many fans I came into contact with, I always received encouragement and good natured backing. But to be honest this was less about me and more about keeping a great club with passionate fans and a devoted Chairman in the Premier League. It didn't matter what a minority felt about me and I very much understood that.

Definitely the odds were stacked against us and though we gained our first home win in my first game at Fratton Park, we were still destined to play catch up for months because that is how badly our season had gone.

Even with the flurry of new players and the arrival of Alexandre Gaydamak, both at a vital period, we needed the time to gel and time was something not on our side. But even in the darker days when we got trounced at Birmingham and produced a wretched performance at Aston Villa, I kept a belief somewhere that we could escape. Maybe that belief came from my strong desire to make it happen.

Then from the Manchester City game onwards, we went on a terrific run that nobody around us could

match. That was one we had to win and no doubt the dramatics of that Pedro Mendes injury time goal was a massive impetus which just propelled us on and on.

Everyone knows what followed at places like West Ham and Fulham and in home games against the likes of Blackburn, Arsenal, Middlesbrough and Sunderland, and the points deficit we made up in the process; an ending you would be hard pressed to make up. It was pretty emotional down in the tunnel for me at Wigan. It was the moment my far fetched vision had come true and a tough mission had been accomplished.

Now what lies ahead is a massively brighter future and a vision to match.

How to Read the Stats

This year's review is better than ever, packed with the sort of in-depth stats which really get you close to the action. If you'd like to know why a particular match turned out the way it did, how a player's form varied over the course of the season, or how Pompey have fared against their biggest rivals, you'll find all the info inside.

To make sure you're getting the most out of the stats, we're including this section to highlight the information presented by some of the charts and tables.

Colours

Pompey vs Opposition
There are lots of comparisons between Pompey and our opponents throughout the book. Pompey stats are shown in blue; opponents are shown in grey:

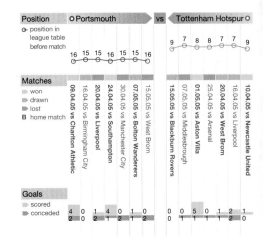

Figure 2: Wins, draws, losses and goals are clearly colour-coded.

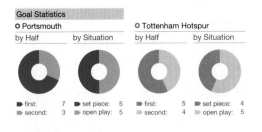

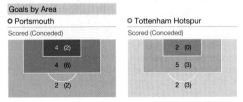

Figure 1: Pompey stats are in blue; opposition stats are grey.

WDL, Scored, Conceded
When reviewing match results, wins, draws and losses are indicated by green, grey and orange blocks, respectively. For goals, green blocks indicate goals scored; orange blocks show goals conceded:

Match Reports

The Match Report section contains reports, quotes, facts and stats from every Pompey match of the 2005/06 season.

Stats Order (Home and Away)
The order of the stats varies depending on whether a match was home or away: for home matches, Pompey stats are shown on the left, for away matches they're on the right:

Premiership Totals	Portsmouth	Tottenham
Premiership Appearances	820	730
Team Appearances	229	338
Goals Scored	55	92
Assists	67	70
Clean Sheets (goalkeepers)	28	30
Yellow Cards	89	59
Red Cards	10	3
Full Internationals	10	11

Figure 3: For home matches, Pompey stats appear on the left.

Premiership Totals	○ West Brom	Portsmouth ○
Premiership Appearances	1,297	816
Team Appearances	413	211
Goals Scored	144	58
Assists	112	66
Clean Sheets (goalkeepers)	9	28
Yellow Cards	115	91
Red Cards	8	10
Full Internationals	5	9

Figure 4: For away matches, Pompey stats appear on the right.

Form Coming into Fixture
Stats are from the previous seven league games. For the first few matches, these stats include games from the end of the previous season.

Team Statistics
Stats are for starters and playing subs. The "Premiership Totals" chart measures performance within the Premiership (with the exception of "Full Internationals").

Premiership Totals	○ Portsmouth	Tottenham ○
Premiership Appearances	820	730
Team Appearances	229	338
Goals Scored	55	92
Assists	67	70
Clean Sheets (goalkeepers)	28	30
Yellow Cards	89	59
Red Cards	10	3
Full Internationals	10	11

Age/Height

Portsmouth Age	Tottenham Hotspur Age
▶ **26 yrs, 5 mo**	▶ **24 yrs, 8 mo**
Portsmouth Height	Tottenham Hotspur Height
▶ **6'**	▶ **5'11"**

Figure 5: Team statistics are for starters and playing subs.

Player Profiles

The Player Profile section provides season reviews and comprehensive stats for Pompey's players. The section is organised by position, starting with goalkeepers. Ages are as of May, 2006.

Pitch Diagram
The diagram shows all positions the player played during 2005/06. The main position is denoted by a dark blue circle; alternative positions are denoted by light blue circles:

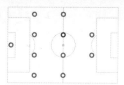

Figure 6: Major positions are shown in dark blue; minor positions are shown in light blue.

Player Performance
All stats show league performance, with the exception of the "Cup Games" table. The "League Performance" chart provides an excellent overview of the player's performance over the course of the season. At a glance, you can see when and how much he played, and how he contributed to the team's overall performance at different stages of the season. Note that outfield players receive a "clean sheet" whenever they played 75 or more minutes in a a game where Pompey didn't concede a goal.

Career History
Due to the difficulties involved in obtaining reliable stats for international clubs, the "Clubs" table is incomplete for players who have played for non-English clubs. The names of all clubs have been included for the reader's interest, but international stats have been left blank.

The Opposition

The Opposition section shows how Pompey sizes up against the other 19 teams in the Premiership.

Points / Position
The points / position chart is a snapshot of the last 10 years' league performance of Pompey and the opponent. For any season when the two teams met in the league, the results of their clashes are shown at the bottom of the chart.

Premiership Head-to-Head
Stats are only for the two teams' meetings in the Premiership.

Season Review 2005/06

0-2

Portsmouth ○
Tottenham Hotspur ○

▶ Gregory Vignal puts future loanee Wayne Routledge under pressure

Event Line

37 ○ ▪	Tainio
45 ○ ⊕	Griffin / LF / OG / IA
	Assist: Defoe
Half time 0-1	
46 ○ ⇄	Pericard > Mornar
58 ○ ▪	Reid
64 ○ ⊕	Defoe / LF / OP / IA
	Assist: Mido
69 ○ ⇄	Taylor > Viafara
70 ○ ⇄	Mendes > Routledge
74 ○ ⇄	Mbesuma > Karadas
81 ○ ⇄	Kanoute > Mido
Full time 0-2	

Pompey succumbed to an opening day defeat against Spurs after matching the London side for much of the game.

Andy O'Brien, Laurent Robert, Sander Westerveld, Azar Karadas, Gregory Vignal and John Viafara all made their debuts as the season began.

The home side were undone by a cruel twist in first half stoppage time when Mido raced onto a Defoe through-ball, but as he shaped to shoot, Andy Griffin's tackle gently sent the ball past his own 'keeper to give Tottenham the lead.

It was all over mid-way through the second half when this time Mido reversed roles by sending Defoe on a clear run after a quick Spurs throw had caught Pompey napping. The striker waltzed past Westerveld and slotted home to leave the home side pointless. Soon afterwards Defoe nearly made the scoreline more emphatic, but Pompey's debutant 'keeper kept his shot out.

At the other end Collins Mbesuma, who came off the bench to become the seventh home debutant, had a chance to add an air of respectability to the score right at the death. But as the ball fell invitingly from a corner, the African striker could only tamely prod at Robinson.

Player of the Match	Quote	Premiership Milestone
7 Gregory Vignal	❝ **Alain Perrin**	▶ **20,215**
	I know the team can play better because we were better in pre-season, but we didn't create enough chances in the second half.	The attendance of 20,215 was a Premiership record at Fratton Park.

Venue:	Fratton Park	Referee:	B.Knight - 05/06
Attendance:	20,215	Matches:	1
Capacity:	20,288	Yellow Cards:	1
		Red Cards:	0

Portsmouth
Tottenham Hotspur

Form Coming into Fixture

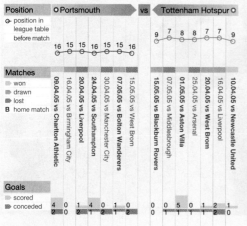

Position	O Portsmouth	vs	Tottenham Hotspur
position in league table before match			

Portsmouth: 16 15 15 16 15 15 16
Tottenham Hotspur: 9 7 8 8 7 7 9

Matches
- won
- drawn
- lost
- B home match

Portsmouth matches:
- 09.04.05 vs Charlton Athletic
- 16.04.05 vs Birmingham City
- 20.04.05 vs Liverpool
- 24.04.05 vs Southampton
- 30.04.05 vs Manchester City
- 07.05.05 vs Bolton Wanderers
- 15.05.05 vs West Brom

Tottenham matches:
- 15.05.05 vs Blackburn Rovers
- 07.05.05 vs Middlesbrough
- 01.05.05 vs Aston Villa
- 25.04.05 vs Arsenal
- 20.04.05 vs West Brom
- 16.04.05 vs Liverpool
- 10.04.05 vs Newcastle United

Goals
- scored
- conceded

Portsmouth: scored 4 0 1 4 0 1 0 / conceded 2 0 2 1 2 1 2
Tottenham: scored 0 0 5 0 1 2 1 / conceded 0 1 1 1 1 2 0

Goal Statistics

O Portsmouth
by Half | by Situation

O Tottenham Hotspur
by Half | by Situation

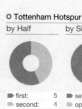

Portsmouth:
- first: 7
- second: 3
- set piece: 5
- open play: 5

Tottenham Hotspur:
- first: 5
- second: 4
- set piece: 4
- open play: 5

Goals by Area

O Portsmouth — Scored (Conceded)
- 4 (2)
- 4 (6)
- 2 (2)

O Tottenham Hotspur — Scored (Conceded)
- 2 (0)
- 5 (3)
- 2 (3)

Team Statistics

Starting Line-Ups

Portsmouth:
Westerveld
Vignal, Robert
Stefanovic, Hughes, LuaLua, Defoe
O'Brien, Viafara (Taylor)
Griffin, Mornar (Pericard)
Karadas (Mbesuma)

Tottenham:
Robinson
Routledge (Mendes), Stalteri
Tainio, Dawson
Mido (Kanoute)
Carrick, Gardner
Reid, Edman

4/4/2 | **4/4/2**

Unused Sub: Ashdown, Skopelitis | Unused Sub: Cerny, Naybet, Kelly

Premiership Totals	O Portsmouth	Tottenham O
Premiership Appearances	820	730
Team Appearances	229	338
Goals Scored	55	92
Assists	67	70
Clean Sheets (goalkeepers)	28	30
Yellow Cards	89	59
Red Cards	10	3
Full Internationals	10	11

Age/Height

Portsmouth Age	Tottenham Hotspur Age
26 yrs, 5 mo	**24 yrs, 8 mo**
Portsmouth Height	Tottenham Hotspur Height
6'	**5'11"**

Match Statistics

League Table after Fixture

		Played	Won	Drawn	Lost	For	Against	Pts
4	Tottenham	1	1	0	0	2	0	3
...		...	...	...	...	...	...	...
14	Chelsea	0	0	0	0	0	0	0
15	Newcastle	0	0	0	0	0	0	0
16	Wigan	0	0	0	0	0	0	0
17	Blackburn	1	0	0	1	1	3	0
18	Sunderland	1	0	0	1	1	3	0
19	Everton	1	0	0	1	0	2	0
20	Portsmouth	1	0	0	1	0	2	0

Statistics	O Portsmouth	Tottenham O
Goals	0	2
Shots on Target	7	6
Shots off Target	4	5
Hit Woodwork	0	0
Possession %	50	50
Corners	7	2
Offsides	7	0
Fouls	13	23
Disciplinary Points	0	8

2-1

West Bromwich Albion ○
Portsmouth ○

▶ Lomana Tresor LuaLua holds off Ronnie Wallwork

Event Line

2 ○ ⊕ Horsfield / H / OP / 6Y	
Assist: Greening	
Half time 1-0	
57 ○ ▪ Viafara	
58 ○ ▪ Karadas	
58 ○ ▪ Campbell	
59 ○ ⊕ Horsfield / LF / OP / IA	
Assist: Gera	
63 ○ ⊕ Robert / LF / DFK / OA	
Assist: O'Neil	
65 ○ ▪ Gera	
66 ○ ⇄ Albrechtsen > Gera	
70 ○ ⇄ Todorov > O'Neil	
81 ○ ⇄ Pericard > Karadas	
83 ○ ⇄ Earnshaw > Watson	
84 ○ ⇄ Skopelitis > Griffin	
87 ○ ▪ Johnson	
90 ○ ▪ Vignal	
90 ○ ▪ Horsfield	
Full time 2-1	

A stunning Laurent Robert free kick failed to stave off a defeat that was a bitter blow even this early on.

Albion, tipped to be amongst the strugglers, made light of such predictions and were ahead after only two minutes when Geoff Horsfield nipped in between Stefanovic and Vignal to head the home side into the lead.

Pompey never really recovered from the early blow and LuaLua was the closest to equalising when he shot just wide. But on the hour Horsfield scored his and Albion's second when he turned Vignal and though his shot appeared to be covered by Westerveld, the 'keeper allowed the ball to squirm under his body before rolling agonisingly over the line.

However, almost immediately Robert curled a wonderful free kick into Kirkland's top right hand corner from twenty yards to give Pompey hope and in stoppage time sub Skopelitis fired over when it seemed easier to score.

Player of the Match	Quote	Premiership Milestone
32 Lomana LuaLua	❝ **Alain Perrin**	▶ **100**

It was always difficult for us after we lost the first goal so early on and although we weren't very good in the first half, we improved in the second.

Andy Griffin made his 100th Premiership appearance.

Venue:	The Hawthorns	Referee:	M.A.Riley - 05/06
Attendance:	24,404	Matches:	1
Capacity:	28,003	Yellow Cards:	2
		Red Cards:	0

West Bromwich Albion
Portsmouth

Form Coming into Fixture

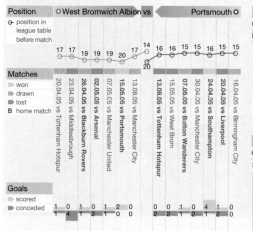

Goal Statistics

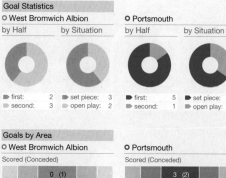

○ West Bromwich Albion

by Half — by Situation

- first: 2
- second: 3
- set piece: 3
- open play: 2

○ Portsmouth

by Half — by Situation

- first: 5
- second: 1
- set piece: 4
- open play: 2

Goals by Area

○ West Bromwich Albion
Scored (Conceded)

| 0 (1) |
| 4 (6) |
| 1 (2) |

○ Portsmouth
Scored (Conceded)

| 3 (2) |
| 1 (7) |
| 2 (1) |

Team Statistics

Starting Line-Ups

4 / 4 / 2   **4 / 4 / 2**

Unused Sub: Kuszczak, Kamara, Ellington

Unused Sub: Ashdown, Taylor

Premiership Totals

	West Brom	Portsmouth
Premiership Appearances	1,297	816
Team Appearances	413	211
Goals Scored	144	58
Assists	112	66
Clean Sheets (goalkeepers)	9	28
Yellow Cards	115	91
Red Cards	8	10
Full Internationals	5	9

Age/Height

West Bromwich Albion Age
▶ 28 yrs

Portsmouth Age
▶ 26 yrs, 5 mo

West Bromwich Albion Height
▶ 6'

Portsmouth Height
▶ 6'

Match Statistics

League Table after Fixture

		Played	Won	Drawn	Lost	For	Against	Pts
↑ 6	West Brom	2	1	1	0	2	1	4
...		...	...	...	...	...	...	...
↓ 14	Fulham	2	0	1	1	1	2	1
↓ 15	Middlesbrough	2	0	1	1	0	2	1
↑ 16	Newcastle	2	0	1	1	0	2	1
↑ 17	Everton	1	0	0	1	0	2	0
↓ 18	Wigan	2	0	0	2	0	2	0
↑ 19	Portsmouth	2	0	0	2	1	4	0
↓ 20	Sunderland	2	0	0	2	1	4	0

Statistics

	West Brom	Portsmouth
Goals	2	1
Shots on Target	2	2
Shots off Target	4	8
Hit Woodwork	0	0
Possession %	48	52
Corners	3	3
Offsides	4	2
Fouls	21	19
Disciplinary Points	16	12

1-1

Portsmouth ○
Aston Villa ○

▶ Laurent Robert tries to escape Aaron Hughes

Event Line

11 ○ ■	Solano
	Violent Conduct
11 ○ ⊕	Hughes / H / OG / IA
	Assist: Barry
11 ○ ■	Hughes
16 ○ ■	Barry
32 ○ ■	Viafara
37 ○ ⇄	De la Cruz > Phillips
42 ○ ⊕	LuaLua / RF / OP / OA
	Assist: Karadas
Half time 1-1	
51 ○ ■	Lua Lua
74 ○ ⇄	Moore > Angel
76 ○ ⇄	Todorov > O'Neil
83 ○ ⇄	Pericard > Karadas
Full time 1-1	

This was a game that Pompey really rued not taking all three points from as they played against an Aston Villa side down to ten men for all of eighty minutes.

The match started explosively when Nolberto Solano elbowed Richard Hughes as he tried to shake off the midfield man's attentions and official Graham Poll had no hesitation in showing the Peruvian a straight red card.

Bizarrely the resulting free kick was awarded to Villa for shirt pulling by Hughes and totally unexpectedly the visitors took the lead through the man whose alleged foul had triggered off events, as Barry's free kick was diverted by Hughes past his own 'keeper.

Pompey huffed and puffed, but couldn't blow the Villa house down, yet with half time approaching they were back in the game through a special effort from LuaLua. The DR Congo international cut across the Villa defence before arrowing a brilliant shot past Sorensen. The home side desperately attacked thereafter, but could not find the cutting edge to earn the first win so desperately sought after.

Player of the Match	Quote	Premiership Milestone
6 Brian Priske	❝ **Alain Perrin**	▶ **Debut**
	We had many chances and could have scored more goals, I think we were unlucky.	Brian Priske made his Premiership debut.

Venue:	Fratton Park	Referee:	G.Poll - 05/06	**Portsmouth**
Attendance:	19,778	Matches:	2	**Aston Villa**
		Yellow Cards:	9	
		Red Cards:	0	

Form Coming into Fixture

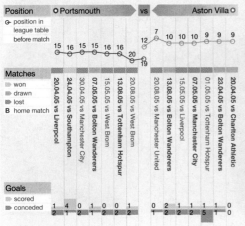

Position

⊙ position in league table before match

Matches
- won
- drawn
- lost
- B home match

Goals
- scored
- conceded

Goal Statistics

○ Portsmouth

by Half		by Situation	
first:	5	set piece:	5
second:	2	open play:	2

○ Aston Villa

by Half		by Situation	
first:	4	set piece:	1
second:	2	open play:	4
		own goals:	1

Goals by Area

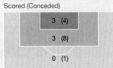

○ Portsmouth — Scored (Conceded)

3 (3) / 1 (8) / 3 (1)

○ Aston Villa — Scored (Conceded)

3 (4) / 3 (8) / 0 (1)

Team Statistics

Starting Line-Ups

4/4/2 (Diamond)

Unused Sub: Ashdown, Griffin, Skopelitis

4/4/2

Unused Sub: Taylor, Cahill, Djemba-Djemba

Premiership Totals	○ Portsmouth	Aston Villa ○
Premiership Appearances	716	1,701
Team Appearances	187	879
Goals Scored	57	197
Assists	66	167
Clean Sheets (goalkeepers)	28	59
Yellow Cards	75	164
Red Cards	9	7
Full Internationals	10	10

Age/Height

Portsmouth Age	Aston Villa Age
26 yrs, 6 mo	**26 yrs, 3 mo**
Portsmouth Height	Aston Villa Height
6'	**5'11"**

Match Statistics

League Table after Fixture

		Played	Won	Drawn	Lost	For	Against	Pts
↓	12 Everton	2	1	0	1	1	2	3
↓	13 Aston Villa	3	0	2	1	3	4	2
↓	14 Bolton	2	0	1	1	2	3	1
●	15 Fulham	2	0	1	1	1	2	1
↑	16 Newcastle	2	0	1	1	0	2	1
↑	17 Portsmouth	3	0	1	2	2	5	1
↓	18 Birmingham	3	0	1	2	1	5	1
↓	19 Wigan	2	0	0	2	0	2	0
●	20 Sunderland	3	0	0	3	2	6	0

Statistics	○ Portsmouth	Aston Villa ○
Goals	1	1
Shots on Target	11	3
Shots off Target	9	4
Hit Woodwork	0	1
Possession %	53	47
Corners	13	4
Offsides	2	1
Fouls	12	10
Disciplinary Points	12	16

2-1

Manchester City ○
Portsmouth ○

➤ Azar Karadas bursts clear of Richard Dunne

Event Line

16 ○ ▨ Sinclair	
Half time 0-0	
46 ○ ⇄ Jihai > Mills D	
52 ○ ⊕ Viafara / H / IFK / 6Y	
Assist: Robert	
66 ○ ⊕ Reyna / RF / OP / IA	
Assist: Barton	
69 ○ ⊕ Cole / RF / OP / IA	
Assist: Sinclair	
71 ○ ▨ Viafara	
76 ○ ⇄ Karadas > O'Neil	
76 ○ ⇄ Taylor > Viafara	
78 ○ ▨ Hughes	
85 ○ ⇄ Skopelitis > Griffin	
Full time 2-1	

Pompey's dismal run continued after they had looked a good bet to at least earn a point in Manchester when they took the lead early in the second half.

Manager Alain Perrin played LuaLua as a lone striker and Pompey absorbed all that City threw at them in the first half of a game in which the home side created few genuine opportunities.

After 52 minutes Pompey took the lead when John Viafara rose to head Robert's pin-point free kick past David James, but it was a goal that only served to rile Manchester City and within 15 minutes they were level when Westerveld failed to deal with Joey Barton's cross and Claudio Reyna hungrily picked up the pieces to fire home.

Another three minutes and victory had been turned quickly into defeat as City laid siege on Pompey. Andy Cole was allowed sufficient room in the area to turn and though his shot took a deflection off Andy O'Brien, it nestled into the net to deflate the visitors. Now Pompey had to react by pushing more men up front, but the oncoming Karadas could not provide the answer or prevent Pompey slipping to another morale sapping defeat.

Player of the Match	Quote	Premiership Milestone
3 Dejan Stefanovic	❝ **Alain Perrin**	➤ **First Goal**

We need to keep the ball when we move it forward, which is something we found difficult to do here.

John Viafara netted his first Premiership goal

Venue:	City of Manchester	Referee:	A.G.Wiley - 05/06		Manchester City
Attendance:	41,022	Matches:	3		Portsmouth
Capacity:	48,000	Yellow Cards:	6		
		Red Cards:	1		

Form Coming into Fixture

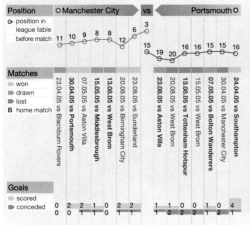

Position ○ Manchester City vs Portsmouth ○
- ○ position in league table before match

Matches
- won
- drawn
- lost
- B home match

Goals
- scored
- conceded

Goal Statistics

○ Manchester City

by Half — by Situation

- first: 7
- second: 2
- set piece: 2
- open play: 7

○ Portsmouth

by Half — by Situation

- first: 5
- second: 2
- set piece: 4
- open play: 3

Goals by Area

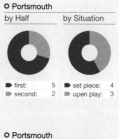

○ Manchester City

Scored (Conceded)

2 (1)
6 (2)
1 (1)

○ Portsmouth

Scored (Conceded)

2 (2)
1 (8)
4 (1)

Team Statistics

Starting Line-Ups

Manchester City
Thatcher, Musampa, Onuoha, Barton, Vassell, James, Dunne, Reyna, Cole, LuaLua, Mills D / Jihai, Sinclair

4 / 4 / 2

Unused Sub: De Vlieger, Jordan, Sibierski, Wright-Phillips

Portsmouth
Griffin, Skopelitis, O'Neil / Karadas, Priske, Viafara / Taylor, O'Brien, Westerveld, Hughes, Stefanovic, Robert, Vignal

5 / 4 / 1

Unused Sub: Ashdown, Todorov

Premiership Totals

Premiership Totals	○ Man City	Portsmouth ○
Premiership Appearances	2,045	880
Team Appearances	488	289
Goals Scored	286	60
Assists	207	71
Clean Sheets (goalkeepers)	126	28
Yellow Cards	236	99
Red Cards	20	10
Full Internationals	9	9

Age/Height

	Manchester City	Portsmouth
Age	28 yrs, 5 mo	26 yrs, 7 mo
Height	5'11"	6'

Match Statistics

League Table after Fixture

		Played	Won	Drawn	Lost	For	Against	Pts
↑	2 Man City	4	3	1	0	6	3	10
...		...	...	...	...	...	...	...
↑	14 Fulham	4	1	1	2	3	6	4
↓	15 West Brom	4	1	1	2	4	8	4
↑	16 Wigan	3	1	0	2	1	2	3
↓	17 Everton	3	1	0	2	1	3	3
↓	18 Portsmouth	4	0	1	3	3	7	1
↓	19 Newcastle	3	0	1	2	0	4	1
●	20 Sunderland	4	0	0	4	2	7	0

Statistics

Statistics	○ Man City	Portsmouth ○
Goals	2	1
Shots on Target	9	2
Shots off Target	7	5
Hit Woodwork	0	0
Possession %	60	40
Corners	12	3
Offsides	0	4
Fouls	13	17
Disciplinary Points	4	8

0-1

Everton ○
Portsmouth ○

▶ Lomana Tresor LuaLua battles with Joseph Yobo

Event Line	
Half time 0-0	
60 ○ ⊕	Ferguson / H / OG / 6Y
	Assist: Robert
65 ○ ▢	Davies
66 ○ ⇄	Beattie > Bent M
66 ○ ⇄	McFadden > Davies
66 ○ ⇄	Osman > Kilbane
70 ○ ⇄	Viafara > Silva
72 ○ ⇄	Vukic > Robert
79 ○ ⇄	Karadas > Lua Lua
81 ○ ▢	Hughes
84 ○ ▢	Valente
Full time 0-1	

Pompey finally cracked it with their first win of the season.

This victory at Goodison Park was reward for a gritty performance which made nonsense of their position and results over the first few matches.

In the end they were beholden to an own goal by Duncan Ferguson in the second half of this contest. There were more debuts as Dario Silva, Zvonimir Vukic and Salif Diao all took their bows after signing before the August transfer window shut.

After comfortably holding their own throughout a first half in which they looked dangerous, with the adventurous Silva buzzing around, the visitors were unlucky not to take in a lead when LuaLua's audacious chip beat Martyn in the Everton goal but came back off the bar.

With the hour mark approaching they deservedly took the lead. Robert floated in a corner which Stefanovic looked to have got his head to, but closer inspection revealed that the Everton striker Ferguson, more renowned for sticking them in at the other end, had given Pompey the lead amidst the challenge. The home side predictably put on the pressure but created little with the recalled Ashdown in goal standing firm.

Player of the Match	Quote	Premiership Milestone
15 Jamie Ashdown	❝ **Dejan Stefanovic**	▶ **Debut**

❝ I am very happy. We played well, especially in the first half. I am pleased for all the lads and the new ones in particular.

Salif Diao made his first Premiership appearance in the colours of Portsmouth

Venue:	Goodison Park	Referee:	M.Atkinson - 05/06
Attendance:	36,831	Matches:	4
Capacity:	40,569	Yellow Cards:	10
		Red Cards:	0

Everton
Portsmouth

Form Coming into Fixture

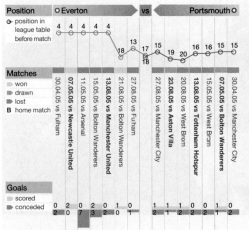

Position
- position in league table before match

Matches
- won
- drawn
- lost
- B home match

Goals
- scored
- conceded

Goal Statistics

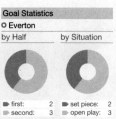

Everton

by Half	by Situation
first: 2	set piece: 2
second: 3	open play: 3

Portsmouth

by Half	by Situation
first: 1	set piece: 3
second: 3	open play: 1

Goals by Area

Everton

Scored (Conceded)

| 3 (2) |
| 2 (13) |
| 0 (0) |

Portsmouth

Scored (Conceded)

| 2 (2) |
| 0 (9) |
| 2 (1) |

Team Statistics

Starting Line-Ups

Everton: Martyn; Valente, Weir, Yobo, Hibbert, Kilbane (Osman), Arteta, Cahill, Davies (McFadden), Ferguson, Silva (Viafara), Bent M (Beattie), LuaLua (Karadas)

4/4/2

Unused Sub: Wright, Ferrari

Portsmouth: Unknown; O'Neil, Priske, Diao, O'Brien, Hughes, Stefanovic, Robert (Vukic), Vignal

4/4/2

Unused Sub: Westerveld, Griffin

Premiership Totals	Everton	Portsmouth
Premiership Appearances	1,764	690
Team Appearances	928	211
Goals Scored	221	59
Assists	137	66
Clean Sheets (goalkeepers)	131	2
Yellow Cards	158	80
Red Cards	16	9
Full Internationals	10	11

Age/Height

Everton Age	Portsmouth Age
28 yrs, 2 mo	**26 yrs, 11 mo**
Everton Height	Portsmouth Height
6'	**6'**

Match Statistics

League Table after Fixture

		Played	Won	Drawn	Lost	For	Against	Pts
●	10 Liverpool	3	1	2	0	1	0	5
↓	11 Aston Villa	4	1	2	1	4	4	5
↑	12 Fulham	5	1	2	2	4	7	5
↓	13 West Ham	3	1	1	1	4	3	4
↓	14 Blackburn	4	1	1	2	3	5	4
↑	15 Portsmouth	5	1	1	3	4	7	4
↓	16 Birmingham	5	1	1	3	4	4	4
↓	17 West Brom	5	1	1	3	5	10	4
↓	18 Everton	4	1	0	3	1	4	3

Statistics	Everton	Portsmouth
Goals	0	1
Shots on Target	6	8
Shots off Target	5	4
Hit Woodwork	0	1
Possession %	54	46
Corners	11	6
Offsides	3	2
Fouls	10	12
Disciplinary Points	8	4

1-1

Portsmouth ○
Birmingham City ○

➡ Dejan Stefanovic weighs up his options

Event Line

4 ○ ⊕ LuaLua / RF / C / 6Y	
Assist: Robert	
6 ○ ⊕ Jarosik / H / IFK / IA	
Assist: Heskey	
42 ○ ⇄ Izzet > Jarosik	
45 ○ ▢ Silva	
45 ○ ▢ Butt	
Violent Conduct	
Half time 1-1	
46 ○ ⇄ Clapham > Forssell	
65 ○ ⇄ Vukic > Hughes	
74 ○ ▢ Diao	
76 ○ ⇄ Karadas > Lua Lua	
90 ○ ⇄ Pandiani > Pennant	
Full time 1-1	

Pompey failed to build on the previous week's victory as once more they were unable to overcome a ten-man side from the Midlands.

It was Nicky Butt who this time received his marching orders for angrily kicking out at Dario Silva as they jostled in the area awaiting a free kick, but with a whole second half to survive Birmingham did so rather comfortably as again a lack of fire power cost the home team.

Early on it looked as if Pompey, refreshed from the win at Everton, were going to take charge and after four minutes they were ahead when LuaLua stabbed home Robert's corner to keep everyone on a high. But the elation lasted just a few minutes as Pompey, still celebrating, were hit by a sucker punch. Jermaine Pennant swung in a free kick from the right and Heskey's flick was met by Jarosik who headed past Ashdown.

The visitors were then reduced to ten men on the brink of half time, but that was only to heighten Pompey's second half frustration. Gary O'Neil, Vukic and LuaLua all came close as the home side staged a finale, but the final whistle brought more disappointment at points lost with the home fans still awaiting a Fratton Park victory.

Player of the Match	Quote
11 Laurent Robert	🔾 **Alain Perrin**

We deserved to win and had a lot of chances to score but had no success.

Venue:	Fratton Park	Referee:	D.J.Gallagher - 05/06		**Portsmouth**
Attendance:	19,319	Matches:	7		**Birmingham City**
		Yellow Cards:	18		
		Red Cards:	2		

Form Coming into Fixture

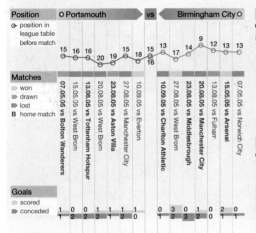

Goal Statistics

○ Portsmouth

by Half — by Situation

- first: 1
- second: 4
- set piece: 3
- open play: 1
- own goals: 1

○ Birmingham City

by Half — by Situation

- first: 4
- second: 2
- set piece: 2
- open play: 4

Goals by Area

○ Portsmouth
Scored (Conceded)

3 (1)
0 (9)
2 (0)

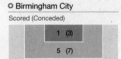

○ Birmingham City
Scored (Conceded)

1 (3)
5 (7)
0 (0)

Team Statistics

Starting Line-Ups

Portsmouth:
Ashdown
Vignal, Stefanovic, O'Brien, Priske
Robert, Hughes (Vukic), LuaLua (Karadas), Diao, O'Neil
Silva
Forssell (Clapham)

4/4/2

Unused Sub: Westerveld, Skopelitis, Viafara

Birmingham City:
Taylor Maik
Pennant (Pandiani), Tebily, Butt, Cunningham, Upson
Heskey, Jarosik (Izzet)
Johnson, Gray

4/4/2

Unused Sub: Vaesen, Taylor Martin

Premiership Totals

	○ Portsmouth	Birmingham ○
Premiership Appearances	699	1,922
Team Appearances	220	672
Goals Scored	58	185
Assists	67	194
Clean Sheets (goalkeepers)	3	36
Yellow Cards	78	220
Red Cards	9	15
Full Internationals	10	11

Age/Height

Portsmouth Age
26 yrs, 11 mo

Birmingham City Age
28 yrs, 7 mo

Portsmouth Height
6'

Birmingham City Height
6'

Match Statistics

League Table after Fixture

		Played	Won	Drawn	Lost	For	Against	Pts
↓	7 Bolton	5	2	2	1	6	4	8
●	8 Middlesbrough	5	2	1	2	5	6	7
●	9 Arsenal	4	2	0	2	7	4	6
●	10 Wigan	4	2	0	2	3	3	6
↑	11 Aston Villa	6	1	3	2	5	9	6
↓	12 Liverpool	3	1	2	0	1	0	5
↓	13 Blackburn	5	1	2	2	3	5	5
↑	14 Portsmouth	6	1	2	3	5	8	5
↑	15 Birmingham	6	1	2	3	5	9	5

Statistics

	○ Portsmouth	Birmingham ○
Goals	1	1
Shots on Target	9	2
Shots off Target	5	1
Hit Woodwork	0	0
Possession %	50	50
Corners	7	3
Offsides	1	2
Fouls	16	14
Disciplinary Points	8	12

3-2

Gillingham ○
Portsmouth ○

➡ Richard Hughes prepares to challenge Matthew Jarvis

Event Line

24 ○ ⊕ O'Neil / RF / OP / IA	
Assist: Silva	
37 ○ ▪ Johnson	
42 ○ ⊕ Byfield / LF / OP / OA	
Half time 1-1	
48 ○ ⊕ Taylor / LF / P / IA	
Assist: O'Neil	
56 ○ ⊕ Ashdown / H / OG / 6Y	
Assist: Byfield	
63 ○ ⇄ Todorov > Silva	
65 ○ ⇄ Williams > Hessenthaler	
70 ○ ⇄ Songo'o > Diao	
76 ○ ▪ Stefanovic	
77 ○ ⇄ Jackman > Hope	
86 ○ ▪ Sancho	
94 ○ ⊕ Crofts / RF / OP / IA	
Assist: Jackman	
95 ○ ▪ Brown	
105 ○ ⇄ Viafara > Taylor	
112 ○ ⇄ Hislop > Shields	
116 ○ ▪ Vignal	
Full time 3-2	

Things took a definite turn for the worse as Pompey were unceremoniously dispatched from the Carling Cup by lower league opposition.

Early on Pompey had looked in control, playing some slick football that earned them the lead after twenty four minutes. Andy O'Brien's long ball found Dario Silva who laid it back for Gary O'Neil to score.

For most of the first half Perrin's side looked comfortable, but a misunderstanding in Pompey's defence gifted the home side an equaliser. 'Keeper Ashdown rolled the ball out to Taylor who seemed unaware that Darren Byfield, previously off the field receiving treatment, had returned. The striker stole the ball and advanced before smashing it home to draw Gillingham level.

Even then there was little hint of what was to come and minutes after the break Pompey promptly regained the lead as Karadas set up O'Neil. The midfield man forced a great save from 'keeper Brown but as he shaped up to hit home the rebound, his legs were taken from underneath him by Sancho. Matt Taylor stepped up to put home the penalty.

However, from what should have been a straightforward position more confusion was to follow: Byfield was allowed time and space to run at the Pompey defence and when he shot, the ball came back off the post, but struck the diving Ashdown's arm and went back into the net.

With ten minutes remaining the perfect chance came to avert extra time following a second penalty award after Gills defender Sancho had again infringed. However, this time Svetoslav Todorov took the kick and fired his effort well wide of the goal. Now there was an extra half hour to play and Pompey's misery was compounded

► Dario Silva closes down the goalkeeper

Match Statistics

Starting Line-Ups

Statistics	Gillingham	Portsmouth
Goals	3	2
Shots on Target	7	8
Shots off Target	8	7
Hit Woodwork	1	0
Possession %	47	53
Corners	6	6
Offsides	5	6
Fouls	14	16
Disciplinary Points	12	8

Age/Height

Gillingham Age	Portsmouth Age
► 26 yrs, 2 mo	► 26 yrs, 1 mo
Gillingham Height	Portsmouth Height
► 5'10"	► 6'

► 4/4/2   ► 4/4/2

Unused Sub: Crichton, Pouton   Unused Sub: Westerveld, Skopelitis

when just four minutes into this period they found themselves behind for the first time in the evening. The defence was completely missing as substitute Danny Jackman pulled the ball back for Andrew Crofts who had time to size his chance up before shooting home.

Pompey piled men forward, but in truth they never looked like pulling the deficit back. Given the start to their Premier League campaign it was the last thing they needed and their dispirited exit from the field told its own story.

Player of the Match

26 Gary O'Neil

Quote

❝ Dejan Stefanovic

Sometimes it's much easier to play against Manchester United than a second division club.

1-0

Bolton Wanderers ○
Portsmouth ○

▶ Andy O'Brien prepares to stop Kevin Davies

Event Line

10 ○ ⇄	O'Brien > Speed
25 ○ ⊕	Nolan / RF / OP / IA
	Assist: Davies
Half time 1-0	
52 ○ ■	Ben Haim
66 ○ ⇄	Karadas > Taylor
73 ○ ⇄	Songo'o > O'Neil
74 ○ ■	Stefanovic
75 ○ ⇄	Giannakopoulos > Okocha
85 ○ ⇄	Todorov > Silva
90 ○ ■	Giannakopoulos
90 ○ ⇄	Diouf > Hunt
90 ○ ■	Priske
Full time 1-0	

Pompey left the Reebok Stadium with a definite sense of injustice after being rocked by a twenty fifth minute Kevin Nolan strike that had more than a hint of offside about it.

To compound their misery the normally mild mannered Alain Perrin was sent from the touchline in the closing stages of the game after sarcastically applauding referee Mark Clattenburg.

Once again Pompey were left ruing a lack of cutting edge which was now threatening to entrench them firmly in relegation trouble. It wasn't exactly great entertainment for Sky television who broadcast the game live.

Nolan's strike came when Pedersen's cross was headed on by Kevin Davies for the midfield man to launch an overhead kick which gave Ashdown little chance. The visitors were pretty enough in their approach work, but had no finish and Bolton posed little more threat. The defeat merely prolonged a gloomy start to the season with Pompey struggling to get a run together.

Player of the Match

5 Andy O'Brien

Quote

❝ Joe Jordan

We had chances to get back in the game after the goal, but failed to take them.

Premiership Milestone

▶ **Debut**

Franck Songo'o made his Premiership debut.

Venue:	Reebok Stadium	Referee:	M.Clattenburg - 05/06		**Bolton Wanderers**
Attendance:	23,134	Matches:	8		**Portsmouth**
Capacity:	28,723	Yellow Cards:	33		
		Red Cards:	2		

Form Coming into Fixture

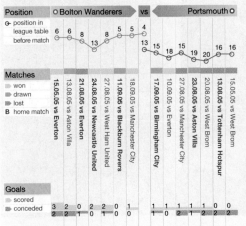

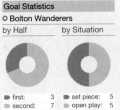

Goal Statistics

○ **Bolton Wanderers**

by Half | by Situation

■ first: 3 ■ set piece: 5
■ second: 7 ■ open play: 5

○ **Portsmouth**

by Half | by Situation

■ first: 2 ■ set piece: 3
■ second: 3 ■ open play: 1
■ own goals: 1

Goals by Area

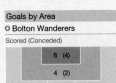

○ **Bolton Wanderers**
Scored (Conceded)

6 (4)
4 (2)
0 (0)

○ **Portsmouth**
Scored (Conceded)

3 (1)
0 (9)
2 (0)

Team Statistics

Starting Line-Ups

4/5/1

Unused Sub: Walker, Borgetti

4/4/1/1

Unused Sub: Westerveld, Skopelitis

Premiership Totals	○ Bolton	Portsmouth ○
Premiership Appearances	1,672	686
Team Appearances	1,075	252
Goals Scored	198	44
Assists	165	68
Clean Sheets (goalkeepers)	38	3
Yellow Cards	218	82
Red Cards	10	8
Full Internationals	10	9

Age/Height

Bolton Wanderers Age
➤ 28 yrs

Portsmouth Age
➤ 26 yrs, 4 mo

Bolton Wanderers Height
➤ 5'11"

Portsmouth Height
➤ 6'

Match Statistics

League Table after Fixture

		Played	Won	Drawn	Lost	For	Against	Pts
↑ 3	Bolton	7	4	2	1	8	4	14
...	...	...	...	...	...	...	...	...
↑ 14	Birmingham	7	1	3	3	7	11	6
↓ 15	Aston Villa	7	1	3	3	6	11	6
● 16	Fulham	6	1	2	3	5	9	5
↓ 17	Portsmouth	7	1	2	4	5	9	5
↓ 18	West Brom	7	1	2	4	7	13	5
● 19	Everton	6	1	0	5	1	7	3
● 20	Sunderland	6	0	1	5	3	10	1

Statistics	○ Bolton	Portsmouth ○
Goals	1	0
Shots on Target	2	4
Shots off Target	9	2
Hit Woodwork	0	0
Possession %	52	48
Corners	7	3
Offsides	4	2
Fouls	9	6
Disciplinary Points	8	8

0-0

Portsmouth ○
Newcastle United ○

▶ Dario Silva lets out his frustrations

Event Line
Half time 0-0
46 ○ ⇄ Elliott > Babayaro
66 ○ ▢ Taylor
69 ○ ⇄ Hughes > Diao
76 ○ ⇄ Songo'o > Griffin
80 ○ ▢ Parker
88 ○ ⇄ Faye > Clark
88 ○ ▢ Vukic
Full time 0-0

Once more Pompey could not be faulted for effort and commitment with in the end only Newcastle 'keeper Shay Given keeping them from registering their first home victory which the performance richly deserved.

For the first time since the opening game against Spurs the home side found themselves with an unusual conundrum: How to break down eleven men at home. But in truth Pompey looked more dangerous than at any time in those two previous games. Newcastle in comparison created very little, whilst the midfield duo of Vukic and O'Neil looked a constant threat for Pompey.

Given denied them in the first half, but the Irish stopper would save his best 'til last when twice thwarting Matthew Taylor in quick succession. He produced a stunning save to keep out the left-back's shot and then from the resulting corner provided one of equal stature to claw away another effort.

Vukic then looked as if he had earned a penalty in the eighty-eighth minute after Given appeared to bring the midfield man down. But referee Steve Bennett booked the Serbian for what he saw as a dive and the home side, heartened by their best display of the season, had to settle for a point.

Player of the Match	Quote	Premiership Milestone
14 Matthew Taylor	❝ **Andy Griffin**	▶ **20,220**

The chances still kept coming and on another day it could have been three-nil.

The attendance of 20,220 was a Premiership record at Fratton Park.

Venue:	Fratton Park	Referee:	S.G.Bennett - 05/06	**Portsmouth**
Attendance:	20,220	Matches:	8	**Newcastle United**
		Yellow Cards:	33	
		Red Cards:	3	

Form Coming into Fixture

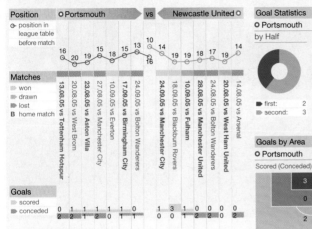

Position — O Portsmouth — vs — Newcastle United O

- O⃝ position in league table before match

Matches
- won
- drawn
- lost
- B home match

Portsmouth matches: 13.08.05 vs Tottenham Hotspur, 20.08.05 vs West Brom, 23.08.05 vs Aston Villa, 27.08.05 vs Manchester City, 10.09.05 vs Everton, 17.09.05 vs Birmingham City, 24.09.05 vs Bolton Wanderers

Newcastle matches: 24.09.05 vs Manchester City, 18.09.05 vs Blackburn Rovers, 10.09.05 vs Fulham, 28.08.05 vs Manchester United, 24.08.05 vs Bolton Wanderers, 20.08.05 vs West Ham United, 14.08.05 vs Arsenal

Goals
- scored
- conceded

Portsmouth Goals scored: 0 1 1 1 1 1 0 / conceded: 2 2 1 2 0 1 1
Newcastle Goals scored: 1 3 1 0 0 0 0 / conceded: 0 0 1 2 2 0 2

Goal Statistics

O Portsmouth

by Half		by Situation	
first:	2	set piece:	3
second:	3	open play:	1
		own goals:	1

O Newcastle United

by Half		by Situation	
first:	1	set piece:	2
second:	4	open play:	3

Goals by Area

O Portsmouth — Scored (Conceded)

3 (1)
0 (8)
2 (0)

O Newcastle United — Scored (Conceded)

0 (3)
3 (4)
2 (0)

Team Statistics

Starting Line-Ups

Portsmouth: Ashdown, Vignal, O'Brien, Stefanovic, Priske, Griffin, Taylor, Vukic, Silva, Diao / Hughes, O'Neil, Songo'o

Newcastle: Given, Bowyer, Carr, Parker, Boumsong, Shearer, Ameobi, Clark / Faye, Taylor, N'Zogbia, Babayaro / Elliott

Portsmouth: ▶ 5/4/1

Newcastle: ▶ 4/4/2

Unused Sub: Westerveld, Skopelitis, Karadas

Unused Sub: Harper, Brittain, Chopra

Premiership Totals	O Portsmouth	Newcastle O
Premiership Appearances	642	2,011
Team Appearances	275	1,062
Goals Scored	22	357
Assists	17	217
Clean Sheets (goalkeepers)	3	71
Yellow Cards	83	267
Red Cards	7	14
Full Internationals	7	8

Age/Height

Portsmouth Age	Newcastle United Age
▶ **26 yrs, 2 mo**	▶ **27 yrs, 5 mo**
Portsmouth Height	Newcastle United Height
▶ **5'11"**	▶ **5'11"**

Match Statistics

League Table after Fixture

	Played	Won	Drawn	Lost	For	Against	Pts
↓ 11 Newcastle	8	2	3	3	5	7	9
↓ 12 Middlesbrough	7	2	2	3	6	9	8
● 13 Liverpool	5	1	4	0	3	2	7
● 14 Birmingham	7	1	3	3	7	11	6
↑ 15 Portsmouth	8	1	3	4	5	9	6
↓ 16 Aston Villa	7	1	3	3	6	11	6
↑ 17 Sunderland	8	1	2	5	6	11	5
↓ 18 Fulham	8	1	2	5	7	13	5
↓ 19 West Brom	8	1	2	5	7	15	5

Statistics	O Portsmouth	Newcastle O
Goals	0	0
Shots on Target	7	4
Shots off Target	4	3
Hit Woodwork	0	0
Possession %	55	45
Corners	5	5
Offsides	2	6
Fouls	12	12
Disciplinary Points	4	8

1-1

Middlesbrough ○
Portsmouth ○

▶ Gary O'Neil in midfield action

Event Line	
Half time 0-0	
46 ○ ⇄	Mendieta > Queudrue
46 ○ ⊕	O'Neil / RF / OP / IA
	Assist: Vukic
46 ○ ⇄	Skopelitis > Griffin
46 ○ ⇄	Todorov > Silva
54 ○ ⊕	Yakubu / H / C / 6Y
	Assist: Rochemback
55 ○ ⇄	Viduka > Maccarone
55 ○ ⇄	Hasselbaink > Rochemback
58 ○ ⇄	Vignal > Robert
66 ○	Skopelitis
70 ○	O'Neil
88 ○	Pogatetz
90 ○	Boateng
90 ○	Vignal
Full time 1-1	

Former Fratton Park marksman Yakubu came back to haunt Pompey with an equaliser that deprived them of the three points which their performance on Teesside probably deserved.

Neither goalkeeper had a first half save to make, but Silva came closest to breaking the stalemate as he just failed to connect with a Robert cross.

Shortly after the interval Pompey forged ahead with a splendid move. Todorov sparked it off, latching onto a through-ball and feeding Vukic whose low cross was swept home by Gary O'Neil. But once more Pompey were pulled back in quick time and within ten minutes Middlesbrough had drawn level.

Rochemback floated over a corner and marker Skopelitis lost Yakubu who arrived to head home with clinical accuracy. The home side sensed they could win the game, but Pompey held firm at the back despite yielding territorial advantage.

Player of the Match

26 Gary O'Neil

Quote

❝ **Alain Perrin**

I'm a little bit disappointed because we led 1-0 but we have won a point against a good team.

Venue:	Riverside Stadium	Referee:	C.J.Foy - 05/06		**Middlesbrough**
Attendance:	26,551	Matches:	9		**Portsmouth**
Capacity:	35,100	Yellow Cards:	20		
		Red Cards:	2		

Form Coming into Fixture

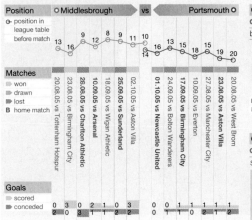

Position
Middlesbrough vs Portsmouth

o- position in league table before match

Matches
- won
- drawn
- lost
- B home match

Goals
- scored
- conceded

Goal Statistics

Middlesbrough

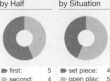

by Half — by Situation

- first: 5
- second: 4
- set piece: 4
- open play: 5

Portsmouth

by Half — by Situation

- first: 2
- second: 3
- set piece: 3
- open play: 1
- own goals: 1

Goals by Area

Middlesbrough — Scored (Conceded)

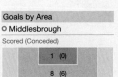

1 (0)
8 (6)
0 (5)

Portsmouth — Scored (Conceded)

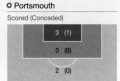

3 (1)
0 (6)
2 (0)

Team Statistics

Starting Line-Ups

4/4/1/1 — **5/4/1**

Unused Sub: Knight, Bates — Unused Sub: Westerveld, Songo'o

Premiership Totals	Boro	Portsmouth
Premiership Appearances	1,833	748
Team Appearances	946	278
Goals Scored	279	46
Assists	192	66
Clean Sheets (goalkeepers)	71	4
Yellow Cards	222	92
Red Cards	12	8
Full Internationals	11	8

Age/Height

Middlesbrough Age: **28 yrs, 5 mo**

Portsmouth Age: **27 yrs, 1 mo**

Middlesbrough Height: **6'**

Portsmouth Height: **5'11"**

Match Statistics

League Table after Fixture

	Played	Won	Drawn	Lost	For	Against	Pts
● 10 Middlesbrough	9	3	3	3	10	12	12
● 11 Blackburn	9	3	2	4	7	10	11
↑ 12 Liverpool	7	2	4	1	5	6	10
↓ 13 Newcastle	9	2	3	4	5	8	9
↑ 14 West Brom	9	2	2	5	9	16	8
↓ 15 Portsmouth	9	1	4	4	6	10	7
↓ 16 Birmingham	8	1	3	4	7	12	6
↓ 17 Aston Villa	8	1	3	4	8	14	6
● 18 Fulham	8	1	2	5	7	13	5

Statistics	Boro	Portsmouth
Goals	1	1
Shots on Target	7	4
Shots off Target	7	5
Hit Woodwork	0	0
Possession %	48	52
Corners	6	3
Offsides	2	2
Fouls	12	12
Disciplinary Points	8	12

1-2

Portsmouth ○
Charlton Athletic ○

➡ Matthew Taylor takes on Luke Young

Event Line

12 ○ ▪	Kishishev
13 ○ ▪	Hreidarsson
14 ○ ⊕	Silva / RF / OP / IA
	Assist: O'Brien
24 ○ ▪	Robert
Half time 1-0	
51 ○ ▪	Vignal
61 ○ ⊕	Ambrose / RF / OP / IA
	Assist: Murphy
77 ○ ⊕	Rommedahl / RF / OP / IA
	Assist: Murphy
83 ○ ⇄	Johansson > Rommedahl
87 ○ ⇄	Todorov > Robert
87 ○ ⇄	Hughes > Taylor
88 ○ ⇄	Mbesuma > Vukic
90 ○ ▪	Ambrose
90 ○ ⇄	El Karkouri > Murphy
Full time 1-2	

Pompey will wonder how they lost this game to an in-form Charlton side after completely dominating the opening forty-five minutes.

The home side headed for the tunnel at half time a goal up and completely in command, but they were hit by a second half revival by the Londoners which wrestled all the points from them and left the Blues still searching vainly for their first home win.

It had all looked so different early on. Dario Silva had put Pompey ahead with a spectacular strike when, after fourteen minutes, he latched on to O'Brien's long ball and sent it rocketing past Andersen in the visiting goal.

But Charlton were not finished off and Pompey were made to pay. Danny Murphy slotted through the eye of a needle for Ambrose to beat Ashdown on the hour and from there the home side deflated like a pricked balloon. Sixteen minutes later Murphy was the architect again as this time he picked out Rommedahl who finished in devastating fashion, giving Ashdown no chance. With five minutes remaining Vukic skied over the bar and a point which had looked the very least Pompey would gain was lost as another home match passed without victory.

Player of the Match	Quote	Premiership Milestone
31 Dario Silva	❝ **Alain Perrin**	➡ **First Goal**

We started very well and had many chances to score in the first half. I think we forgot to play, we stopped playing, there was no movement.

Dario Silva netted his first Premiership goal.

Venue:	Fratton Park	Referee:	H.M.Webb - 05/06	Portsmouth
Attendance:	19,030	Matches:	9	Charlton Athletic
		Yellow Cards:	27	
		Red Cards:	1	

Form Coming into Fixture

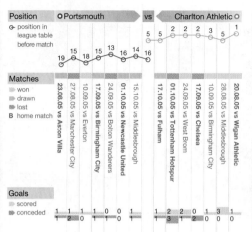

Position ○ Portsmouth vs Charlton Athletic ○

○ position in league table before match

Portsmouth: 19, 15, 18, 15, 13, 16, 14
Charlton: 5, 5, 2, 2, 2, 3, 5, 1, 16

Matches
- won
- drawn
- lost
- B home match

Portsmouth:
23.08.05 vs Aston Villa
27.08.05 vs Manchester City
10.09.05 vs Everton
17.09.05 vs Birmingham City
24.09.05 vs Bolton Wanderers
01.10.05 vs Newcastle United
15.10.05 vs Middlesbrough

Charlton Athletic:
17.10.05 vs Fulham
01.10.05 vs Tottenham Hotspur
24.09.05 vs West Brom
17.09.05 vs Chelsea
10.09.05 vs Birmingham City
28.08.05 vs Middlesbrough
20.08.05 vs Wigan Athletic

Goals
- scored: 1 1 1 1 0 0 1 | 1 2 2 0 1 3 1
- conceded: 1 2 0 1 1 0 1 | 1 3 1 2 0 0 0

Goal Statistics

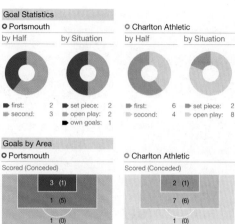

○ Portsmouth

by Half | by Situation
- first: 2
- second: 3
- set piece: 2
- open play: 2
- own goals: 1

○ Charlton Athletic

by Half | by Situation
- first: 6
- second: 4
- set piece: 2
- open play: 8

Goals by Area

○ Portsmouth
Scored (Conceded)

3 (1)
1 (5)
1 (0)

○ Charlton Athletic
Scored (Conceded)

2 (1)
7 (6)
1 (0)

Team Statistics

Starting Line-Ups

Portsmouth:
Ashdown
Stefanovic, Vignal, Priske, O'Brien
Taylor Hughes, O'Neil, Vukic Mbesuma
Robert Todorov, Viafara, Silva, Bent D

Charlton Athletic:
Andersen
Young, Perry, Spector, Hreidarsson
Smertin, Murphy El Karkouri, Ambrose
Rommedahl Johansson, Kishishev

▶ 4/5/1 **▶ 4/5/1**

Unused Sub: Westerveld, Griffin

Unused Sub: Kiely, Hughes, Bothroyd

Premiership Totals

	○ Portsmouth	Charlton ○
Premiership Appearances	680	1,424
Team Appearances	285	689
Goals Scored	45	100
Assists	66	89
Clean Sheets (goalkeepers)	4	3
Yellow Cards	83	174
Red Cards	7	5
Full Internationals	10	10

Age/Height

Portsmouth Age	Charlton Athletic Age
▶ **26 yrs, 8 mo**	▶ **27 yrs, 4 mo**
Portsmouth Height	Charlton Athletic Height
▶ **5'11"**	▶ **6'**

Match Statistics

League Table after Fixture

		Played	Won	Drawn	Lost	For	Against	Pts
↑ 2	Charlton	9	6	1	2	15	9	19
...		...	...	...	...	...	...	...
↑ 14	Fulham	10	2	3	5	10	14	9
↓ 15	Aston Villa	10	2	3	5	9	16	9
↓ 16	West Brom	9	2	2	5	9	16	8
↓ 17	Portsmouth	10	1	4	5	7	12	7
● 18	Birmingham	10	1	3	6	7	15	6
● 19	Sunderland	9	1	2	6	7	14	5
● 20	Everton	8	1	0	7	1	11	3

Statistics

	○ Portsmouth	Charlton ○
Goals	1	2
Shots on Target	6	7
Shots off Target	9	4
Hit Woodwork	0	0
Possession %	45	55
Corners	6	5
Offsides	3	1
Fouls	10	15
Disciplinary Points	8	12

33

▶ Matthew Taylor is mobbed by exuberant teammates

Event Line

4 ○ ⊕ Whitehead / RF / P / IA	
Assist: Gray	
35 ○ ▇ Griffin	
Half time 1-0	
48 ○ ⊕ Vukic / LF / OP / IA	
Assist: Taylor	
50 ○ ⇄ Robinson > Miller	
59 ○ ⊕ Taylor / RF / IFK / IA	
Assist: Silva	
62 ○ ⇄ Stead > Lawrence	
67 ○ ⊕ Taylor / LF / OP / OA	
Assist: Vukic	
68 ○ ⇄ Viafara > Vukic	
74 ○ ⊕ Silva / H / OP / 6Y	
Assist: Taylor	
77 ○ ⇄ Mbesuma > Silva	
84 ○ ⇄ Todorov > Taylor	
Full time 1-4	

Pompey trounced Sunderland at The Stadium of Light to truly kick-start their season.

Sunderland, who like Pompey were searching for a first home win, forged ahead after just four minutes. Gray's header struck Priske's hand on the way towards goal and Mark Halsey had no hesitation in pointing to the spot.

Within three minutes of the re-start Pompey were level when Vukic scored his first goal in a blue shirt after good work by Vignal and Taylor.

On fifty-nine minutes Pompey took the lead as Sunderland gifted them the second. Keeper Davies and Stubbs made a mess of clearing Silva's header between them and Matt Taylor was on hand to sweep home from their error.

If that goal was scrappy, Taylor's second and Pompey's third was a candidate for 'goal of the season'. Striker Silva was hurt in an incident which left him prostrate, but when the ball came to Taylor, only marginally in the attacking half, he blasted an effort that flew high over the head of the bemused Davies and into the net.

There was now no stopping the man of the match as he marauded down the right to put in a perfect cross for Silva who headed home to cap the scoring.

Player of the Match	Quote	Premiership Milestone
14 Matthew Taylor	⓴ **Matthew Taylor**	▶ **100**

It was nice personally to get a couple of goals, but the main thing was that the team got a win.

Matthew Taylor's spectacular second goal was the 100th scored by Portsmouth in the Premiership.

Venue:	Stadium of Light	Referee:	M.R.Halsey - 05/06		Sunderland
Attendance:	34,926	Matches:	13		Portsmouth
Capacity:	48,300	Yellow Cards:	18		
		Red Cards:	3		

Form Coming into Fixture

Position

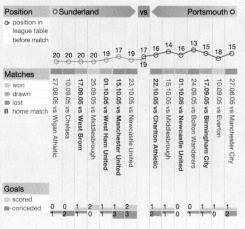

- ⊙ position in league table before match

Matches
- won
- drawn
- lost
- B home match

Goal Statistics

○ Sunderland
- by Half
- by Situation

○ Portsmouth
- by Half
- by Situation

○ Sunderland			
first:	5	set piece:	2
second:	2	open play:	5

○ Portsmouth			
first:	2	set piece:	2
second:	3	open play:	2
		own goals:	1

Goals by Area

○ Sunderland — Scored (Conceded)
- 1 (1)
- 2 (7)
- 4 (3)

○ Portsmouth — Scored (Conceded)
- 3 (1)
- 2 (6)
- 0 (0)

Goals
- scored
- conceded

Team Statistics

Starting Line-Ups

Sunderland: Davis; Nosworthy, Stubbs, Caldwell, Hoyte; Whitehead, Miller Robinson, Elliott, Welsh; Gray, Lawrence Stead

Formation: ▶ 4/4/2

Unused Sub: Alnwick, Woods, Murphy D

Portsmouth: Ashdown; Vignal, Priske, Primus, Griffin; Taylor Todorov, Stefanovic, Vukic Viafara, Silva Mbesuma, O'Neil; Hughes

Formation: ▶ 5/4/1

Unused Sub: Westerveld

Premiership Totals

	○ Sunderland	Portsmouth ○
Premiership Appearances	381	531
Team Appearances	102	363
Goals Scored	23	19
Assists	13	19
Clean Sheets (goalkeepers)	1	4
Yellow Cards	38	77
Red Cards	2	4
Full Internationals	4	8

Age/Height

Sunderland Age	Portsmouth Age
▶ 25 yrs, 6 mo	▶ 26 yrs, 10 mo
Sunderland Height	Portsmouth Height
▶ 5'11"	▶ 5'11"

Match Statistics

League Table after Fixture

		Played	Won	Drawn	Lost	For	Against	Pts
↑	12 Liverpool	9	3	4	2	7	8	13
↓	13 Newcastle	10	3	3	4	8	10	12
↑	14 Portsmouth	11	2	4	5	11	13	10
↓	15 Fulham	11	2	3	6	10	15	9
↓	16 Aston Villa	10	2	3	5	9	16	9
↓	17 West Brom	10	2	2	6	9	18	8
↑	18 Everton	10	2	1	7	3	16	7
↓	19 Birmingham	11	1	3	7	7	16	6
↓	20 Sunderland	11	1	2	8	10	21	5

Statistics

	○ Sunderland	Portsmouth ○
Goals	1	4
Shots on Target	3	5
Shots off Target	3	0
Hit Woodwork	0	0
Possession %	49	51
Corners	11	2
Offsides	0	4
Fouls	11	9
Disciplinary Points	0	4

0-2

Portsmouth ○
Wigan Athletic ○

▶ Zvonimir Vukic is challenged by Stephane Henchoz

Event Line
Half time 0-0

48 ○ ⊕	Chimbonda / H / C / 6Y	
	Assist: Bullard	
60 ○ ⇄	Robert > Vignal	
68 ○ ⇄	LuaLua > Vukic	
76 ○ ⇄	Diao > Griffin	
79 ○ ⊕	Roberts / RF / OP / IA	
	Assist: Chimbonda	
84 ○	Francis	
86 ○	Stefanovic	
87 ○	De Zeeuw	
88 ○ ⇄	Jackson > Roberts	
89 ○ ⇄	Taylor > Camara	

Full time 0-2

Pompey were brought crashing back to earth with a tame display against Premier League newcomers Wigan, who chalked up an easy win.

Not that this game was ever expected to be a walk in the park. Wigan had so far not only defied, but astounded their many critics by rising to second place in the league with only Chelsea in front of them.

The first half produced few clear cut chances and former Pompey striker Jason Roberts was the closest when he fired wide after finding himself in a good position, but after the break the visitors took control and never looked back.

They took the lead on 48 minutes when Jimmy Bullard's corner was met by Pascal Chimbonda whose header went in at the far post. Jamie Ashdown tipped over Camara's header as the home side clung on, and with twelve minutes remaining any hope of coming back into a game in which the Blues had created few openings was lost. Full-back Chimbonda collected the ball deep in his own half but ran the complete length of the field virtually unchallenged before squaring a ball to Jason Roberts who had the simple task of sweeping home.

Player of the Match

2 Linvoy Primus

Quote

❝ Alain Perrin

We just have to play better if we want to win. It was not a good day.

Venue:	Fratton Park	Referee:	M.Clattenburg - 05/06		Portsmouth
Attendance:	19,102	Matches:	14		Wigan Athletic
		Yellow Cards:	48		
		Red Cards:	3		

Form Coming into Fixture

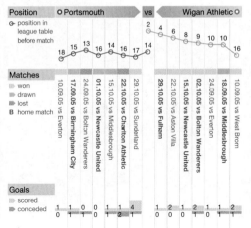

Goal Statistics

Portsmouth

by Half		by Situation	
first:	2	set piece:	2
second:	6	open play:	5
		own goals:	1

Wigan Athletic

by Half		by Situation	
first:	3	set piece:	1
second:	7	open play:	8
		own goals:	1

Goals by Area

Portsmouth
Scored (Conceded)

3 (1)
4 (5)
1 (0)

Wigan Athletic
Scored (Conceded)

1 (0)
7 (2)
2 (1)

Team Statistics

Starting Line-Ups

5/4/1

4/4/2

Unused Sub: Westerveld, Mbesuma

Unused Sub: Pollitt, McMillan, Mahon

Premiership Totals

	Portsmouth	Wigan
Premiership Appearances	799	703
Team Appearances	418	102
Goals Scored	62	38
Assists	80	34
Clean Sheets (goalkeepers)	4	16
Yellow Cards	100	84
Red Cards	8	2
Full Internationals	8	7

Age/Height

Portsmouth Age

27 yrs, 5 mo

Portsmouth Height

5'11"

Wigan Athletic Age

28 yrs, 10 mo

Wigan Athletic Height

5'11"

Match Statistics

League Table after Fixture

		Played	Won	Drawn	Lost	For	Against	Pts
●	2 Wigan	11	8	1	2	13	5	25
...	...	...	...	...	...	...	...	...
↑	14 Fulham	12	3	3	6	12	16	12
↓	15 Portsmouth	12	2	4	6	11	15	10
●	16 Aston Villa	12	2	3	7	10	21	9
●	17 West Brom	12	2	2	8	9	22	8
●	18 Everton	10	2	1	7	3	12	7
●	19 Birmingham	12	1	3	8	7	17	6
●	20 Sunderland	12	1	2	9	11	24	5

Statistics

	Portsmouth	Wigan
Goals	0	2
Shots on Target	4	5
Shots off Target	3	2
Hit Woodwork	0	0
Possession %	43	57
Corners	5	8
Offsides	1	2
Fouls	11	13
Disciplinary Points	4	8

3-0

Liverpool ○
Portsmouth ○

▶ Gary O'Neil keeps Boudewijn Zenden in focus

Event Line

22 ○ ⇄	Morientes > Garcia
23 ○ ⊕	Zenden / H / P / IA
	Assist: Crouch
39 ○ ⊕	Cisse / RF / OP / OA
Half time 2-0	
62 ○	Viafara
64 ○ ⇄	Vukic > Robert
69 ○ ⇄	Alonso > Cisse
70 ○ ⇄	Mbesuma > LuaLua
74 ○ ⇄	Skopelitis > Hughes
75 ○	Hamann
80 ○ ⊕	Morientes / RF / OP / IA
	Assist: Hyypia
83 ○ ⇄	Josemi > Gerrard
Full time 3-0	

Pompey were ruthlessly swept aside by a slick Liverpool with the result rarely in much doubt.

Former Fratton Park striker Peter Crouch was looking for his first goal in red and only a fine save from Jamie Ashdown prevented it when he impressively clawed his header away. Yet the chance for Crouch to break his duck was even greater minutes later after Griffin was somewhat controversially judged to have pushed Zenden to the floor as he burst into the penalty area. Crouch stepped up to the spot, but once more Pompey's 'keeper reacted brilliantly by keeping the spot-kick out with a low save to his right. However, a lurking Zenden forced home the rebound and Ashdown was left cursing his and his side's luck.

Pompey's heroic goalkeeper then produced a brilliant point-blank save from Morientes. But minutes later he was deceived as Cissé ghosted past Vignal on the right wing before putting in a high cross that sailed over Ashdown's head.

The second half was almost damage limitation for Pompey as they intermittently struggled to cope with the speed and pace of the home side. With ten minutes remaining Morientes took advantage of defensive hesitation to strike home the third.

Player of the Match	Quote
15 Jamie Ashdown	❝ **Alain Perrin**

We did not play well in the first half but we were better in the second half.

Venue:	Anfield	Referee:	P.Walton - 05/06		Liverpool
Attendance:	44,394	Matches:	14		Portsmouth
Capacity:	45,362	Yellow Cards:	48		
		Red Cards:	3		

Form Coming into Fixture

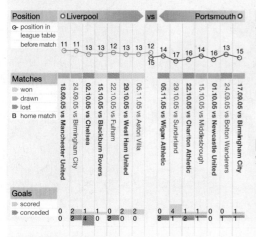

Goal Statistics

Liverpool by Half — first: 2, second: 6; by Situation — set piece: 5, open play: 3

Portsmouth by Half — first: 2, second: 5; by Situation — set piece: 2, open play: 5

Goals by Area

Liverpool Scored (Conceded)

0 (5)
5 (3)
3 (0)

Portsmouth Scored (Conceded)

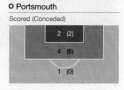

2 (2)
4 (6)
1 (0)

Team Statistics

Starting Line-Ups

Liverpool: Reina; Warnock, Hyypia, Carragher, Finnan; Zenden, Gerrard, Josemi, Hamann, Garcia Morientes; Crouch, Cisse Alonso

4/4/2

Unused Sub: Dudek, Traore

Portsmouth: Vukic; O'Neil, O'Brien, Priske, Vignal; Viafara, Griffin, LuaLua Mbesuma, Hughes Skopelitis, Taylor, Robert; Ashdown

4/5/1

Unused Sub: Westerveld, Primus

Premiership Totals

	Liverpool	Portsmouth
Premiership Appearances	1,386	772
Team Appearances	1,119	322
Goals Scored	117	59
Assists	124	75
Clean Sheets (goalkeepers)	7	4
Yellow Cards	160	85
Red Cards	12	6
Full Internationals	12	8

Age/Height

	Liverpool	Portsmouth
Age	27 yrs, 1 mo	25 yrs, 10 mo
Height	6'	5'11"

Match Statistics

League Table after Fixture

		Played	Won	Drawn	Lost	For	Against	Pts
↑ 8	Liverpool	11	5	4	2	12	8	19
...		...	...	...	...	...	...	...
● 14	Fulham	12	3	3	6	12	16	12
↑ 15	Aston Villa	13	3	3	7	13	22	12
↑ 16	West Brom	13	3	2	8	13	22	11
↓ 17	Portsmouth	13	2	4	7	11	18	10
↓ 18	Everton	12	3	1	8	4	16	10
● 19	Birmingham	12	1	3	8	7	17	6
● 20	Sunderland	13	1	2	10	12	27	5

Statistics

	Liverpool	Portsmouth
Goals	3	0
Shots on Target	11	6
Shots off Target	4	2
Hit Woodwork	0	0
Possession %	66	34
Corners	7	6
Offsides	3	1
Fouls	7	8
Disciplinary Points	4	4

0-2

Portsmouth ○
Chelsea ○

▶ Andy O'Brien demonstrates his defensive strengths

Event Line

27 ○ ⊕ Crespo / RF / OP / IA	
	Assist: Ferreira
38 ○ ⇄ Cole C > Crespo	
Half time 0-1	
52 ○ ▪ Diao	
57 ○ ▪ Cole C	
60 ○ ▪ Hughes	
63 ○ ⇄ Todorov > Silva	
64 ○ ▪ Griffin	
66 ○ ▪ Stefanovic	
67 ○ ⊕ Lampard / RF / P / IA	
	Assist: Cole J
78 ○ ⇄ Viafara > Hughes	
79 ○ ⇄ Wright-Phillips > Duff	
83 ○ ⇄ Geremi > Cole J	
87 ○ ▪ Taylor	
Full time 0-2	

Alain Perrin had paid the price in the week for a Pompey run that still saw the Blues without a home win with December just around the corner and Joe Jordan took temporary charge.

Though Pompey put up a gutsy display, the nouveau riche Londoners proved too much of a challenge for a side short on confidence, goals and home wins.

On seventeen minutes 'keeper Cech reacted brilliantly to turn LuaLua's volley away and ten minutes later the visitors took a lead that would be rarely threatened. The goal was somewhat fortunate when Hernan Crespo got behind Pompey's defence and stuck a foot out as Paulo Ferreira's shot was fizzing wide. It was enough to divert the ball past a bewildered Ashdown though who was a helpless spectator.

With twenty minutes of the second half gone Joe Cole was allegedly brought down by Stefanovic as he advanced into the area and Frank Lampard dispatched the penalty. Ashdown then saved well from Gudjohnson and Geremi grazed the post, but a more emphatic victory would have been harsh on Pompey.

Player of the Match	Quote
32 Lomana LuaLua	❝ **Joe Jordan**
	The players tried very hard and were committed but unfortunately there was to be no breaking them.

Venue:	Fratton Park	Referee:	P.Dowd - 05/06		Portsmouth
Attendance:	20,182	Matches:	14		Chelsea
		Yellow Cards:	52		
		Red Cards:	2		

Form Coming into Fixture

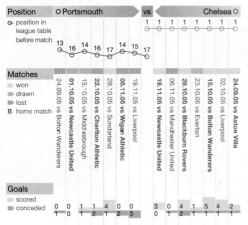

Position
- position in league table before match

Portsmouth vs Chelsea

Portsmouth: 13, 16, 14, 16, 17, 14, 15, 17
Chelsea: 1, 1, 1, 1, 1, 1, 1, 1

Matches
- won
- drawn
- lost
- B home match

Portsmouth: 24.09.05 vs Bolton Wanderers, 01.10.05 vs Newcastle United, 15.10.05 vs Middlesbrough, 22.10.05 vs Charlton Athletic, 29.10.05 vs Sunderland, 05.11.05 vs Wigan Athletic, 19.11.05 vs Liverpool

Chelsea: 19.11.05 vs Newcastle United, 06.11.05 vs Manchester United, 29.10.05 vs Everton, 23.10.05 vs Blackburn Rovers, 15.10.05 vs Bolton Wanderers, 02.10.05 vs Liverpool, 24.09.05 vs Aston Villa

Goals
- scored
- conceded

Portsmouth: 0/1, 0/0, 1/1, 1/2, 4/1, 0/2, 0/3
Chelsea: 3/0, 0/1, 4/2, 1/1, 5/1, 4/1, 2/1

Goal Statistics

Portsmouth

by Half
- first: 1
- second: 5

by Situation
- set piece: 1
- open play: 5

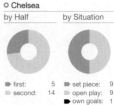

Chelsea

by Half
- first: 5
- second: 14

by Situation
- set piece: 9
- open play: 9
- own goals: 1

Goals by Area

Portsmouth

Scored (Conceded)
- 1 (2)
- 4 (7)
- 1 (1)

Chelsea

Scored (Conceded)
- 3 (1)
- 11 (6)
- 5 (0)

Team Statistics

Starting Line-Ups

Portsmouth:
Ashdown
Griffin, Taylor, Stefanovic, Hughes (Viafara), O'Brien, Diao, Priske, O'Neil, LuaLua, Silva (Todorov)

Chelsea:
Cech
Cole J (Geremi), Ferreira, Gudjohnsen, Carvalho, Crespo (Cole C), Essien, Terry, Lampard, Duff (Wright-Phillips), Gallas

▶ 4/4/1/1

▶ 4/3/3

Unused Sub: Westerveld, Vignal, Vukic

Unused Sub: Cudicini, Del Horno

Premiership Totals	O Portsmouth	Chelsea O
Premiership Appearances	808	1,576
Team Appearances	379	994
Goals Scored	46	247
Assists	34	208
Clean Sheets (goalkeepers)	4	30
Yellow Cards	95	134
Red Cards	8	6
Full Internationals	9	13

Age/Height

Portsmouth Age
▶ 27 yrs, 1 mo

Chelsea Age
▶ 25 yrs, 11 mo

Portsmouth Height
▶ 5'11"

Chelsea Height
▶ 6'

Match Statistics

League Table after Fixture

		Played	Won	Drawn	Lost	For	Against	Pts
●	1 Chelsea	14	12	1	1	33	7	37
...	...	...	...	...	...	...	...	...
↑	14 Aston Villa	14	4	3	7	14	22	15
↓	15 Fulham	13	3	3	7	14	19	12
●	16 West Brom	13	3	2	8	13	22	11
●	17 Portsmouth	14	2	4	8	11	20	10
●	18 Everton	12	3	1	8	4	16	10
●	19 Birmingham	13	2	3	8	8	17	9
●	20 Sunderland	14	1	2	11	12	28	5

Statistics	O Portsmouth	Chelsea O
Goals	0	2
Shots on Target	2	7
Shots off Target	4	6
Hit Woodwork	0	0
Possession %	38	62
Corners	2	1
Offsides	1	1
Fouls	22	7
Disciplinary Points	20	4

3-0

Manchester United ○
Portsmouth ○

▶ Gary O'Neil slides in on Wayne Rooney

Event Line

20 ○ ⊕	Scholes / H / C / IA
	Assist: Giggs
Half time 1-0	
46 ⇄	Richardson > O'Shea
59 ○ ⇄	Todorov > Silva
65 ○ ⇄	Ronaldo > Giggs
68 ○	Griffin
72 ○ ⇄	Robert > Taylor
79 ⇄	Saha > Park
80 ○ ⊕	Rooney / RF / OP / IA
84 ○ ⊕	van Nistelrooy / RF / OP / IA
	Assist: Ronaldo
Full time 3-0	

Old Trafford is not the ideal place to visit at the best of times, but when you are struggling it can be akin to a 'theatre of nightmares' as opposed to one of 'dreams'.

After bossing the opening twenty minutes the hosts took the lead that seemed to be on the cards when Giggs flighted over a corner which was headed home by an unmarked Paul Scholes for his first goal of the season.

Pompey rallied at the start of the second half and Van der Sar had to be at his best to tip Taylor's effort over the bar, but it was hardly concerted pressure and both Rooney and van Nistelrooy missed chances to let Pompey further off the hook at the other end.

Ten minutes from time the game was wrapped up when Griffin seemed to have averted immediate danger by dispossessing Saha, but the ball ran kindly into the path of Rooney who needed no second invitation to gobble up the chance. Four minutes later Pompey were hit again as van Nistelrooy latched on to Ronaldo's cross to chip Jamie Ashdown.

Player of the Match	Quote	Premiership Milestone
15 Jamie Ashdown	❻ **Joe Jordan**	▶ **50**
	I enjoyed the build-up and preparation and taking that responsibility but I didn't enjoy the result and I certainly didn't enjoy the last 15 minutes.	Lomana Tresor LuaLua made his 50th Premiership appearance in the colours of Portsmouth.

Venue:	Old Trafford	Referee:	C.J.Foy - 05/06		Manchester United
Attendance:	67,684	Matches:	16		Portsmouth
Capacity:	73,006	Yellow Cards:	38		
		Red Cards:	4		

Form Coming into Fixture

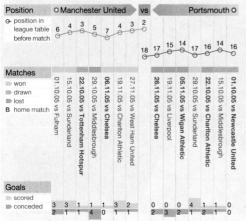

Goal Statistics

Manchester United

by Half — by Situation

- first: 7
- second: 7
- set piece: 4
- open play: 10

Portsmouth

by Half — by Situation

- first: 1
- second: 5
- set piece: 1
- open play: 5

Goals by Area

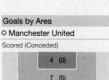

Manchester United — Scored (Conceded)

- 4 (0)
- 7 (5)
- 3 (5)

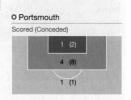

Portsmouth — Scored (Conceded)

- 1 (2)
- 4 (8)
- 1 (1)

Team Statistics

Starting Line-Ups

Manchester United: O'Shea, Richardson, Giggs, Ronaldo, Viafara, Priske, Silvestre, Scholes, van Nistelrooy, LuaLua, Diao, O'Brien, van der Sar, Ferdinand, Smith, Rooney, Silva/Todorov, O'Neil, Stefanovic, Anderson, Brown, Park/Saha, Taylor/Robert, Griffin

4/4/2 — Manchester United

4/4/2 — Portsmouth

Unused Sub: Howard, Fletcher

Unused Sub: Westerveld, Primus, Vukic

Premiership Totals	Man Utd	Portsmouth
Premiership Appearances	2,277	920
Team Appearances	1,634	363
Goals Scored	397	69
Assists	351	82
Clean Sheets (goalkeepers)	47	4
Yellow Cards	230	106
Red Cards	11	10
Full Internationals	14	9

Age/Height

	Manchester United	Portsmouth
Age	26 yrs, 8 mo	27 yrs, 5 mo
Height	6'	5'11"

Match Statistics

League Table after Fixture

		Played	Won	Drawn	Lost	For	Against	Pts
● 2	Man Utd	14	9	3	2	24	13	30
...	...	...	...	...	...	...	...	...
● 14	Fulham	15	4	4	7	16	20	16
● 15	Aston Villa	15	4	4	7	15	23	16
● 16	Everton	14	5	1	8	7	16	16
● 17	West Brom	15	3	4	8	15	24	13
● 18	Portsmouth	15	2	4	9	11	23	10
● 19	Birmingham	13	2	3	8	8	17	9
● 20	Sunderland	16	1	2	13	14	33	5

Statistics	Man Utd	Portsmouth
Goals	3	0
Shots on Target	12	4
Shots off Target	7	4
Hit Woodwork	0	0
Possession %	58	42
Corners	11	4
Offsides	1	0
Fouls	9	16
Disciplinary Points	0	4

3-1

Tottenham Hotspur ○
Portsmouth ○

Premiership
12.12.05

▶ Lomana Tresor LuaLua takes on Ledley King

The second coming of Harry Redknapp dominated the pre-match focus of this Monday night clash and his first game back in charge saw a spirited display spoiled by a contentious decision from referee Uriah Rennie.

If ever a manager needed to get off to a winning start it was Harry and LuaLua gave the side just that with a terrific trademark goal. From twenty yards out he struck home an instinctive out of the blue drive that flew past Robinson mid-way through the first half.

On fifty-seven minutes though Tottenham drew level when Ledley King powered home Carrick's cross. Pompey continued to contest an equally balanced match, but on eighty-five minutes they were cruelly undone. Spurs won themselves a debatable free kick on the edge of the area, but Reid's drive was blocked by the defensive wall. However, official Rennie ruled that it had been the hand of O'Neil which had stopped the effort and pointed to the spot, with Mido converting.

In injury time Defoe got the better of Griffin to fire under Ashdown and give the scoreline a thoroughly flattering look.

Player of the Match

22 Richard Hughes

Quote

🎙 **Harry Redknapp**

It was always going to be hard, the way things were going but if the players show the same spirit and effort they will do well for me.

Venue:	White Hart Lane	Referee:	U.D.Rennie - 05/06		Tottenham Hotspur
Attendance:	36,141	Matches:	17		Portsmouth
Capacity:	36,247	Yellow Cards:	28		
		Red Cards:	2		

Form Coming into Fixture

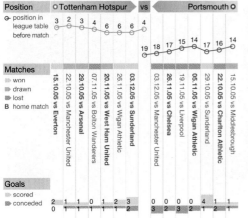

Position — position in league table before match

Tottenham Hotspur: 3 2 3 4 6 6 6 4
Portsmouth: 19 18 17 15 14 17 16 14

Matches
- won
- drawn
- lost
- B home match

Tottenham matches:
15.10.05 vs Everton
22.10.05 vs Manchester United
29.10.05 vs Arsenal
07.11.05 vs Bolton Wanderers
20.11.05 vs West Ham United
26.11.05 vs Sunderland
03.12.05 vs Manchester United

Portsmouth matches:
26.11.05 vs Chelsea
19.11.05 vs Liverpool
05.11.05 vs Wigan Athletic
29.10.05 vs Sunderland
22.10.05 vs Charlton Athletic
15.10.05 vs Middlesbrough

Goals
- scored
- conceded

Tottenham: scored 2 1 1 0 1 2 3 / conceded 0 1 1 1 1 1 2
Portsmouth: scored 0 0 0 0 4 1 1 / conceded 3 2 3 2 1 2 1

Goal Statistics

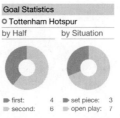

Tottenham Hotspur

by Half		by Situation	
first:	4	set piece:	3
second:	6	open play:	7

Portsmouth

by Half		by Situation	
first:	1	set piece:	1
second:	5	open play:	5

Goals by Area

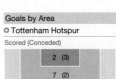

Tottenham Hotspur — Scored (Conceded)

2 (3)
7 (2)
1 (2)

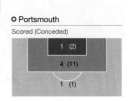

Portsmouth — Scored (Conceded)

1 (2)
4 (11)
1 (1)

Team Statistics

Starting Line-Ups

Tottenham Hotspur: Robinson; Stalteri, Dawson, King, Carrick, Davids, Tainio/Routledge, Keane/Defoe, Mido, Jenas, Lee

Portsmouth: Ashdown; Griffin, Stefanovic, Hughes, O'Brien, O'Neil, Viafara, Pericard, Taylor/Robert, Primus, LuaLua

4/4/2 (Diamond)

4/5/1

Unused Sub: Cerny, Kelly

Unused Sub: Westerveld, Cisse, Priske, Todorov

Premiership Totals

	Tottenham	Portsmouth
Premiership Appearances	1,038	949
Team Appearances	543	444
Goals Scored	141	66
Assists	109	77
Clean Sheets (goalkeepers)	36	4
Yellow Cards	73	107
Red Cards	3	9
Full Internationals	12	6

Age/Height

Tottenham Hotspur Age	Portsmouth Age
25 yrs, 1 mo	**26 yrs, 9 mo**
Tottenham Hotspur Height	Portsmouth Height
5'11"	**5'11"**

Match Statistics

League Table after Fixture

		Played	Won	Drawn	Lost	For	Against	Pts
● 4	Tottenham	16	8	6	2	22	13	30
...		...	...	...	...	...	...	...
● 14	Aston Villa	16	4	5	7	16	24	17
● 15	Everton	15	5	2	8	8	17	17
● 16	Fulham	16	4	4	8	16	21	16
● 17	West Brom	16	4	4	8	17	24	16
● 18	Birmingham	15	3	3	9	10	19	12
● 19	Portsmouth	16	2	4	10	12	26	10
● 20	Sunderland	17	1	2	14	14	35	5

Statistics

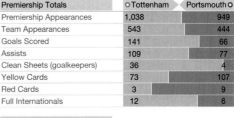

Statistics	Tottenham	Portsmouth
Goals	3	1
Shots on Target	10	5
Shots off Target	7	3
Hit Woodwork	0	0
Possession %	54	46
Corners	6	3
Offsides	2	2
Fouls	6	19
Disciplinary Points	0	0

1-0

Portsmouth ○
West Bromwich Albion ○

▶ Harry Redknapp makes an emotional return to Fratton Park

Event Line

6 ○ ⇄ Todorov > Pericard
7 ○ ▢ Wallwork
Half time 0-0
56 ○ ⊕ Todorov / RF / OP / IA
    Assist: LuaLua
59 ○ ▢ Taylor
65 ○ ⇄ Earnshaw > Kamara
89 ○ ⇄ Priske > Todorov
90 ○ ⇄ Campbell > Greening
Full time 1-0

It was imperative for Pompey to get something from this clash and they followed up their spirited showing at Spurs five days previously by finally putting the home supporters out of their misery.

Harry Redknapp's first home match in charge had created a buzz of anticipation and the crowd were not to be disappointed.

Fittingly it was a Svetoslav Todorov goal after fifty-six minutes which settled this tense affair. The Bulgarian striker who had endured a two year injury nightmare on the sidelines was only on the field after Vincent Pericard had been forced off through injury after six minutes. It had been a blow, but Todorov changed the script and his moment came when LuaLua burst down the right and delivered a low cross for the striker who deftly chipped Kuszczak in the West Brom goal.

The game was played out to its conclusion before a sea of nerves as the first home win came within touching distance. West Brom failed to threaten however and joy exploded around Fratton Park as Christmas came early with the best ever present.

Player of the Match	Quote	Premiership Milestone
11 Laurent Robert	🔘 **Svetoslav Todorov**	▶ **First Goal**

It was good to score, but it was a difficult game and we needed the three points so it was good to take them.

Svetoslav Todorov netted his first Premiership goal for Portsmouth.

Venue:	Fratton Park	Referee:	M.R.Halsey - 05/06		**Portsmouth**
Attendance:	20,052	Matches:	16		**West Bromwich Albion**
		Yellow Cards:	24		
		Red Cards:	4		

Form Coming into Fixture

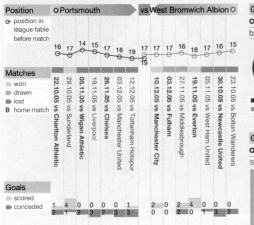

Goal Statistics

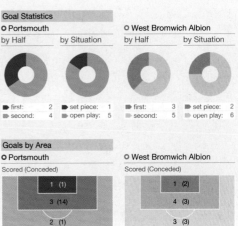

○ Portsmouth

by Half		by Situation	
► first:	2	► set piece:	1
► second:	4	► open play:	5

○ West Bromwich Albion

by Half		by Situation	
► first:	3	► set piece:	2
► second:	5	► open play:	6

Goals by Area

○ Portsmouth
Scored (Conceded)

1 (1)
3 (14)
2 (1)

○ West Bromwich Albion
Scored (Conceded)

1 (2)
4 (3)
3 (3)

Team Statistics

Starting Line-Ups

► 4/5/1

► 4/4/2

Unused Sub: Westerveld, Cisse, Viafara

Unused Sub: Kirkland, Moore, Carter

Premiership Totals

	○ Portsmouth	West Brom ○
Premiership Appearances	985	1,065
Team Appearances	466	435
Goals Scored	67	153
Assists	81	118
Clean Sheets (goalkeepers)	4	4
Yellow Cards	107	89
Red Cards	9	2
Full Internationals	7	6

Age/Height

Portsmouth Age	West Bromwich Albion Age
► **26 yrs, 11 mo**	► **26 yrs, 7 mo**
Portsmouth Height	West Bromwich Albion Height
► **5'11"**	► **6'**

Match Statistics

League Table after Fixture

		Played	Won	Drawn	Lost	For	Against	Pts
●	12 Blackburn	17	6	3	8	19	24	21
●	13 Middlesbrough	16	5	4	7	20	23	19
↑	14 Fulham	17	5	4	8	18	22	19
↓	15 Aston Villa	17	4	5	8	16	26	17
↓	16 Everton	17	5	2	10	9	23	17
●	17 West Brom	17	4	4	9	17	25	16
↑	18 Portsmouth	17	3	4	10	13	26	13
↓	19 Birmingham	16	3	3	10	11	23	12
●	20 Sunderland	17	1	2	14	14	35	5

Statistics

	○ Portsmouth	West Brom ○
Goals	1	0
Shots on Target	4	2
Shots off Target	1	2
Hit Woodwork	0	0
Possession %	55	45
Corners	6	8
Offsides	5	1
Fouls	15	7
Disciplinary Points	4	4

1-1

Portsmouth ○
West Ham United ○

Premiership
26.12.05

➡ Richard Hughes goes in strongly on Carl Fletcher

Event Line

12 ○ ⇄ Fletcher > Mullins	
17 ○ ⊕ O'Neil / RF / OP / IA	
Assist: Robert	
20 ○ ⇄ Priske > Primus	
33 ○ ⇄ Gabbidon > Repka	
33 ○ ▢ Taylor	
39 ○ ⇄ Dailly > Gabbidon	
Half time 1-0	
56 ○ ⊕ Collins / RF / IFK / IA	
Assist: Ferdinand	
63 ○ ▢ Hughes	
64 ○ ▢ Reo-Coker	
84 ○ ◢ Robert	
2nd Bookable Offence	
86 ○ ⇄ Viafara > Silva	
Full time 1-1	

Harry Redknapp will have been content with a point against his former club whom he managed against for the first time since leaving Upton Park.

This draw allowed Pompey to move within two points of West Brom having trailed them by six just a week previously.

After a bright beginning to clear the Christmas cobwebs Pompey took the lead on 17 minutes when LuaLua fed Laurent Robert whose low cross was converted by Gary O'Neil. West Ham shook off their slumbers and Harewood brought a great save from Ashdown who turned his twenty-five yard effort away. But minutes later the Hammers were level when Collins latched onto Ferdinand's header from a Newton free kick to fire home.

Robert received his marching orders six minutes from time for a second bookable offence when fouling Konchesky and in the end Pompey were grateful for the point which brought them closer to their relegation rivals.

Player of the Match

32 Lomana LuaLua

Quote

🍺 **Harry Redknapp**

At half time the points were there for the taking, but we didn't get hold of the ball in the second half and made lots of wrong decisions. We worked so hard that we seemed to run out of steam in the second half.

Venue:	Fratton Park	Referee:	A.G.Wiley - 05/06		**Portsmouth**
Attendance:	20,168	Matches:	21		**West Ham United**
		Yellow Cards:	61		
		Red Cards:	3		

Form Coming into Fixture

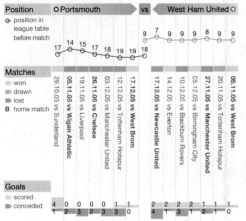

Position
G- position in league table before match

Matches
- won
- drawn
- lost
- B home match

Goals
- scored
- conceded

Goal Statistics

O Portsmouth
by Half | by Situation

- first: 1
- second: 5
- set piece: 1
- open play: 5

O West Ham United
by Half | by Situation

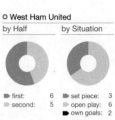

- first: 6
- second: 5
- set piece: 3
- open play: 6
- own goals: 2

Goals by Area

O Portsmouth
Scored (Conceded)

O West Ham United
Scored (Conceded)

Team Statistics

Starting Line-Ups

Ashdown
Griffin — Taylor — Newton — Repka / Gabbidon
Stefanovic — Hughes — Silva / Viafara — Harewood — Reo-Coker — Ferdinand — Carroll
O'Brien — O'Neil — LuaLua — Zamora — Mullins / Fletcher — Collins
Primus / Priske — Robert — Etherington — Konchesky

▶ 4/4/2   ▶ 4/4/2

Unused Sub: Westerveld, Karadas, Todorov

Unused Sub: Hislop, Bellion

Premiership Totals

	O Portsmouth	West Ham O
Premiership Appearances	985	742
Team Appearances	480	322
Goals Scored	69	26
Assists	79	44
Clean Sheets (goalkeepers)	5	27
Yellow Cards	109	94
Red Cards	9	6
Full Internationals	8	7

Age/Height

Portsmouth Age	West Ham United Age
▶ **27 yrs, 8 mo**	▶ **26 yrs, 3 mo**
Portsmouth Height	West Ham United Height
▶ **5'11"**	▶ **5'11"**

Match Statistics

League Table after Fixture

	Played	Won	Drawn	Lost	For	Against	Pts
● 9 West Ham	18	7	5	6	26	23	26
...	...	...	...	...	...	...	...
↑ 14 Aston Villa	18	5	5	8	20	26	20
↓ 15 Fulham	18	5	4	9	20	25	19
● 16 Everton	18	5	2	11	9	27	17
● 17 West Brom	18	4	4	10	17	28	16
● 18 Portsmouth	18	3	5	10	14	27	14
● 19 Birmingham	17	3	3	11	11	25	12
● 20 Sunderland	18	1	3	14	14	35	6

Statistics

	O Portsmouth	West Ham O
Goals	1	1
Shots on Target	9	4
Shots off Target	2	10
Hit Woodwork	0	1
Possession %	51	49
Corners	6	5
Offsides	3	0
Fouls	14	10
Disciplinary Points	18	4

4-0

Arsenal ○
Portsmouth ○

▶ Aliou Cisse plays a simple pass

Event Line	
7 ○ ⊕ Bergkamp / RF / OP / IA	
Assist: Reyes	
13 ○ ⊕ Reyes / LF / OP / IA	
Assist: Henry	
37 ○ ⊕ Henry / LF / OP / IA	
Assist: Flamini	
39 ○ ▢ Hughes	
43 ○ ⊕ Henry / RF / P / IA	
Assist: Reyes	
Half time 4-0	
46 ○ ⇄ Todorov > Vukic	
67 ○ ⇄ Eboue > Reyes	
72 ○ ⇄ Fabregas > Gilberto Silva	
83 ○ ⇄ Mornar > LuaLua	
90 ○ ⇄ Skopelitis > Hughes	
Full time 4-0	

This was a Highbury horror show on Pompey's last ever league visit to the famous ground.

Effectively Pompey were out of the contest within fifteen minutes. Dennis Bergkamp set the ball rolling after just seven minutes when Reyes fed the Dutch forward to hit home after the Spaniard had burst down the left. Six minutes later Thierry Henry advanced on Pompey's threadbare defence and awaited his moment to play through Reyes who made it 2-0.

Two became three on thirty six minutes when Flamini sent Henry racing through the centre to waltz round Ashdown and plant the ball home and just before half time matters worsened. Referee Mark Clattenburg spotted an infringement, adjudging Griffin to have pushed Reyes, and Henry audaciously swept the spot kick home.

After the break LuaLua so nearly scored when he struck the bar, but normal service was quickly resumed though thankfully Pompey were far more resolute and Arsenal far less irresistible. In the end avoiding conceding more goals to add to an ever worsening goal difference became a moral victory in itself.

Player of the Match	Quote
32 Lomana LuaLua	❝ **Richard Hughes**

It was a very proud moment to be the captain and lead out a Portsmouth team in a Premiership game at Highbury, where it all started for me. But that's where it ended.

Venue:	Highbury	Referee:	M.Clattenburg - 05/06	**Arsenal**
Attendance:	38,223	Matches:	20	**Portsmouth**
Capacity:	38,419	Yellow Cards:	71	
		Red Cards:	4	

Form Coming into Fixture

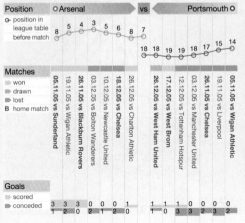

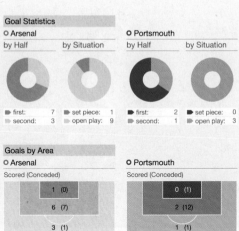

Goal Statistics

○ Arsenal

by Half | by Situation

- first: 7
- second: 3
- set piece: 1
- open play: 9

○ Portsmouth

by Half | by Situation

- first: 2
- second: 1
- set piece: 0
- open play: 3

Goals by Area

○ Arsenal

Scored (Conceded)

| 1 (0) |
| 6 (7) |
| 3 (1) |

○ Portsmouth

Scored (Conceded)

| 0 (1) |
| 2 (12) |
| 1 (1) |

Team Statistics

Starting Line-Ups

Lehmann

Cygan, Reyes / Eboue, Campbell, Flamini, Henry, LuaLua / Mornar, Bergkamp, Toure, Gilberto Silva / Fabregas, Vukic / Todorov, Lauren, Pires

Viafara, Griffin, Cisse, O'Brien, Ashdown, Hughes / Skopelitis, Priske, Taylor, Vignal

▶ 4/4/2

▶ 4/4/1/1

Unused Sub: Almunia, Senderos, Ljungberg

Unused Sub: Westerveld, Karadas

Premiership Totals

	○ Arsenal	Portsmouth ○
Premiership Appearances	1,721	729
Team Appearances	1,466	358
Goals Scored	339	35
Assists	291	29
Clean Sheets (goalkeepers)	33	5
Yellow Cards	170	93
Red Cards	6	5
Full Internationals	10	9

Age/Height

Arsenal Age	Portsmouth Age
▶ **28 yrs, 1 mo**	▶ **27 yrs**
Arsenal Height	Portsmouth Height
▶ **6'**	▶ **6'**

Match Statistics

League Table after Fixture

	Played	Won	Drawn	Lost	For	Against	Pts
↑ 6 Arsenal	18	10	2	6	27	15	32
...	...	...	...	...	...	...	...
↑ 14 Fulham	19	5	5	9	23	28	20
↓ 15 Middlesbrough	18	5	5	8	23	28	20
↑ 16 West Brom	19	5	4	10	19	28	19
↓ 17 Everton	19	5	2	12	10	30	17
● 18 Portsmouth	19	3	5	11	14	31	14
● 19 Birmingham	18	3	4	11	13	27	13
● 20 Sunderland	18	1	3	14	14	35	6

Statistics

	○ Arsenal	Portsmouth ○
Goals	4	0
Shots on Target	5	4
Shots off Target	2	2
Hit Woodwork	0	1
Possession %	65	35
Corners	3	1
Offsides	1	8
Fouls	12	13
Disciplinary Points	0	4

1-0 Portsmouth ○
Fulham ○

➤ Gary O'Neil confronts Tomasz Radzinski

Event Line

28 ○ ⇄ John > Helguson
41 ○ ▢ Rosenior
43 ○ ⊕ O'Neil / LF / OP / IA
    Assist: Silva

Half time 1-0

59 ○ ⇄ Bocanegra > Elrich
85 ○ ▢ Bocanegra
86 ○ ⇄ Karadas > Silva
87 ○ ▢ Karadas
90 ○ ⇄ Cisse > Robert

Full time 1-0

Pompey ended 2005 on a note of high optimism by securing their second home win of the season and making it seven points out of a possible nine at Fratton Park since Harry Redknapp's return.

A Gary O'Neil strike late in the first half settled a drab contest and though the victory was not enough to pull Pompey out of the relegation zone, it kept them in touch, with just two points between them and West Brom.

The goal, like the match, was scrappy. Silva's cross was prodded on by LuaLua and the bobbling ball seemed to come off O'Neil's arm as it evaded Warner in the Fulham goal.

Forwards LuaLua and Silva both caused problems in a first half that Pompey controlled without ever threatening to break loose. In the second half they were content to hold on to what they had and look for the break against a Fulham side who were hardly raising the blood pressure to any great extent. Striker LuaLua looked certain to make the breathing easier after fine work by Silva and O'Neil, but with only Warner to beat, he blasted high into the Fratton End. It was not to prove costly.

Player of the Match

26 Gary O'Neil

Quote

❝ **Harry Redknapp**

It was a great performance and three great points.

Venue:	Fratton Park	Referee:	M.A.Riley - 05/06		Portsmouth
Attendance:	19,101	Matches:	19		Fulham
		Yellow Cards:	67		
		Red Cards:	4		

Form Coming into Fixture

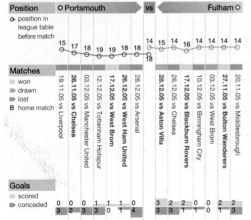

Position
o- position in league table before match

Portsmouth: 15 17 18 19 19 18 18 18
Fulham: 14 15 14 16 14 14 14 14

Matches
- won
- drawn
- lost
- B home match

Portsmouth fixtures: 19.11.05 vs Liverpool, 26.11.05 vs Chelsea, 03.12.05 vs Manchester United, 12.12.05 vs Tottenham Hotspur, 17.12.05 vs West Brom, 26.12.05 vs West Ham United, 28.12.05 vs Arsenal

Fulham fixtures: 28.12.05 vs Aston Villa, 26.12.05 vs Chelsea, 17.12.05 vs Blackburn Rovers, 10.12.05 vs Birmingham City, 03.12.05 vs West Brom, 27.11.05 vs Bolton Wanderers, 20.11.05 vs Middlesbrough

Goals
- scored
- conceded

Portsmouth: scored 0 0 0 1 1 1 0 / conceded 3 2 3 3 0 1 4
Fulham: scored 3 2 2 0 0 2 2 / conceded 3 3 1 1 0 1 3

Goal Statistics

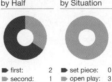

Portsmouth
by Half / by Situation
- first: 2
- second: 1
- set piece: 0
- open play: 3

Fulham
by Half / by Situation
- first: 7
- second: 4
- set piece: 5
- open play: 6

Goals by Area

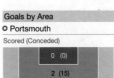

Portsmouth — Scored (Conceded)
0 (0)
2 (15)
1 (1)

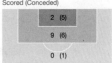

Fulham — Scored (Conceded)
2 (5)
9 (6)
0 (1)

Team Statistics

Starting Line-Ups

Portsmouth: Westerveld; Griffin, Taylor, Stefanovic, Hughes, Silva Karadas, Helguson John, O'Brien, O'Neil, LuaLua, McBride, Priske, Robert Cisse

Fulham: Elrich Bocanegra, Leacock, Legwinski, Knight, Warner, Boa Morte, Goma, Radzinski, Rosenior

4/4/2 (Portsmouth)   **4/4/2** (Fulham)

Unused Sub: Guatelli, Viafara, Todorov

Unused Sub: Drobny, Jensen N, Pearce

Premiership Totals

	o Portsmouth	Fulham o
Premiership Appearances	1,043	948
Team Appearances	427	761
Goals Scored	68	108
Assists	83	87
Clean Sheets (goalkeepers)	28	2
Yellow Cards	124	129
Red Cards	12	11
Full Internationals	10	9

Age/Height

Portsmouth Age	Fulham Age
27 yrs, 9 mo	**27 yrs, 8 mo**
Portsmouth Height	Fulham Height
5'11"	**5'11"**

Match Statistics

League Table after Fixture

	Played	Won	Drawn	Lost	For	Against	Pts
● 12 Charlton	18	8	1	9	23	27	25
● 13 Aston Villa	20	5	7	8	23	29	22
↑ 14 Middlesbrough	19	5	6	8	23	28	21
↓ 15 Fulham	20	5	5	10	23	29	20
↑ 16 Everton	20	6	2	12	11	30	20
↓ 17 West Brom	20	5	4	11	19	29	19
● 18 Portsmouth	20	4	5	11	15	31	17
● 19 Birmingham	19	3	4	12	13	29	13
● 20 Sunderland	19	1	3	15	14	36	6

Statistics

	o Portsmouth	Fulham o
Goals	1	0
Shots on Target	7	4
Shots off Target	10	5
Hit Woodwork	0	0
Possession %	54	46
Corners	8	8
Offsides	5	2
Fouls	14	7
Disciplinary Points	4	8

2-1

Blackburn Rovers ○
Portsmouth ○

▶ Salif Diao is a pillar of strength in midfield

Event Line

3 ○ ⊕	Taylor	/ LF / DFK / OA
9 ○ ⊕	Pedersen	/ LF / DFK / OA
	Assist: Dickov	
13 ○	Diao	
34 ○	Cisse	
39 ○ ⊕	Dickov	/ H / OP / 6Y
	Assist: Reid	

Half time 2-1

46 ○ ⇄	Todorov > Silva	
47 ○	Stefanovic	
60 ○	Griffin	
62 ○	Pedersen	
66 ○ ⇄	Emerton > Bentley	
66 ○ ⇄	Bellamy > Dickov	
76 ○ ⇄	Robert > Cisse	
82 ○ ⇄	Karadas > Taylor	
90 ○ ⇄	Tugay > Kuqi	

Full time 2-1

The news on the first away trip of the New Year was all concentrated on the emergence of Alexandre Gaydamak who was later to be officially confirmed as Pompey's new co-owner.

The side made the perfect start after just three minutes when they took the lead with a marvellous strike. Ryan Nelsen was ruled to have handled the ball outside the area and from the resulting free kick Matthew Taylor curled a delectable free kick around the wall and past Brad Friedel.

It was a lead that was only to last six minutes however as Blackburn won a free kick of their own in similar territory after Andy O'Brien had brought down the waspish Paul Dickov. Morten Gamst Pedersen produced an almost identical strike which flew past Westerveld in the Pompey goal.

Things took a turn for the worse shortly before half time when Pompey's 'keeper failed to hold onto Steven Reid's long strike, Dickov nodding the rebound home.

After the break both sides created chances as one looked for consolidation and the other for a way back. Neither found the answer as Pompey faced a long trip home pointless.

Player of the Match	Quote
5 Andy O'Brien	❝ **Harry Redknapp**

I thought that in the second half we did well and had some good opportunities to have perhaps got something from the game.

Venue:	Ewood Park	Referee:	M.L.Dean - 05/06		Blackburn Rovers
Attendance:	19,521	Matches:	19		Portsmouth
Capacity:	31,367	Yellow Cards:	51		
		Red Cards:	4		

Form Coming into Fixture

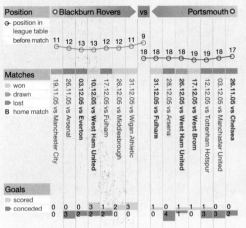

Position
- position in league table before match

Blackburn Rovers: 11 12 13 13 12 12 11
Portsmouth: 9 18 18 18 18 19 19 18 17

Matches
- won
- drawn
- lost
- B home match

Blackburn Rovers:
- 19.11.05 vs Manchester City
- 26.11.05 vs Arsenal
- **03.12.05 vs Everton**
- **10.12.05 vs West Ham United**
- 17.12.05 vs Fulham
- 26.12.05 vs Middlesbrough
- 31.12.05 vs Wigan Athletic

Portsmouth:
- **31.12.05 vs Fulham**
- 28.12.05 vs Arsena
- **26.12.05 vs West Ham United**
- **17.12.05 vs West Brom**
- 12.12.05 vs Tottenham Hotspur
- 03.12.05 vs Manchester United
- **26.11.05 vs Chelsea**

Goals
- scored
- conceded

Blackburn scored: 0 0 0 3 1 2 3
Blackburn conceded: 0 3 2 2 2 0 0
Portsmouth scored: 1 0 1 1 1 0 0
Portsmouth conceded: 0 4 0 3 3 2

Goal Statistics

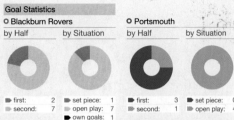

Blackburn Rovers

by Half
- first: 2
- second: 7

by Situation
- set piece: 1
- open play: 7
- own goals: 1

Portsmouth

by Half
- first: 3
- second: 1

by Situation
- set piece: 0
- open play: 4

Goals by Area

Blackburn Rovers
Scored (Conceded)

3 (2)
5 (5)
1 (2)

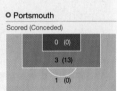

Portsmouth
Scored (Conceded)

0 (0)
3 (13)
1 (0)

Team Statistics

Starting Line-Ups

Matteo, Pedersen
Nelson, Savage
Dickov Bellamy, LuaLua
Friedel
Kuqi Tugay, Silva Todorov
Khizanishvili, Reid
Neill, Bentley Emerton

O'Neil, Priske
Diao, O'Brien
Westerveld
Cisse Robert, Stefanovic
Taylor Karadas, Griffin

4/4/2 **4/4/2**

Unused Sub: Enckelman, Mokoena
Unused Sub: Guatelli, Viafara

	Blackburn	Portsmouth
Premiership Totals		
Premiership Appearances	1,600	1,081
Team Appearances	829	413
Goals Scored	133	72
Assists	145	89
Clean Sheets (goalkeepers)	58	29
Yellow Cards	258	124
Red Cards	13	13
Full Internationals	13	11

Age/Height

Blackburn Rovers Age	Portsmouth Age
28 yrs, 6 mo	**27 yrs, 11 mo**
Blackburn Rovers Height	Portsmouth Height
5'11"	**5'11"**

Match Statistics

League Table after Fixture

		Played	Won	Drawn	Lost	For	Against	Pts
↑ 8	Blackburn	20	9	3	8	26	25	30
...		...	...	...	...	...	...	...
↑ 14	Fulham	21	6	5	10	25	30	23
↑ 15	Everton	21	7	2	12	14	31	23
↓ 16	Middlesbrough	20	5	7	8	25	30	22
● 17	West Brom	21	5	4	12	20	31	19
● 18	Portsmouth	21	4	5	12	16	33	17
● 19	Birmingham	20	4	4	12	15	29	16
● 20	Sunderland	20	1	3	16	15	38	6

Statistics

Statistics	Blackburn	Portsmouth
Goals	2	1
Shots on Target	7	4
Shots off Target	5	4
Hit Woodwork	0	0
Possession %	58	42
Corners	4	6
Offsides	4	6
Fouls	11	12
Disciplinary Points	4	16

0-1

Ipswich Town ○
Portsmouth ○

➤ Dario Silva challenges Darren Currie

Event Line

37 ○ ⊕ Silva / H / OP / 6Y	
Assist: Taylor	

Half time 0-1

56 ○ ⇄ Sito > Magilton	
56 ○ ⇄ Garvan > Richards	
63 ○ ▇ Priske	
68 ○ ▇ Silva	
68 ○ ⇄ Todorov > Silva	
74 ○ ▇ Williams	
81 ○ ⇄ Juan > Westlake	
89 ○ ⇄ Karadas > Lua Lua	

Full time 0-1

Dario Silva's first half header was enough to take Pompey through to the FA Cup 4th Round as the Blues emerged unscathed from this tricky tie.

With the emphasis on Premier League survival Harry Redknapp rested some of his first team choices, but in the final analysis his side still had a little too much for their Championship opponents. That was not before an opening scare had shaken the side out of any complacency they might have had. Scott Barron sent in a powerful cross that bypassed everyone and required Gregory Vignal to clear off his own line. Even then the ball fell invitingly for Gavin Williams who looked certain to score but shot wide of the post.

Pompey took the lead on thirty-seven minutes with a neatly worked goal which was somehow out of context with an otherwise scrappy game. Silva had begun the move by laying the ball off to Taylor and when the left-sider delivered his cross into the area there was the striker again to dispatch a neatly cushioned header past Supple in the Ipswich goal.

Certainly the clear cut chances were falling to Pompey and just before the break LuaLua might have doubled the lead but curled a chance just wide after some good approach play. The DR Congo striker looked certain to finally hit the net ten minutes into the second half, but defender Fabian Wilnis got in an inch perfect tackle.

Ipswich got up a head of steam and Danny Haynes thought he had drawn the home side level when he got the better of Vignal, but rolled the ball agonisingly wide of the post. Then the hosts came even closer following a goalmouth scramble before Pompey finally got the ball to safety. After this the game settled back into a lull with Pompey happy to settle for what they had, whilst Ipswich huffed and

Venue:	Portman Road
Attendance:	15,593
Capacity:	30,300

Referee:	D.J.Gallagher - 05/06
Matches:	23
Yellow Cards:	56
Red Cards:	6

Ipswich Town
Portsmouth

▶ Dejan Stefanovic halts the run of Ian Westlake

Match Statistics

Starting Line-Ups

| Barron | Williams | | | O'Neil | Priske |

De Vos, Westlake, Juan, Haynes, LuaLua Karadas, Diao, O'Brien, Westerveld, Supple, Currie, Silva Todorov, Naylor, Richards Garvan, Hughes, Stefanovic, Wilnis, Magilton Sito, Taylor, Vignal

▶ 4/4/1/1   ▶ 4/4/2

Unused Sub: Price, Horlock   Unused Sub: Guatelli, Cisse, Songo'o

Statistics	○ Ipswich	Portsmouth ○
Goals	0	1
Shots on Target	3	6
Shots off Target	8	5
Hit Woodwork	0	0
Possession %	52	48
Corners	4	6
Offsides	3	12
Fouls	2	18
Disciplinary Points	4	8

Age/Height

Ipswich Town Age	Portsmouth Age
▶ 25 yrs, 5 mo	▶ 27 yrs, 3 mo

Ipswich Town Height	Portsmouth Height
▶ 5'11"	▶ 6'

puffed without really threatening to break the door down. However, with two minutes remaining they came close to taking the tie back to Fratton Park when Westerveld's attempted clearance cannoned off the back of Naylor who had turned to retreat back up the field. However, to the keeper's immense relief, the ball fell kindly for him. With that Pompey had booked their passage into the next round, but Harry Redknapp still remained more concerned with fortunes in the Premier League.

Player of the Match

31 Dario Silva

Quote

❝ **Harry Redknapp**

It was a good result and I was pleased to get home without having to go to a replay. There are no games which are easy.

0-1

Portsmouth ○
Everton ○

▶ Matthew Taylor is just too quick for Leon Osman

Event Line

27 ○ ▢	Mendes
31 ○ ⊕	O'Brien / LF / OG / IA
	Assist: Osman
Half time 0-1	
53 ○ ▢	Davis
61 ○ ⇄	Olisadebe > Hughes
62 ○ ▢	Ferrari
65 ○ ▢	Kilbane
73 ○ ⇄	Diao > Mendes
87 ○ ⇄	Karadas > Davis
88 ○ ⇄	Weir > Beattie
90 ○ ⇄	Bent M > Arteta
Full time 0-1	

This was the mid-winter beginning of a new era at Fratton Park with the first home match for new co-owner Alexandre Gaydamak and a host of new faces brought in during the January transfer window.

Sean Davis, Pedro Mendes, Noé Pamarot and Benjani Mwaruwari were all making their debuts, but the Merseysiders left with their third consecutive Premier League victory at Fratton Park to gain revenge for Pompey's win at Goodison earlier in the season.

The goal, which came on the half hour mark, was a comedy of errors with Yobo's long ball out of defence bouncing in the area before Osman's half hit shot appeared to cannon off both Hughes and O'Brien, wrong-footing Ashdown. It was a blow that deflated the mood of expectancy and the debutant players in blue shirts were naturally finding things tough on their baptism. In fact the visitors created more clear-cut opportunities to extend their lead with Ashdown making several important stops.

Player of the Match	Quote	Premiership Milestone
16 Andy Griffin	❝ **Harry Redknapp**	▶ **Debut**
	I thought we started well, but Everton set their stall out to play a certain way and when they get ahead they make it very difficult.	Sean Davis, Pedro Mendes and Noe Pamarot all made their first Premiership appearances in the colours of Portsmouth.

Venue:	Fratton Park	Referee:	A.Marriner - 05/06	**Portsmouth**
Attendance:	20,094	Matches:	13	**Everton**
		Yellow Cards:	43	
		Red Cards:	6	

Form Coming into Fixture

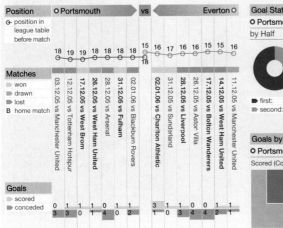

Position ○ Portsmouth vs Everton ○
○- position in league table before match

18 19 19 18 18 18 18 15 16 17 16 16 15 15 16
18

Matches
won
drawn
lost
B home match

03.12.05 vs Manchester United
17.12.05 vs Tottenham Hotspur
17.12.05 vs West Brom
26.12.05 vs West Ham United
28.12.05 vs Arsenal
31.12.05 vs Fulham
02.01.06 vs Blackburn Rovers
02.01.06 vs Charlton Athletic
31.12.05 vs Sunderland
28.12.05 vs Liverpool
26.12.05 vs Aston Villa
17.12.05 vs Bolton Wanderers
14.12.05 vs West Ham United
11.12.05 vs Manchester United

Goals
scored
conceded

| 0 | 1 | 1 | 1 | 0 | 1 | 1 | | 3 | 1 | 1 | 0 | 0 | 1 | 1 |
| 3 | 3 | 0 | 1 | 4 | 0 | 2 | | 1 | 0 | 3 | 4 | 4 | 2 | 1 |

Goal Statistics

○ **Portsmouth**

by Half | by Situation
▶ first: 4 | ▶ set piece: 1
▶ second: 1 | ▶ open play: 4

○ **Everton**

by Half | by Situation
▶ first: 5 | ▶ set piece: 4
▶ second: 2 | ▶ open play: 3

Goals by Area

○ **Portsmouth**
Scored (Conceded)

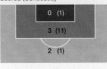

0 (1)
3 (11)
2 (1)

○ **Everton**
Scored (Conceded)

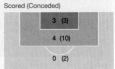

3 (3)
4 (10)
0 (2)

Team Statistics

Starting Line-Ups

Taylor
Hughes
Olisadebe
O'Brien
Davis Karadas
Mwaruwari
Beattie Weir
Ashdown
Pamarot
Mendes Diao
LuaLua
Griffin
O'Neil

Osman
Hibbert
Arteta
Bent M
Yobo
Cahill
Neville
Martyn
Ferrari
Kilbane
Valente

▶ 4/4/2   ▶ 4/4/1/1

Unused Sub: Westerveld, Priske

Unused Sub: Wright, Davies, McFadden

Premiership Totals	○ Portsmouth	Everton ○
Premiership Appearances	832	1,797
Team Appearances	331	850
Goals Scored	49	155
Assists	42	102
Clean Sheets (goalkeepers)	5	135
Yellow Cards	99	175
Red Cards	5	11
Full Internationals	8	9

Age/Height

Portsmouth Age | Everton Age
▶ **26 yrs, 1 mo** | ▶ **28 yrs, 6 mo**

Portsmouth Height | Everton Height
▶ **5'11"** | ▶ **6'**

Match Statistics

League Table after Fixture

		Played	Won	Drawn	Lost	For	Against	Pts
↑	12 Fulham	22	7	5	10	26	30	26
↓	13 Newcastle	21	7	5	9	20	24	26
↑	14 Everton	22	8	2	12	15	31	26
↓	15 Aston Villa	22	6	7	9	26	32	25
●	16 Middlesbrough	21	5	7	9	25	37	22
●	17 West Brom	21	5	4	12	20	31	19
●	18 Portsmouth	22	4	5	13	16	34	17
●	19 Birmingham	21	4	4	13	15	31	16
●	20 Sunderland	20	1	3	16	15	38	6

Statistics	○ Portsmouth	Everton ○
Goals	0	1
Shots on Target	8	3
Shots off Target	6	6
Hit Woodwork	0	0
Possession %	53	47
Corners	4	8
Offsides	4	3
Fouls	21	13
Disciplinary Points	8	8

5-0

Birmingham City ○
Portsmouth ○

▶ Andy O'Brien battles with Chris Sutton

Event Line

5 ○ ⊕ Jarosik / H / OP / 6Y	
Assist: Melchiot	
37 ○ ⊕ Pennant / LF / OP / IA	
Assist: Heskey	
Half time 2-0	
53 ○ ⇄ Olisadebe > Pericard	
55 ○ ⊕ Upson / H / C / IA	
Assist: Pennant	
71 ○ ☐ Johnson	
74 ○ ⇄ Dunn > Jarosik	
76 ○ ☐ Griffin	
78 ○ ⇄ Forssell > Heskey	
81 ○ ⇄ Kilkenny > Cunningham	
83 ○ ⇄ Priske > Stefanovic	
90 ○ ⇄ Karadas > Pamarot	
90 ○ ⊕ Forssell / RF / P / IA	
Assist: Forssell	
90 ○ ⊕ Dunn / RF / OP / IA	
Assist: Sutton	
Full time 5-0	

This was a bitter result that left even the optimists amongst Pompey's faithful staring down the barrels of relegation.

As six pointers go this was up there with the best of them and what ensued on a glum day in the Midlands moved Birmingham above Pompey in the table, whilst bestowing on the visitors grave goal difference damage in the process.

In truth the display was not half as bad as the score-line suggested, but that did not make the pill any less bitter to swallow. Birmingham landed the first blow after only five minutes when Mario Melchiot crossed for Jiri Jarosik to head home at the far post. With half time approaching Pompey were mortally wounded when Heskey's cross was taken by the impressive Pennant who slid past Ashdown.

It was all up ten minutes after the break when Upson headed in Pennant's cross from close range and in injury time it got worse as Forssell converted from the spot after a supposed foul by Pamarot. David Dunn then made it all the more comprehensive as Pompey wilted.

Player of the Match	Quote	Premiership Milestone
14 Matthew Taylor	❝ **Harry Redknapp**	▶ **150**
	We're bitterly disappointed.	Dejan Stefanovic made his 150th Premiership appearance.

Venue:	St Andrew's	Referee:	C.J.Foy - 05/06	**Birmingham City**
Attendance:	29,138	Matches:	22	**Portsmouth**
Capacity:	30,016	Yellow Cards:	51	
		Red Cards:	6	

Form Coming into Fixture

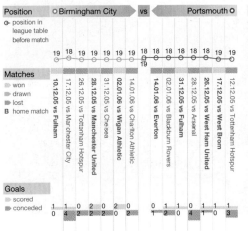

Goal Statistics

○ Birmingham City

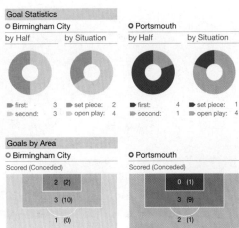

by Half	by Situation
▶ first: 3	▶ set piece: 2
▶ second: 3	▶ open play: 4

○ Portsmouth

by Half	by Situation
▶ first: 4	▶ set piece: 1
▶ second: 1	▶ open play: 4

Goals by Area

○ Birmingham City — Scored (Conceded)

- 2 (2)
- 3 (10)
- 1 (0)

○ Portsmouth — Scored (Conceded)

- 0 (1)
- 3 (9)
- 2 (1)

Team Statistics

Starting Line-Ups

Birmingham City: Lazaridis, Jarosik (Dunn), Upson, Izzet, Sutton, Mwaruwari, Taylor Maik, Cunningham (Kilkenny), Johnson, Heskey (Forssell), Pericard (Olisadebe), Melchiot, Pennant

Portsmouth: O'Neil, Pamarot (Karadas), Mendes, O'Brien, Ashdown, Davis, Stefanovic (Priske), Taylor, Griffin

▶ 4/4/2   ▶ 4/4/2

Unused Sub: Vaesen, Gray   Unused Sub: Westerveld, Hughes

Premiership Totals

	○ Birmingham	Portsmouth ○
Premiership Appearances	2,186	813
Team Appearances	785	345
Goals Scored	270	37
Assists	266	33
Clean Sheets (goalkeepers)	37	5
Yellow Cards	244	104
Red Cards	15	6
Full Internationals	12	7

Age/Height

Birmingham City Age	Portsmouth Age
▶ 28 yrs, 7 mo	▶ 26 yrs, 3 mo

Birmingham City Height	Portsmouth Height
▶ 6'	▶ 6'

Match Statistics

League Table after Fixture

		Played	Won	Drawn	Lost	For	Against	Pts
↓	12 Charlton	20	9	1	10	26	30	28
↓	13 Fulham	22	7	5	10	26	30	26
↓	14 Newcastle	22	7	5	10	20	25	26
●	15 Aston Villa	23	6	8	9	26	32	26
●	16 West Brom	23	6	4	13	21	32	22
●	17 Middlesbrough	22	5	7	10	27	40	22
↑	18 Birmingham	22	5	4	13	20	31	19
↓	19 Portsmouth	23	4	5	14	16	39	17
●	20 Sunderland	22	2	3	17	17	40	9

Statistics

	○ Birmingham	Portsmouth ○
Goals	5	0
Shots on Target	7	4
Shots off Target	3	6
Hit Woodwork	0	0
Possession %	53	47
Corners	7	2
Offsides	2	2
Fouls	11	23
Disciplinary Points	4	4

1-2

Portsmouth ○
Liverpool ○

➡ Vincent Pericard shields the ball from Jamie Carragher

Event Line

11 ○	▣	Pericard
12 ○	▣	Hughes
37 ○	⊕	Gerrard / RF / P / IA
41 ○	⊕	Riise / LF / OP / OA
		Assist: Morientes
42 ○		Davis

Half time 0-2

46 ○	⇄	Todorov > Vignal
54 ○	⊕	Davis / H / IFK / IA
		Assist: O'Neil
64 ○		Sissoko
66 ○	⇄	Karadas > Pericard
72 ○	⇄	Crouch > Morientes
80 ○	⇄	Finnan > Gerrard
83 ○	⇄	Kewell > Cisse
88 ○	⇄	Priske > Primus

Full time 1-2

Pompey bowed out of the FA Cup, but at least they regained some pride after their mauling at Birmingham eight days previously.

Dean Kiely, bought from Charlton in the week, made his Fratton Park debut. Again Harry Redknapp's priority was Premier League survival, but he knew the importance of putting in a performance which restored some confidence.

The first half saw a scrappy encounter, but Pompey's packed midfield managed to stifle the attacking flair of Liverpool. Yet having done so it was the visitors who took the lead on thirty seven minutes in controversial style. In attempting to clear the ball, Linvoy Primus hit his own defender's arm when Dejan Stefanovic got in the way. Referee Phil Dowd pointed to the spot to the dismay of Pompey's players and Steven Gerrard stepped up to hit home the harshly awarded penalty.

Worse was to follow when four minutes later Liverpool tightened their grip with a spectacular effort. John Arne Riise advanced down the left before unleashing a rocket of a shot which seared into Kiely's bottom left hand corner. The new 'keeper barely had a save to make in the opening half yet found himself picking the ball out of the net twice. It was the last thing Pompey needed but they showed great character to rally and erase the Birmingham blues.

On 54 minutes they pulled a goal back when Sean Davis scored his first for the club by rising highest to head home Gary O'Neil's free kick. That signalled an onslaught and bayed on by the crowd, Stefanovic sent a fierce free kick dipping just over the bar. Then, with time running out, Karadas was denied by the outcoming Reina as he attempted to connect with Todorov's low cross.

Portsmouth
Liverpool

▶ Sean Davis celebrates reducing the deficit

Match Statistics

Starting Line-Ups

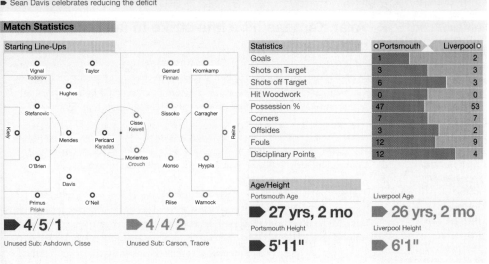

Vignal, Taylor, Todorov, Gerrard, Kromkamp, Finnan, Hughes, Stefanovic, Sissoko, Carragher, Kidy, Cisse, Kewell, Mendes, Pericard, Karadas, Reina, O'Brien, Morientes, Crouch, Alonso, Hyypia, Davis, Primus, Priske, O'Neil, Riise, Warnock

▶ 4/5/1   ▶ 4/4/2

Unused Sub: Ashdown, Cisse

Unused Sub: Carson, Traore

Statistics	○ Portsmouth	Liverpool ○
Goals	1	2
Shots on Target	3	3
Shots off Target	6	3
Hit Woodwork	0	0
Possession %	47	53
Corners	7	7
Offsides	3	2
Fouls	12	9
Disciplinary Points	12	4

Age/Height

Portsmouth Age
▶ **27 yrs, 2 mo**

Liverpool Age
▶ **26 yrs, 2 mo**

Portsmouth Height
▶ **5'11"**

Liverpool Height
▶ **6'1"**

Pompey kept going but in the end the two goal deficit they had faced had been a bridge too far. But the important thing was that they had restored their pride and confidence for the tough league programme that lay ahead. In truth, a potent Liverpool side had been well contained and in the second half it had been important not to be caught by an onslaught. In that respect Pompey's FA Cup exit could be looked on as a blessing and their performance had certainly given hope for the weeks ahead.

Player of the Match

28 Sean Davis

Quote

❝ **Harry Redknapp**

If we continue to work as hard as that we've got a real chance of staying in the Premiership.

1-1

Portsmouth ○
Bolton Wanderers ○

▶ Andres d'Alessandro welcomes Svetoslav Todorov onto the pitch

Event Line

15 ○ ⇄ Griffin > Stefanovic	
Half time 0-0	
46 ○ ⇄ Todorov > O'Neil	
60 ○ ⇄ Vaz Te > Hunt	
69 ○ ⊕ Fadiga / LF / DFK / OA	
Assist: Giannakopoulos	
81 ○ ⇄ Karadas > Mwaruwari	
85 ○ ⊕ Karadas / RF / OP / IA	
Assist: Routledge	
86 ○ ⇄ Fojut > Fadiga	
Full time 1-1	

Azar Karadas hit a late strike to keep Pompey in with a hope.

With Argentine midfielder Andres d'Alessandro making his debut on loan from German club Wolfsburg this was a far more positive and wholehearted display. Wayne Routledge was another debutant after his loan move from Spurs.

With a tough batch of fixtures coming up Pompey essentially needed a win from this game but in the end the lateness of the eighty-fifth minute equaliser made even a point seem welcome, snatched as it was from the jaws of defeat.

Pompey survived on the stroke of half time when Stelios was brought down by Dean Kiely in the area. The spot kick was awarded but Fadiga blasted it high and wide to the relief of the Fratton End, but after some exerted Pompey pressure in which Davis had come close, the visitors took the lead. Fadiga whipped in a free kick from the right which evaded everyone to sneak in with twenty minutes remaining.

However Pompey got their reward when Karadas connected beautifully with Routledge's cross to send the ball screaming into the net to earn a point.

Player of the Match	Quote	Premiership Milestone
4 A. d'Alessandro	🗨 **Harry Redknapp**	▶ **100**
	All the new lads were terrific and it was a smashing performance after half-time.	Sean Davis made his 100th Premiership appearance.

Venue:	Fratton Park	Referee:	D.J.Gallagher - 05/06		Portsmouth
Attendance:	19,128	Matches:	26		Bolton Wanderers
		Yellow Cards:	63		
		Red Cards:	7		

Form Coming into Fixture

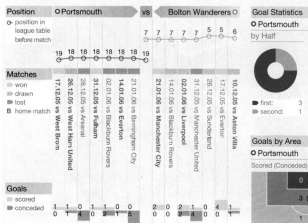

Position ○ Portsmouth vs Bolton Wanderers ○

○- position in league table before match

7 7 7 7 7 5 5 6
19 18 18 18 18 18 18 19

Matches
- won
- drawn
- lost
- B home match

17.12.05 vs West Brom
26.12.05 vs West Ham United
28.12.05 vs Arsenal
31.12.05 vs Fulham
02.01.06 vs Blackburn Rovers
14.01.06 vs Everton
21.01.06 vs Birmingham City
21.01.06 vs Manchester City
14.01.06 vs Blackburn Rovers
02.01.06 vs Liverpool
31.12.05 vs Manchester United
26.12.05 vs Sunderland
17.12.05 vs Everton
10.12.05 vs Aston Villa

Goals
- scored
- conceded

| scored | 1 | 1 | 0 | 1 | 1 | 0 | 0 | | 2 | 0 | 2 | 1 | 0 | 4 | 1 |
| conceded | 0 | 1 | 4 | 0 | 2 | 1 | 5 | | 0 | 0 | 2 | 4 | 0 | 0 | 1 |

Goal Statistics

○ Portsmouth

by Half   by Situation

- first: 3   set piece: 1
- second: 1   open play: 3

○ Bolton Wanderers

by Half   by Situation

- first: 5   set piece: 4
- second: 5   open play: 6

Goals by Area

○ Portsmouth — Scored (Conceded)

0 (2)
3 (10)
1 (1)

○ Bolton Wanderers — Scored (Conceded)

3 (4)
7 (3)
0 (0)

Team Statistics

Starting Line-Ups

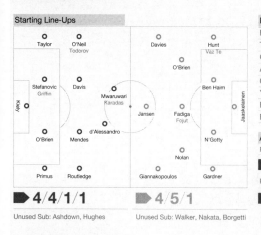

Taylor O'Neil
Todorov
Davies Hunt
Vaz Te
O'Brien
Stefanovic Davis
Griffin
Mwaruwari
Karadas
Ben Haim
Kiely
Jansen Fadiga
Fojut
Jaaskelainen
O'Brien Mendes d'Alessandro
N'Gotty
Nolan
Primus Routledge Giannakopoulos Gardner

▶ 4/4/1/1   ▶ 4/5/1

Unused Sub: Ashdown, Hughes

Unused Sub: Walker, Nakata, Borgetti

Premiership Totals

Premiership Totals	○ Portsmouth	Bolton ○
Premiership Appearances	1,039	1,147
Team Appearances	364	928
Goals Scored	39	113
Assists	49	95
Clean Sheets (goalkeepers)	52	47
Yellow Cards	108	153
Red Cards	7	9
Full Internationals	8	6

Age/Height

Portsmouth Age

▶ **27 yrs**

Portsmouth Height

▶ **5'11"**

Bolton Wanderers Age

▶ **26 yrs, 2 mo**

Bolton Wanderers Height

▶ **6'**

Match Statistics

League Table after Fixture

	Played	Won	Drawn	Lost	For	Against	Pts
● 7 Bolton	22	10	7	5	28	21	37
...	...	...	...	...	...	...	...
↑ 14 Aston Villa	24	6	9	9	27	33	27
↓ 15 Newcastle	23	7	5	11	20	28	26
● 16 Middlesbrough	23	6	7	10	30	40	25
● 17 West Brom	24	6	5	13	21	32	23
● 18 Birmingham	23	5	5	13	21	32	20
● 19 Portsmouth	24	4	6	14	17	40	18
● 20 Sunderland	23	2	3	18	17	43	9

Statistics

Statistics	○ Portsmouth	Bolton ○
Goals	1	1
Shots on Target	5	2
Shots off Target	8	7
Hit Woodwork	0	0
Possession %	50	50
Corners	6	4
Offsides	1	5
Fouls	12	9
Disciplinary Points	0	0

2-0 Newcastle United ○
Portsmouth ○

Premiership
04.02.06

▶ Benjani keeps a close eye on Kieron Dyer

Event Line

31 ○ ▯ Griffin
41 ○ ⊕ N'Zogbia / LF / OP / IA
    Assist: Shearer

Half time 1-0

46 ○ ⇄ Pamarot > Griffin
46 ○ ⇄ Todorov > Routledge
64 ○ ⊕ Shearer / RF / OP / IA
    Assist: Ameobi
74 ○ ⇄ Bowyer > Emre
74 ○ ⇄ Dyer > Solano
76 ○ ⇄ Diao > Davis
86 ○ ⇄ Clark > Parker

Full time 2-0

Pompey sunk deeper into the relegation mire with this defeat that left them seven points from safety as the home side played their first game after the sacking of Graeme Souness earlier in the week.

It was a day for Geordies as Alan Shearer took all the headlines by breaking the all time goal-scoring record of Newcastle legend Jackie Milburn. Only the heroics of Dean Kiely saved Pompey from a heavier defeat and he also did brilliantly to keep Shearer at bay by clawing away his header, but this time the ball fell for N'Zogbia to drill home on forty-one minutes.

Pompey's 'keeper again denied Shearer his record, holding his powerful shot, but on sixty-five minutes the master marksman was sent clear by Ameobi's back heel and despite the close attentions of former team-mate Andy O'Brien, Shearer raced away to clinch his personal feat and victory for Newcastle.

Pompey had disappointed by creating little to trouble Shay Given in the home goal as they slipped to another defeat with Manchester United and Chelsea awaiting next.

Player of the Match	Quote	Premiership Milestone
33 Dean Kiely	ⓖ **Harry Redknapp**	▶ **50**

It was interesting they could put in a performance like that after such a bad run. But they have a team full of good players and it was difficult for us.

Gary O'Neil made his 50th Premiership appearance.

Venue:	St James' Park	Referee:	M.R.Halsey - 05/06		Newcastle United
Attendance:	51,627	Matches:	22		Portsmouth
Capacity:	52,327	Yellow Cards:	35		
		Red Cards:	5		

Form Coming into Fixture

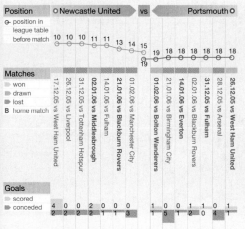

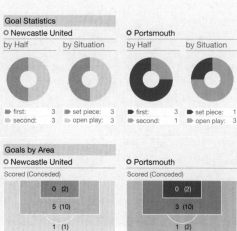

Goal Statistics

Newcastle United

by Half · by Situation

first: 3 · set piece: 3
second: 3 · open play: 3

Portsmouth

by Half · by Situation

first: 3 · set piece: 1
second: 1 · open play: 3

Goals by Area

Newcastle United
Scored (Conceded)

| 0 (2) |
| 5 (10) |
| 1 (1) |

Portsmouth
Scored (Conceded)

| 0 (2) |
| 3 (10) |
| 1 (2) |

Team Statistics

Starting Line-Ups

Newcastle United:
Given; Babayaro, N'Zogbia; Boumsong, Emre (Bowyer); Ameobi, Mwaruwari; Bramble, Parker (Clark); Shearer, d'Alessandro; Ramage, Solano (Dyer)

Portsmouth:
Routledge (Todorov), Griffin (Pamarot); Mendes, Primus; Kiely; Davis (Diao), O'Brien; O'Neil, Taylor

▶ 4/4/2   ▶ 4/4/1/1

Unused Sub: Harper, Elliott

Unused Sub: Ashdown, Karadas

Premiership Totals

	Newcastle	Portsmouth
Premiership Appearances	2,213	965
Team Appearances	1,448	292
Goals Scored	405	34
Assists	294	48
Clean Sheets (goalkeepers)	75	52
Yellow Cards	257	92
Red Cards	17	5
Full Internationals	9	7

Age/Height

Newcastle United Age
▶ **27 yrs, 3 mo**

Portsmouth Age
▶ **27 yrs**

Newcastle United Height
▶ **5'10"**

Portsmouth Height
▶ **5'10"**

Match Statistics

League Table after Fixture

		Played	Won	Drawn	Lost	For	Against	Pts
↑	12 Aston Villa	25	7	9	9	31	33	30
↓	13 Charlton	22	9	3	10	27	31	30
↓	14 Fulham	25	8	5	12	30	36	29
●	15 Newcastle	24	8	5	11	22	28	29
↑	16 West Brom	25	7	5	13	23	32	26
↓	17 Middlesbrough	24	6	7	11	30	44	25
●	18 Birmingham	24	5	5	14	21	34	20
●	19 Portsmouth	25	4	6	15	17	42	18
●	20 Sunderland	24	2	3	19	17	45	9

Statistics

	Newcastle	Portsmouth
Goals	2	0
Shots on Target	10	1
Shots off Target	4	2
Hit Woodwork	0	0
Possession %	63	37
Corners	7	1
Offsides	6	3
Fouls	9	8
Disciplinary Points	0	4

1-3

Portsmouth ○
Manchester United ○

▶ Matthew Taylor clears the danger

Event Line

18 ○ ⊕ van Nistelrooy / H / OP / 6Y	
Assist: Giggs	
38 ○ ⊕ Ronaldo / LF / OP / OA	
45 ○ ⊕ Ronaldo / RF / OP / IA	
Assist: Rooney	

Half time 0-3

46 ○ ⇄ Smith > Giggs	
46 ○ ⇄ Howard > van der Sar	
46 ○ ⇄ Routledge > d'Alessandro	
55 ○ ⇄ Griffin > Davis	
82 ○ ⇄ Saha > Rooney	
87 ○ ⊕ Taylor / H / C / 6Y	
Assist: Routledge	

Full time 1-3

This defeat against the might of Manchester United left Pompey eight points adrift of safety.

The home side showed a tremendous spirit to battle back against a United side who had showed their class by ruthlessly taking chances that came their way.

They had taken the lead on eighteen minutes when Giggs swapped passes with van Nistelrooy before rounding Kiely. The angle left the Welshman with a lot still to do, but his shot came back off the bar and his Dutch companion headed home.

Lomana Tresor LuaLua so nearly levelled when he turned Ferdinand before screwing just wide, but then the home side received a second blow when Cristiano Ronaldo advanced and let fly with a superb strike which flew over Kiely and into the net. It was then the Portuguese who made it three just before half time as his shot from Rooney's pass took a deflection off O'Brien on its way in.

Pompey were down but not out and produced a series of chances to make United fight. Striker LuaLua rolled a shot just wide of the post, Routledge did the same and then Howard in the United goal had to make superb saves from LuaLua and Mendes. Pompey finally got a just consolation when Matt Taylor headed home from Routledge's cross.

Player of the Match	Quote
32 Lomana LuaLua	🎙 **Harry Redknapp**

Every time they had an attack they stuck it in the net, but in the second half we showed great pride and created plenty of chances.

Venue:	Fratton Park	Referee:	U.D.Rennie - 05/06	Portsmouth
Attendance:	20,206	Matches:	29	Manchester United
		Yellow Cards:	52	
		Red Cards:	4	

Form Coming into Fixture

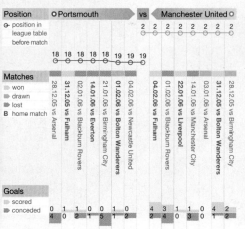

Position: Portsmouth vs Manchester United

- position in league table before match
- Matches: won / drawn / lost / B home match
- Goals: scored / conceded

Goal Statistics

Portsmouth

by Half / by Situation

- first: 2
- second: 1
- set piece: 1
- open play: 2

Manchester United

by Half / by Situation

- first: 7
- second: 8
- set piece: 4
- open play: 9
- own goals: 2

Goals by Area

Portsmouth — Scored (Conceded)

- 0 (2)
- 2 (11)
- 1 (2)

Manchester United — Scored (Conceded)

- 5 (5)
- 9 (7)
- 1 (0)

Team Statistics

Starting Line-Ups

Portsmouth: Taylor, d'Alessandro (Routledge), O'Brien, Mendes, LuaLua, van Nistelrooy... Kiely, Primus, Davis (Griffin), Mwaruwari, Pamarot, O'Neil

Manchester United: Ronaldo, Brown, Fletcher, Ferdinand, Rooney (Saha), Giggs (Smith), Vidic, Park, Silvestre, van der Sar, Howard

Portsmouth: **4/4/2**

Manchester United: **4/4/2**

Unused Sub: Ashdown, Hughes, Karadas

Unused Sub: Evra, Richardson

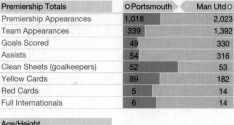

Premiership Totals	Portsmouth	Man Utd
Premiership Appearances	1,018	2,023
Team Appearances	339	1,392
Goals Scored	49	330
Assists	54	316
Clean Sheets (goalkeepers)	52	53
Yellow Cards	89	182
Red Cards	5	14
Full Internationals	6	14

Age/Height

Portsmouth Age	Manchester United Age
26 yrs, 8 mo	**26 yrs, 6 mo**

Portsmouth Height	Manchester United Height
5'10"	**6'**

Match Statistics

League Table after Fixture

		Played	Won	Drawn	Lost	For	Against	Pts
●	2 Man Utd	26	16	6	4	52	27	54
...		...	...	...	...	...	...	...
↑	14 Newcastle	25	9	5	11	24	29	32
↓	15 Aston Villa	26	7	9	10	32	35	30
↑	16 Middlesbrough	25	7	7	11	33	44	28
↓	17 West Brom	26	7	5	14	24	38	26
●	18 Birmingham	24	5	5	14	21	34	20
●	19 Portsmouth	26	4	6	16	18	45	18
●	20 Sunderland	24	2	3	19	17	54	9

Statistics	Portsmouth	Man Utd
Goals	1	3
Shots on Target	6	4
Shots off Target	9	2
Hit Woodwork	2	1
Possession %	50	50
Corners	16	2
Offsides	1	1
Fouls	13	16
Disciplinary Points	0	0

2-0

Chelsea ○
Portsmouth ○

▶ Pedro Mendes keeps tabs on Joe Cole

Event Line

31 ○ ⇄ Duff > Del Horno	
Half time 0-0	
60 ○ ⇄ Gudjohnsen > Cole J	
60 ○ ⇄ Makelele > Wright-Phillips	
65 ○ ⊕ Lampard / RF / OP / IA	
Assist: Drogba	
68 ○ ⇄ Routledge > Koroman	
72 ○ ⇄ Davis > Hughes	
78 ○ ⊕ Robben / LF / OP / IA	
Assist: Gudjohnsen	
86 ○ LuaLua	
Full time 2-0	

Pompey frustrated Chelsea in their charge towards a second successive Premier League title but in the end they were the ones who left Stamford Bridge with the ultimate frustration after caving in to two second half goals.

Strikes from Frank Lampard and Arjen Robben kept Pompey deeply in the relegation zone with games beginning to run out. Indeed the visitors had held Chelsea rather comfortably until the sixty-fifth minute when Drogba fed Lampard who drilled home to break the brave resistance. Even then Pompey might have been on level terms within five minutes when Richard Hughes got on the end of Routledge's cross, but he headed wide.

Chelsea finally confirmed victory in the 78th minute when substitute Gudjohnsen lofted a ball over the Pompey defence for Robben to run onto and slot home past Kiely. Midfielder Lampard came close to piling more misery on the visitors in the final minutes but he hooked over the bar after Duff had set him up. That would have been cruel.

Player of the Match	Quote	Premiership Milestone
33 Dean Kiely	🔵 **Harry Redknapp**	▶ **Debut**

It was no surprise Frank Lampard scored was it? Frank is always likely to score a goal. You give him one opportunity and he will take it.

Ognjen Koroman made his Premiership debut.

Venue:	Stamford Bridge	Referee:	M.A.Riley - 05/06
Attendance:	42,254	Matches:	30
Capacity:	42,449	Yellow Cards:	99
		Red Cards:	7

Chelsea
Portsmouth

Form Coming into Fixture

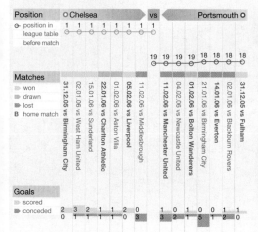

Position	○ Chelsea	vs	Portsmouth ○
○ position in league table before match	1 1 1 1 1 1 1 1		19 19 19 19 18 18 18 18

Matches
- won
- drawn
- lost
- B home match

31.12.05 vs Birmingham City
02.01.06 vs West Ham United
15.01.06 vs Sunderland
22.01.06 vs Charlton Athletic
01.02.06 vs Aston Villa
05.02.06 vs Liverpool
11.02.06 vs Middlesbrough

11.02.06 vs Manchester United
04.02.06 vs Newcastle United
01.02.06 vs Bolton Wanderers
21.01.06 vs Birmingham City
14.01.06 vs Everton
02.01.06 vs Blackburn Rovers
31.12.05 vs Fulham

Goals
- scored
- conceded

scored	2	3	2	1	1	2	0		1	0	1	0	0	1	1
conceded	0	1	1	1	1	0	3		3	2	1	5	1	2	0

Goal Statistics

○ Chelsea

by Half | by Situation

- first: 7
- second: 4
- set piece: 2
- open play: 9

○ Portsmouth

by Half | by Situation

- first: 2
- second: 2
- set piece: 2
- open play: 2

Goals by Area

○ Chelsea
Scored (Conceded)

4 (1)
6 (6)
1 (0)

○ Portsmouth
Scored (Conceded)

1 (3)
2 (8)
1 (3)

Team Statistics

Starting Line-Ups

Del Horno
Duff
Robben
O'Neil
Primus
Lampard
Terry
Mendes
Karadas
Mwaruwari
Cech
Essien
Drogba
Kiely
LuaLua
Huth
Hughes
Davis
O'Brien
Cole J
Gudjohnsen
Ferreira
Wright-Phillips
Makelele
Koroman
Routledge
Taylor

▶ 4/3/3

▶ 4/4/2

Unused Sub: Cudicini, Johnson

Unused Sub: Ashdown, d'Alessandro, Todorov

Premiership Totals	○ Chelsea	Portsmouth ○
Premiership Appearances	1,553	939
Team Appearances	1,052	360
Goals Scored	244	48
Assists	234	55
Clean Sheets (goalkeepers)	36	52
Yellow Cards	155	74
Red Cards	7	4
Full Internationals	14	8

Age/Height

Chelsea Age
▶ **25 yrs, 8 mo**

Portsmouth Age
▶ **26 yrs, 9 mo**

Chelsea Height
▶ **5'11"**

Portsmouth Height
▶ **5'10"**

Match Statistics

League Table after Fixture

		Played	Won	Drawn	Lost	For	Against	Pts
● 1	Chelsea	27	22	3	2	54	16	69
...		...	...	...	...	...	...	...
● 14	Fulham	26	9	5	12	36	37	32
● 15	Aston Villa	27	7	10	10	32	35	31
● 16	Middlesbrough	25	7	7	11	33	44	28
● 17	West Brom	26	7	5	14	24	38	26
● 18	Birmingham	26	6	5	15	22	37	23
● 19	Portsmouth	27	4	6	17	18	47	18
● 20	Sunderland	27	2	4	21	18	49	10

Statistics	○ Chelsea	Portsmouth ○
Goals	2	0
Shots on Target	8	1
Shots off Target	9	4
Hit Woodwork	0	0
Possession %	51	49
Corners	6	7
Offsides	3	4
Fouls	7	13
Disciplinary Points	0	4

1-0

Aston Villa ○
Portsmouth ○

▶ It's Davis at the double as Sean and Steven compete in midfield

Event Line

23 ○ ⇄ De la Cruz > Samuel
36 ○ ⊕ Baros / H / IFK / 6Y
　　　Assist: Milner
Half time 1-0
55 ○ ⇄ Karadas > Todorov
59 ○ ⇄ Moore > Baros
68 ○ ⇄ Koroman > Davis
79 ○ ⇄ Priske > Griffin
90 ○ 　 Ridgewell
90 ○ 　 Karadas
Full time 1-0

Perhaps the most disappointing defeat of all. After showing fighting qualities against Chelsea and Manchester United in previous weeks despite defeat, Pompey went down at Villa Park with barely a whimper.

This game had marked the start of a series that the club had seriously targeted for a late push to pick up some points, but in truth they never looked like doing so from a match that was settled by a sloppy goal in the first half. That came on thirty-five minutes when Milner crossed a free kick in from the left and Milan Baros, in acres of space and unmarked, headed the home side into the lead.

Villa had looked a constant danger down the flanks and one run by Kevin Phillips took him all the way to goal where he was denied by a Dean Kiely block. Pompey gave Villa more to think about in the second half, but Sorensen was not really called upon to make a save of any note. At the other end Kiely made a superb point blank stop to deny Phillips as relegation loomed ever nearer.

Player of the Match

32 Lomana LuaLua

Quote

⑥ Harry Redknapp

It's going to be very difficult to catch West Brom and Birmingham but it's not over. We've got to keep going.

Premiership Milestone

▶ 200

Andy O'Brien made his 200th Premiership appearance.

Venue:	Villa Park		Referee:	M.L.Dean - 05/06
Attendance:	30,194		Matches:	27
Capacity:	42,573		Yellow Cards:	74
			Red Cards:	7

Aston Villa
Portsmouth

Form Coming into Fixture

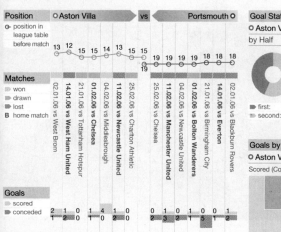

Position
○ Aston Villa vs Portsmouth ○

○ position in league table before match

13 12 15 15 14 13 15 15 — 19 19 19 19 18 18 18
19

Matches
- won
- drawn
- lost
- B home match

02.01.06 vs West Brom
14.01.06 vs West Ham United
21.01.06 vs Tottenham Hotspur
01.02.06 vs Chelsea
04.02.06 vs Middlesbrough
11.02.06 vs Newcastle United
25.02.06 vs Charlton Athletic

25.02.06 vs Chelsea
11.02.06 vs Manchester United
04.02.06 vs Newcastle United
01.02.06 vs Bolton Wanderers
21.01.06 vs Birmingham City
14.01.06 vs Everton
02.01.06 vs Blackburn Rovers

Goals
- scored
- conceded

2 1 0 1 4 1 0 | 0 1 0 1 0 0 1
1 2 0 1 0 2 0 | 2 3 2 1 5 1 2

Goal Statistics

○ Aston Villa
by Half   by Situation

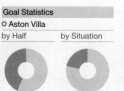

- first: 4   - set piece: 2
- second: 5   - open play: 7

○ Portsmouth
by Half   by Situation

- first: 1   - set piece: 2
- second: 2   - open play: 1

Goals by Area

○ Aston Villa
Scored (Conceded)

3 (1)
6 (5)
0 (0)

○ Portsmouth
Scored (Conceded)

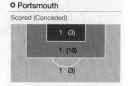

1 (3)
1 (10)
1 (3)

Team Statistics

Starting Line-Ups

Bouma Barry   Routledge Griffin
                                  Priske
Ridgewell Davis   Davis   Primus
          Baros Todorov Koroman
Sorensen Moore Karadas   Kiely
       Phillips LuaLua
Hughes McCann   Mendes O'Brien

Samuel Milner   O'Neil Taylor
De la Cruz

▶ 4/4/2   ▶ 4/4/2

Unused Sub: Taylor, Hendrie, Angel   Unused Sub: Guatelli, Songo'o

Premiership Totals	○ Aston Villa	Portsmouth ○
Premiership Appearances	1,696	1,064
Team Appearances	902	396
Goals Scored	169	52
Assists	137	59
Clean Sheets (goalkeepers)	67	52
Yellow Cards	171	91
Red Cards	6	5
Full Internationals	9	8

Age/Height

	Aston Villa	Portsmouth
Age	▶ 25 yrs, 8 mo	▶ 26 yrs, 11 mo
Height	▶ 5'10"	▶ 5'10"

Match Statistics

League Table after Fixture

		Played	Won	Drawn	Lost	For	Against	Pts
●	12 Everton	28	11	4	13	21	36	37
●	13 Charlton	28	10	6	12	32	37	36
↑	14 Aston Villa	28	8	10	10	33	35	34
↑	15 Middlesbrough	27	9	7	11	36	44	34
↓	16 Fulham	28	9	5	14	37	43	32
●	17 West Brom	28	7	5	16	25	42	26
●	18 Birmingham	27	6	5	16	22	38	23
●	19 Portsmouth	28	4	6	18	18	48	18
●	20 Sunderland	27	2	4	21	18	49	10

Statistics	○ Aston Villa	Portsmouth ○
Goals	1	0
Shots on Target	8	6
Shots off Target	9	5
Hit Woodwork	1	0
Possession %	52	48
Corners	16	10
Offsides	0	4
Fouls	15	14
Disciplinary Points	4	4

2-1 Portsmouth ○
Manchester City ○

▶ Pedro Mendes is the hero for Portsmouth

Event Line	
Half time 0-0	
46 ○ ⇄ Croft > Sinclair	
60 ○ ⊕ Mendes / RF / C / OA	
63 ○ ⇄ Todorov > Mwaruwari	
69 ○ ⇄ Wright-Phillips > Reyna	
75 ○ ⇄ Ireland > Jordan	
83 ○ ⊕ Dunne / H / C / 6Y	
Assist: Samaras	
88 ○ ⇄ Routledge > Davis	
90 ○ ⊕ Mendes / RF / C / OA	
Full time 2-1	

This was without doubt the game that changed the course of Pompey's season as Pedro Mendes wrote himself into Fratton Park folklore.

Pompey showed a courage of conviction absent at Villa Park that gave them at least hope for the weeks ahead. Both goals were special but the dramatic winner, with virtually the last kick of the ball, eclipsed all else.

The first half had been frustrating for Pompey who played some cultured football, but without really threatening the visitors. The frustration was alleviated on the hour when d'Alessandro's corner was cleared only as far as Mendes, who from twenty-five yards out, hit a dipping low volley which left James wrong-footed.

The importance of the first victory of the year was immense, but with seven minutes to go Dunne got in at the near post to head home a corner after City had been allowed to play head tennis in the area.

Then, with all hope apparently lost, Mendes picked up another half-cleared corner deep into injury time and his swerving volley from outside the area left David James a standing spectator as it flew into his top right hand corner to pull off the most dramatic of victories.

Player of the Match	Quote	Premiership Milestone
30 Pedro Mendes	❝ **Harry Redknapp**	▶ **First Goal**

If we didn't win today we were dead and buried. It was no more than Pedro Mendes deserved, he hits balls like that in training and we said 'save one for Saturday Pedro', well he saved two!

Pedro Mendes netted his first Premiership goals for Portsmouth.

Venue:	Fratton Park	Referee:	M.R.Halsey - 05/06	Portsmouth
Attendance:	19,556	Matches:	27	Manchester City
		Yellow Cards:	41	
		Red Cards:	6	

Form Coming into Fixture

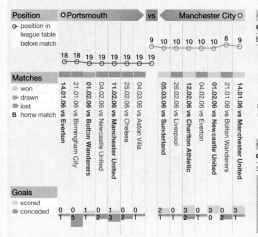

Position — O Portsmouth vs Manchester City O

o- position in league table before match

9 10 10 10 10 10 8 9
18 18 19 19 19 19 19 19

Matches
- won
- drawn
- lost
- B home match

14.01.06 vs Everton
21.01.06 vs Birmingham City
01.02.06 vs Bolton Wanderers
04.02.06 vs Newcastle United
11.02.06 vs Manchester United
25.02.06 vs Chelsea
04.03.06 vs Aston Villa
05.03.06 vs Sunderland
26.02.06 vs Liverpool
12.02.06 vs Charlton Athletic
04.02.06 vs Everton
01.02.06 vs Newcastle United
21.01.06 vs Bolton Wanderers
14.01.06 vs Manchester United

Goals
- scored
- conceded

| 0 | 0 | 1 | 0 | 1 | 0 | 0 | | 2 | 0 | 3 | 0 | 3 | 0 | 3 |
| 1 | 5 | 1 | 2 | 3 | 2 | 1 | | 1 | 1 | 2 | 1 | 0 | 2 | 1 |

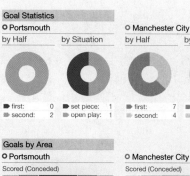

Goal Statistics

O Portsmouth

by Half | by Situation

| first: | 0 | set piece: | 1 |
| second: | 2 | open play: | 1 |

O Manchester City

by Half | by Situation

| first: | 7 | set piece: | 2 |
| second: | 4 | open play: | 9 |

Goals by Area

O Portsmouth — Scored (Conceded)

1 (3)
1 (10)
0 (2)

O Manchester City — Scored (Conceded)

0 (2)
9 (6)
2 (0)

Team Statistics

Starting Line-Ups

Taylor
O'Neil
O'Brien
Kiely
Mendes
d'Alessandro
LuaLua
Samaras
Primus
Mwaruwari
Todorov
Vassell
Davis
Routledge
Priske

Sinclair
Croft
Jihai
Barton
Dunne
James
Reyna
Wright-Phillips
Richards
Musampa
Jordan
Ireland

▶ 4/3/1/2   ▶ 4/4/2

Unused Sub: Ashdown, Koroman, Karadas

Unused Sub: Weaver, Thatcher

Premiership Totals

	O Portsmouth	Man City O
Premiership Appearances	951	1,567
Team Appearances	359	693
Goals Scored	49	123
Assists	57	120
Clean Sheets (goalkeepers)	52	130
Yellow Cards	66	148
Red Cards	4	11
Full Internationals	8	8

Age/Height

Portsmouth Age
▶ **26 yrs, 11 mo**

Manchester City Age
▶ **25 yrs, 8 mo**

Portsmouth Height
▶ **5'10"**

Manchester City Height
▶ **5'11"**

Match Statistics

League Table after Fixture

	Played	Won	Drawn	Lost	For	Against	Pts
↓ 10 Man City	29	12	4	13	39	34	40
...	...	...	...	...	...	...	...
• 14 Aston Villa	29	8	10	11	33	37	34
• 15 Middlesbrough	27	9	7	11	36	44	34
• 16 Fulham	29	9	5	15	38	46	32
• 17 West Brom	29	7	6	16	26	43	27
• 18 Birmingham	28	6	6	16	23	39	24
• 19 Portsmouth	29	5	6	18	20	49	21
• 20 Sunderland	29	2	4	23	19	52	10

Statistics

	O Portsmouth	Man City O
Goals	2	1
Shots on Target	5	4
Shots off Target	7	5
Hit Woodwork	0	0
Possession %	53	47
Corners	8	1
Offsides	8	3
Fouls	11	7
Disciplinary Points	0	0

2-4 West Ham United ○
Portsmouth ○

▶ Pedro Mendes celebrates finding the net again

Event Line

19 ○ ⊕ LuaLua / RF / C / 6Y	
Assist: Taylor	
25 ○ ⊕ Davis / RF / OP / 6Y	
Assist: Priske	
42 ○ ⊕ Mendes / RF / OP / OA	
Assist: d'Alessandro	
Half time 0-3	
46 ○ ⇄ Benayoun > Clarke	
46 ○ ⇄ Harewood > Katan	
57 ○ ⇄ Todorov > Mwaruwari	
69 ○ ⊕ Sheringham / RF / OP / IA	
Assist: Konchesky	
71 ○ ⇄ Fletcher > Ferdinand	
77 ○ ⊕ Todorov / RF / OP / 6Y	
Assist: LuaLua	
84 ○ ▪ Mendes	
85 ○ ▪ Harewood	
90 ○ ⊕ Benayoun / LF / OP / IA	
Assist: Zamora	
Full time 2-4	

Suddenly the heat was on as Pompey followed up their first win of the year with another.

The performance was immense and suddenly Harry Redknapp's January signings were beginning to click, giving his side a potent look. This marauding victory in East London suddenly took Pompey to within three points of the safety zone when just a fortnight previously they had been eight adrift.

In the first half there was only one team in it as Pompey made a nonsense of their position. Lomana Tresor LuaLua put the visitors ahead as he hit high into the net after nineteen minutes from Taylor's cross. On twenty-five minutes it became 2-0 as Sean Davis bundled the ball over the line from Priske's initial cross and before half time Mendes followed up the previous week's spectacular strikes with another, shooting past Walker from outside the area as a disbelieving Upton Park looked on.

With twenty minutes remaining former Pompey striker Sheringham hauled West Ham back, but it was a former Hammers striker Svetoslav Todorov who repaid the complement at the other end as he swept home from LuaLua's dazzling run. An injury time strike by Benayoun could not halt the Pompey party in East London.

Player of the Match	Quote	Premiership Milestone
30 Pedro Mendes	❝ **Harry Redknapp**	▶ **First Goal**

We needed that result. It was a good time to play them, but we still had to perform and we did that. We scored goals when, up until last week, we had only scored more than one goal in one game all season.

Sean Davis netted his first Premiership goal for Portsmouth.

Venue:	Upton Park
Attendance:	34,837
Capacity:	35,647

Referee:	A.G.Wiley - 05/06
Matches:	36
Yellow Cards:	109
Red Cards:	7

West Ham United
Portsmouth

Form Coming into Fixture

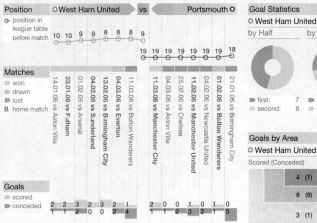

Position

○ West Ham United vs Portsmouth ○

○- position in league table before match

West Ham United: 10 10 9 9 8 8 8 9
Portsmouth: 19 19 19 19 19 19 19 18

Matches
- won
- drawn
- lost
- B home match

West Ham matches: 14.01.06 vs Aston Villa | 23.01.06 vs Fulham | 01.02.05 vs Arsenal | 04.02.06 vs Sunderland | 13.02.06 vs Birmingham City | 04.03.06 vs Everton | 11.03.06 vs Bolton Wanderers

Portsmouth matches: 11.03.06 vs Manchester City | 04.03.06 vs Aston Villa | 25.02.06 vs Chelsea | 11.02.06 vs Manchester United | 04.02.06 vs Newcastle United | 01.02.06 vs Bolton Wanderers | 21.01.06 vs Birmingham City

Goals
scored	2	2	3	2	3	2	1		2	0	0	1	0	1	0
conceded	1	1	2	0	0	2	4		1	1	2	3	2	1	5

Goal Statistics

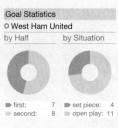

○ West Ham United

by Half	by Situation

| ▶ first: | 7 | ▶ set piece: | 4 |
| ▶ second: | 8 | ▶ open play: | 11 |

○ Portsmouth

by Half	by Situation

| ▶ first: | 0 | ▶ set piece: | 3 |
| ▶ second: | 4 | ▶ open play: | 1 |

Goals by Area

○ West Ham United — Scored (Conceded)

| 4 (1) |
| 8 (8) |
| 3 (1) |

○ Portsmouth — Scored (Conceded)

| 1 (4) |
| 1 (9) |
| 2 (2) |

Team Statistics

Starting Line-Ups

West Ham United:
Konchesky, Clarke, Benayoun, Gabbidon, Dailly, Zamora, Mwaruwari/Todorov, Walker, Ferdinand/Fletcher, Reo-Coker, Sheringham, LuaLua, Scaloni, Katan/Harewood

Portsmouth:
d'Alessandro, Priske, Davis, Primus, Kiely, Mendes, O'Brien, O'Neil, Taylor

▶ 4 / 4 / 2   ▶ 4 / 4 / 2

Unused Sub: Bywater, Ashton

Unused Sub: Ashdown, Pamarot, Routledge, Karadas

Premiership Totals

	○ West Ham	Portsmouth ○
Premiership Appearances	951	917
Team Appearances	303	366
Goals Scored	181	51
Assists	129	44
Clean Sheets (goalkeepers)	0	52
Yellow Cards	114	65
Red Cards	4	4
Full Internationals	9	8

Age/Height

West Ham United Age	Portsmouth Age
▶ 27 yrs, 4 mo	▶ 27 yrs, 5 mo

West Ham United Height	Portsmouth Height
▶ 5'11"	▶ 5'11"

Match Statistics

League Table after Fixture

		Played	Won	Drawn	Lost	For	Against	Pts
↓	10 West Ham	29	12	6	11	44	44	42
...	...	...	...	...	...	...	...	...
●	14 Aston Villa	30	8	10	12	34	41	34
●	15 Middlesbrough	29	9	7	13	49	34	34
●	16 Fulham	30	9	5	16	39	51	32
●	17 West Brom	30	7	6	17	27	45	27
●	18 Birmingham	29	6	6	17	23	41	24
●	19 Portsmouth	30	6	6	18	24	51	24
●	20 Sunderland	30	2	4	24	19	54	10

Statistics

	○ West Ham	Portsmouth ○
Goals	2	4
Shots on Target	6	8
Shots off Target	7	4
Hit Woodwork	2	0
Possession %	49	51
Corners	5	4
Offsides	0	5
Fouls	14	12
Disciplinary Points	4	4

1-3

Fulham ○
Portsmouth ○

▶ Svetoslav Todorov rises with Zat Knight

Event Line

1 ○ ⊕ O'Neil / RF / OP / IA	
Assist: Mwaruwari	
10 ○ ⊕ Malbranque / RF / OP / OA	
24 ○ ⊕ LuaLua / RF / OP / IA	
Assist: Mwaruwari	
34 ○ ⇄ Christanval > Pearce	
Half time 1-2	
55 ○ ■ O'Neil	
62 ○ ⊕ O'Neil / RF / IFK / OA	
Assist: LuaLua	
66 ○ ⇄ Stefanovic > d'Alessandro	
66 ○ ⇄ Helguson > John	
69 ○ ⇄ Todorov > Mwaruwari	
69 ○ ■ Malbranque	
70 ○ ■ Mendes	
72 ○ ⇄ Radzinski > Pembridge	
74 ○ ■ Brown	
Foul	
89 ○ ⇄ Karadas > LuaLua	
90 ○ ■ Helguson	
Full time 1-3	

Another week in London and another win as Pompey's irresistible form continued against a club with one of the best home records in the Premier League.

Incredibly, given their perilous position just a few weeks prior, this victory took the Blues to within goal difference of a place outside the bottom three, with a game in hand.

The Pompey performance was as irresistible as two weeks earlier at Upton Park. Gary O'Neil took just a minute to put Pompey ahead when he took advantage of a Wayne Bridge error, but it was to be a performance of courage after Steed Malbranque fired the home side level with a spectacular effort on ten minutes.

Pompey gritted their teeth, taking the game to Fulham once more, and LuaLua was rewarded when he suddenly found himself running clear to nonchalantly beat Crossley after outpacing Zat Knight.

Early in the second half O'Neil's dipping, out of the blue volley took a wicked deflection to fly into the top corner and for Pompey the streets of London were paved with gold once more.

Player of the Match

26 Gary O'Neil

Quote

⓫ Harry Redknapp

That was a big result. We were in desperate trouble a couple of weeks back but we're starting to score goals and play very well. It's still tough but with that support from the fans, we've got a chance.

Venue:	Craven Cottage	Referee:	C.J.Foy - 05/06		**Fulham**
Attendance:	22,322	Matches:	34		**Portsmouth**
Capacity:	22,646	Yellow Cards:	78		
		Red Cards:	8		

Form Coming into Fixture

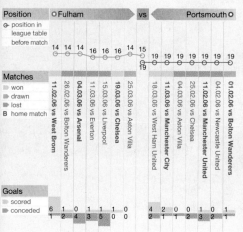

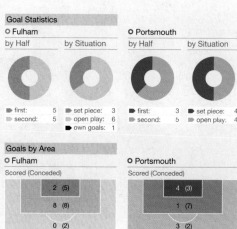

Goal Statistics

○ Fulham

by Half | by Situation

▶ first: 5 ▶ set piece: 3
▶ second: 5 ▶ open play: 6
▶ own goals: 1

○ Portsmouth

by Half | by Situation

▶ first: 3 ▶ set piece: 4
▶ second: 5 ▶ open play: 4

Goals by Area

○ Fulham — Scored (Conceded)

| 2 (5) |
| 8 (8) |
| 0 (2) |

○ Portsmouth — Scored (Conceded)

| 4 (3) |
| 1 (7) |
| 3 (2) |

Team Statistics

Starting Line-Ups

Fulham — 4/4/2 (Diamond)

- Crossley
- Volz, Pearce Christanval, Knight, Pembridge Radziński
- Brown
- Malbranque, John Helguson, McBride
- Boa Morte
- Bridge

Unused Sub: Warner, Rosenior

Portsmouth — 4/4/2

- Kiely
- Taylor, O'Brien, Primus, d'Alessandro Stefanovic
- Mendes
- LuaLua Karadas, Davis
- Mwaruwari Todorov
- O'Neil, Priske

Unused Sub: Ashdown, Routledge

Premiership Totals

	○ Fulham	Portsmouth ○
Premiership Appearances	1,828	1,094
Team Appearances	855	477
Goals Scored	173	63
Assists	184	52
Clean Sheets (goalkeepers)	52	52
Yellow Cards	163	96
Red Cards	12	7
Full Internationals	10	10

Age/Height

Fulham Age	Portsmouth Age
▶ **28 yrs, 11 mo**	▶ **27 yrs, 7 mo**
Fulham Height	Portsmouth Height
▶ **5'10"**	▶ **5'11"**

Match Statistics

League Table after Fixture

	Played	Won	Drawn	Lost	For	Against	Pts
↑ 12 Newcastle	32	12	6	14	34	39	42
↓ 13 Man City	31	12	4	15	39	37	40
● 14 Middlesbrough	30	10	7	13	43	52	37
● 15 Fulham	33	10	6	17	41	54	36
● 16 Aston Villa	32	8	11	13	34	46	35
● 17 West Brom	32	7	6	19	28	49	27
↑ 18 Portsmouth	31	7	6	18	27	52	27
↓ 19 Birmingham	31	6	7	18	23	44	25
● 20 Sunderland	32	2	5	25	21	57	11

Statistics

	○ Fulham	Portsmouth ○
Goals	1	3
Shots on Target	4	7
Shots off Target	6	3
Hit Woodwork	1	0
Possession %	51	49
Corners	7	8
Offsides	4	5
Fouls	9	16
Disciplinary Points	20	8

2-2

Portsmouth ○
Blackburn Rovers ○

Premiership
08.04.06

▶ Lomana Tresor LuaLua celebrates in trademark fashion

Event Line

32 ○ ⊕ Bellamy / LF / OP / IA	
41 ○ ⊕ LuaLua / RF / C / OA	
Half time 1-1	
46 ○ ⇄ Mokoena > Gray	
54 ○ ▢ Dickov	
54 ○ ▢ Mendes	
62 ○ ⊕ Bellamy / LF / OP / IA	
Assist: Bentley	
68 ○ ⇄ Routledge > Davis	
68 ○ ⇄ Todorov > Mwaruwari	
73 ○ ▢ Bellamy	
78 ○ ⊕ Todorov / H / OP / 6Y	
Assist: Taylor	
82 ○ ⇄ Emerton > Pedersen	
90 ○ ▢ Emerton	
Full time 2-2	

Pompey showed their grit and determination to twice fight back from behind to rescue a point.

Twice Craig Bellamy had given Blackburn the lead with spectacular strikes, but twice Pompey equalised to keep them firmly in the mix to escape relegation after what was another impressive display.

Blackburn's Welsh wizard had taken the ball from the halfway line to put Rovers 1-0 up with a scything effort, but LuaLua drew the home side level with a great shot of his own which went into the corner of the net.

Another Bellamy strike after half time restored Blackburn's lead when he latched onto Bentley's ball to sharply shoot past Kiely, but Svetoslav Todorov came off the bench to rescue a point for Pompey which was the very least they deserved, Matt Taylor producing the perfect cross for the striker to ghost in and head home. The home side might have even picked up all three points when a rasping drive by Stefanovic was well held by Friedel in the Blackburn goal.

Player of the Match

9 Svetoslav Todorov

Quote

🎙 **Linvoy Primus**

It was a hard fought game; we definitely deserved more than a point.

Venue:	Fratton Park	Referee:	S.G.Bennett - 05/06	**Portsmouth**
Attendance:	20,048	Matches:	36	**Blackburn Rovers**
		Yellow Cards:	124	
		Red Cards:	11	

Form Coming into Fixture

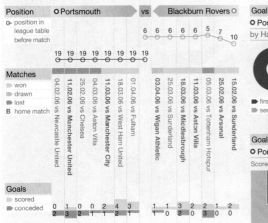

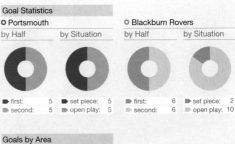

Goal Statistics

○ Portsmouth

by Half — first: 5, second: 5
by Situation — set piece: 5, open play: 5

○ Blackburn Rovers

by Half — first: 6, second: 6
by Situation — set piece: 2, open play: 2

Goals by Area

○ Portsmouth
Scored (Conceded)
4 (3)
2 (7)
4 (2)

○ Blackburn Rovers
Scored (Conceded)
4 (4)
7 (2)
1 (0)

Team Statistics

Starting Line-Ups

Portsmouth: Taylor, d'Alessandro, Stefanovic, Mendes, LuaLua, Bellamy, Kiely, Primus, Davis Routledge, Mwaruwari Todorov, Dickov, Priste, O'Neil

Blackburn: Bentley, Neill, Savage, Khizanishvili, Friedel, Reid, Nelson, Pedersen Emerton, Gray Mokoena

▶ 4/4/2   **▶ 4/4/2**

Unused Sub: Ashdown, Hughes, Karadas

Unused Sub: Enckelman, Kuqi, Sinama-Pongolle

Premiership Totals	○ Portsmouth	Blackburn ○
Premiership Appearances	937	1,535
Team Appearances	453	836
Goals Scored	58	139
Assists	66	144
Clean Sheets (goalkeepers)	52	64
Yellow Cards	84	226
Red Cards	5	10
Full Internationals	8	12

Age/Height

Portsmouth Age
▶ 27 yrs, 5 mo

Blackburn Rovers Age
▶ 27 yrs, 11 mo

Portsmouth Height
▶ 5'11"

Blackburn Rovers Height
▶ 5'11"

Match Statistics

League Table after Fixture

			Played	Won	Drawn	Lost	For	Against	Pts
↑	5	Blackburn	33	16	6	11	45	39	54
...		...	...	...	...	...	...	...	...
●	14	Middlesbrough	31	11	7	13	44	52	40
●	15	Fulham	33	10	6	17	41	54	36
●	16	Aston Villa	32	8	11	13	34	46	35
●	17	Birmingham	33	7	8	18	25	45	29
↑	18	Portsmouth	32	7	7	18	29	54	28
↓	19	West Brom	32	7	6	19	28	49	27
●	20	Sunderland	32	2	5	25	21	57	11

Statistics	○ Portsmouth	Blackburn ○
Goals	2	2
Shots on Target	12	3
Shots off Target	11	1
Hit Woodwork	0	0
Possession %	55	45
Corners	7	3
Offsides	8	5
Fouls	12	12
Disciplinary Points	4	12

1-1

Portsmouth ○
Arsenal ○

Premiership
12.04.06

▶ Sean Davis dispossesses Mathieu Flamini

Event Line

23 ○ ▨	Ljungberg
35 ○ ▨	Mwaruwari
36 ○ ⊕	Henry / RF / OP / OA
	Assist: Adebayor

Half time 0-1

57 ○ ⇄	Routledge > Davis
66 ○ ⊕	LuaLua / H / IFK / IA
	Assist: d'Alessandro
66 ○ ⇄	Todorov > Mwaruwari
69 ○ ⇄	Hughes > LuaLua
75 ○ ⇄	van Persie > Adebayor
80 ○ ⇄	Hleb > Reyes
89 ○ ⇄	Eboue > Campbell

Full time 1-1

This almost tasted like a victory as Pompey fought back against Arsenal to take a deserved share of the spoils.

Though the point was not enough to elevate them from the relegation zone, only inferior goal difference to Birmingham prevented it and given the performance there was every hope of a great escape.

Arsenal had been at their aristocratic best early on, showing their sublime skills, but Pompey had been far from spectators. Almost inevitably when Arsenal took the lead it was from the magical Thierry Henry. He dispossessed Davis and swapped passes with Adebayor, before drilling past Kiely.

The Gunners might have put the game beyond Pompey, but Adebayor somehow contrived to miss the target in front of goal when set up by Henry, but Fratton Park rocked on sixty-five minutes when the home side drew level through Pompey's own magician, LuaLua. Andres d'Alessandro supplied the perfect cross from a free kick and the DR Congo man rose in the area to head home. Pompey held on for a precious point and the finale to the season became even more enthralling.

Player of the Match	Quote	Premiership Milestone
2 Linvoy Primus	🅚 **Harry Redknapp**	▶ **20,230**

It was a great point, a fantastic point. To take a point off Arsenal is a great result and we came back from behind again which shows the spirit and the character in the team.

The attendance of 20,230 was a Premiership record at Fratton Park.

Venue:	Fratton Park	Referee:	U.D.Rennie - 05/06		Portsmouth
Attendance:	20,230	Matches:	38		Arsenal
Capacity:	20,288	Yellow Cards:	76		
		Red Cards:	4		

Form Coming into Fixture

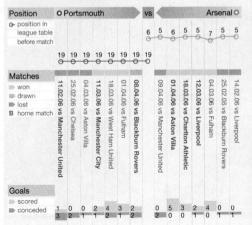

| Position | O Portsmouth | vs | Arsenal O |

G- position in league table before match

Matches
- won
- drawn
- lost
- B home match

Goals
- scored
- conceded

Goal Statistics

O Portsmouth

by Half | by Situation

- first: 6
- second: 6
- set piece: 6
- open play: 6

O Arsenal

by Half | by Situation

- first: 7
- second: 7
- set piece: 0
- open play: 14

Goals by Area

O Portsmouth — Scored (Conceded)

5 (3)
2 (7)
5 (2)

O Arsenal — Scored (Conceded)

1 (3)
12 (2)
1 (0)

Team Statistics

Starting Line-Ups

Portsmouth 4/4/2

Kiely, Stefanovic, Mendes, Primus, Davis Routledge, O'Neil, Priske, LuaLua Hughes, Mwaruwari Todorov, Taylor, d'Alessandro

Unused Sub: Ashdown, O'Brien

Arsenal 4/4/2

Lehmann, Song, Toure, Henry, Diaby, Campbell Eboue, Reyes Hleb, Flamini, Adebayor van Persie, Ljungberg, Djourou

Unused Sub: Poom, Bergkamp

Premiership Totals

	O Portsmouth	Arsenal O
Premiership Appearances	998	1,250
Team Appearances	513	995
Goals Scored	60	256
Assists	67	183
Clean Sheets (goalkeepers)	52	41
Yellow Cards	96	99
Red Cards	5	6
Full Internationals	9	11

Age/Height

Portsmouth Age	Arsenal Age
27 yrs, 4 mo	24 yrs, 9 mo

Portsmouth Height	Arsenal Height
5'11"	6'

Match Statistics

League Table after Fixture

		Played	Won	Drawn	Lost	For	Against	Pts
↑ 5	Arsenal	33	16	6	11	54	26	54
...		...	...	...	...	...	...	...
• 14	Middlesbrough	32	11	7	14	45	54	40
• 15	Aston Villa	33	8	12	13	34	46	36
• 16	Fulham	33	10	6	17	41	54	36
• 17	Birmingham	33	7	8	18	25	45	29
↑ 18	Portsmouth	33	7	8	18	30	55	29
↓ 19	West Brom	33	7	7	19	28	49	28
• 20	Sunderland	32	2	5	25	21	57	11

Statistics	O Portsmouth	Arsenal O
Goals	1	1
Shots on Target	4	3
Shots off Target	6	6
Hit Woodwork	0	0
Possession %	52	48
Corners	3	10
Offsides	4	0
Fouls	9	9
Disciplinary Points	4	4

1-0

Portsmouth ○
Middlesbrough ○

➤ Benjani is spoken to by referee Andre Marriner

Event Line
Half time 0-0
46 ○ ⇄ Routledge > Davis
54 ○ ⊕ O'Neil / RF / OP / IA
Assist: Mwaruwari
59 ○ ⇄ Christie > Doriva
67 ○ ⇄ Karadas > Mwaruwari
77 ○ ⇄ Johnson > Morrison
78 ○ ⇄ Hughes > Todorov
85 ○ ⇄ Wheater > Bates
Full time 1-0

Pompey finally moved out of the relegation zone and gave themselves the impetus to make the great escape a reality as they made it thirteen points from the last five matches.

This was a vital victory for Harry Redknapp's side on Easter Saturday and once more it was a case of 'never mind the quality, but feel the width'.

Gary O'Neil's strike early in the second half was enough to earn this hard fought victory against a Middlesbrough side still in Europe and the FA Cup. It was ten minutes into the second half when Benjani did all the hard work, making his way along the edge of the area before slipping the ball to O'Neil who gratefully shot home in a game where few chances had been created.

Pompey fans had to suffer before O'Neil's goal could be crowned as the match winner with Middlesbrough staging a late rally. First David Wheater shot inches wide and then George Boateng failed to hit the target late on when the ball fell invitingly to him in the area. But this was a massive three points for Pompey who were now piling pressure on the two Midlands teams Birmingham and West Brom who were now below them at this critical stage.

Player of the Match	Quote	Premiership Milestone
26 Gary O'Neil	**❝** **Harry Redknapp**	➤ **50**

Quote: It's a fantastic run that we've been on but it's still all to play for, it's still tight. We've given ourselves a great chance and when you look at our run it's incredible, fourteen points from eighteen, unbelievable.

Premiership Milestone: Wayne Routledge made his 50th Premiership appearance.

Venue:	Fratton Park	Referee:	A.Marriner - 05/06	Portsmouth
Attendance:	20,204	Matches:	23	Middlesbrough
		Yellow Cards:	71	
		Red Cards:	7	

Form Coming into Fixture

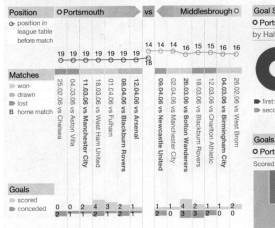

Position — ○ Portsmouth vs Middlesbrough ○
G- position in league table before match

19 19 19 19 19 19 19 18 → 14 14 14 16 15 15 16 16

Matches
- won
- drawn
- lost
B home match

25.02.06 vs Chelsea / 04.03.06 vs Aston Villa / 11.03.06 vs Manchester City / 18.03.06 vs West Ham United / 01.04.06 vs Fulham / 08.04.06 vs Blackburn Rovers / 12.04.06 vs Arsenal / 09.04.06 vs Newcastle United / 02.04.06 vs Manchester City / 26.03.06 vs Bolton Wanderers / 18.03.06 vs Blackburn Rovers / 12.03.06 vs Charlton Athletic / 04.03.06 vs Birmingham City / 26.02.06 vs West Brom

Goals
- scored
- conceded

| 0 | 0 | 2 | 4 | 3 | 2 | 1 | | 1 | 1 | 4 | 2 | 1 | 1 | 2 |
| 2 | 1 | 1 | 2 | 1 | 2 | 1 | | 2 | 0 | 3 | 3 | 2 | 0 | 0 |

Goal Statistics

○ **Portsmouth** — by Half / by Situation

▶ first: 6   ▶ set piece: 6
▶ second: 6   ▶ open play: 6

○ **Middlesbrough** — by Half / by Situation

▶ first: 7   ▶ set piece: 3
▶ second: 5   ▶ open play: 8
          ▶ own goals: 1

Goals by Area

○ **Portsmouth** — Scored (Conceded)

4 (2)
3 (6)
5 (2)

○ **Middlesbrough** — Scored (Conceded)

2 (5)
7 (4)
3 (1)

Team Statistics

Starting Line-Ups

Taylor — d'Alessandro   Morrison / Johnson — Parnaby
Boateng
Stefanovic — Mendes — Todorov / Hughes   Ehiogu
Kiely   Yakubu   Doriva / Christie   Jones
Primus — Davis / Routledge — Mwaruwari / Karadas — Bates / Wheater
Priske — O'Neil   Rochemback   Downing — Taylor

▶ **4/4/2**   ▶ **4/5/1**

Unused Sub: Ashdown, O'Brien   Unused Sub: Knight, Kennedy

Premiership Totals	○ Portsmouth	Boro ○
Premiership Appearances	903	1,141
Team Appearances	477	603
Goals Scored	40	114
Assists	56	86
Clean Sheets (goalkeepers)	52	3
Yellow Cards	92	143
Red Cards	4	7
Full Internationals	9	6

Age/Height

Portsmouth Age   ▶ **27 yrs, 4 mo**
Middlesbrough Age   ▶ **24 yrs, 3 mo**
Portsmouth Height   ▶ **5'11"**
Middlesbrough Height   ▶ **5'11"**

Match Statistics

League Table after Fixture

	Played	Won	Drawn	Lost	For	Against	Pts
● 12 Charlton	34	12	8	14	38	44	44
● 13 Man City	34	12	4	18	40	41	40
● 14 Middlesbrough	33	11	7	15	45	55	40
↑ 15 Fulham	34	11	6	17	43	55	39
↓ 16 Aston Villa	33	8	12	13	34	46	36
↑ 17 Portsmouth	34	8	8	18	31	55	32
↓ 18 Birmingham	33	7	8	18	25	45	29
● 19 West Brom	34	7	7	20	29	52	28
● 20 Sunderland	33	2	6	25	21	57	12

Statistics	○ Portsmouth	Boro ○
Goals	1	0
Shots on Target	11	9
Shots off Target	5	4
Hit Woodwork	0	0
Possession %	46	54
Corners	7	5
Offsides	1	0
Fouls	12	10
Disciplinary Points	0	0

2-1

Charlton Athletic ○
Portsmouth ○

➡ Andres d'Alessandro celebrates his spectacular strike

Event Line

25 ○ ⇄	Bothroyd > Bent M
38 ○ ⇄	Sankofa > Spector
40 ○ ⊕	d'Alessandro / LF / OP / IA
Half time 0-1	
46 ○ ⇄	Ambrose > Thomas
76 ○ ⊕	Hughes / RF / OP / IA
	Assist: Bent D
78 ○ ⇄	Karadas > Todorov
82 ○	Karadas
83 ○ ⊕	Bent D / RF / OP / IA
	Assist: Hreidarsson
84 ○ ⇄	Routledge > Hughes
84 ○	Bent D
Full time 2-1	

Pompey suffered their first defeat in six games at The Valley as they blew a golden opportunity to put intense pressure on those below them.

A win would have taken the Blues six points ahead of Birmingham who were not in action until the Wednesday evening and for much of this game it looked as if Pompey were about to grab that opportunity with both hands and continue their magnificent run.

In the end the amount of games in the week caught up with Harry's side and two goals in the last fifteen minutes proved their undoing. Andres d'Alessandro had given the visitors the lead with a spectacular effort on forty minutes. He ran diagonally across the area before unleashing an effort that flew into Myhre's top corner. It was a goal worthy of winning any match and it looked like doing so, but the home side turned the game on its head with fourteen minutes to go.

Firstly Bent burst into the area and squared for Hughes who stabbed home from close range. Then, with seven minutes remaining, Bent again raced down the right wing before cutting into the area and unleashing a stinging shot past Kiely. That condemned Pompey to a defeat which kept them in the melting pot of relegation trouble.

Player of the Match	Quote	Premiership Milestone
4 A. d'Alessandro	❻ **Dean Kiely**	➡ **First Goal**

Regardless of the result, the effort from the lads was fantastic and it's that ingredient that has got us on a decent run of late and it's that ingredient that will kick us on for the last three games.

Andres d'Alessandro netted his first Premiership goal.

Venue:	The Valley	Referee:	H.M.Webb - 05/06
Attendance:	25,419	Matches:	39
Capacity:	27,111	Yellow Cards:	103
		Red Cards:	4

Charlton Athletic
Portsmouth

Form Coming into Fixture

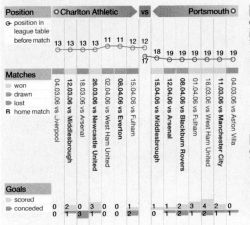

Position — Charlton Athletic vs Portsmouth

O position in league table before match

13 13 13 13 11 11 12 12
18 19 19 19 19 19 19 19
17

Matches
- won
- drawn
- lost
- R home match

04.03.06 vs Liverpool
12.03.06 vs Middlesbrough
18.03.06 vs Arsenal
26.03.06 vs Newcastle United
02.04.06 vs West Ham United
08.04.06 vs Everton
15.04.06 vs Fulham
15.04.06 vs Middlesbrough
12.04.06 vs Arsenal
08.04.06 vs Blackburn Rovers
01.04.06 vs Fulham
18.03.06 vs West Ham United
11.03.06 vs Manchester City
04.03.06 vs Aston Villa

Goals
- scored
- conceded

| scored | 0 | 2 | 0 | 3 | 0 | 0 | 1 | 1 | 1 | 2 | 3 | 4 | 2 | 0 |
| conceded | 0 | 1 | 3 | 1 | 0 | 0 | 2 | 0 | 1 | 2 | 1 | 2 | 1 | 1 |

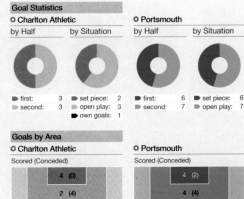

Goal Statistics

O Charlton Athletic

by Half | by Situation
- first: 3 | set piece: 2
- second: 3 | open play: 3
- | own goals: 1

O Portsmouth

by Half | by Situation
- first: 6 | set piece: 6
- second: 7 | open play: 7

Goals by Area

O Charlton Athletic
Scored (Conceded)

4 (0)
2 (4)
0 (3)

O Portsmouth
Scored (Conceded)

4 (2)
4 (4)
5 (2)

Team Statistics

Starting Line-Ups

Powell — Thomas Ambrose — O'Neil — Priske

Hreidarsson — Hughes — Bent D / Todorov Karadas — Davis — Primus

Myhre — Kiely

Sorondo — Holland — Bent M Bothroyd — Mwaruwari — Hughes Routledge — Pamarot

Spector Sankofa — Kishishev — d'Alessandro — Taylor

4 / 4 / 2

4 / 4 / 2

Unused Sub: Andersen, Euell

Unused Sub: Ashdown, Koroman

Premiership Totals	O Charlton	Portsmouth O
Premiership Appearances	1,370	748
Team Appearances	753	393
Goals Scored	100	31
Assists	84	53
Clean Sheets (goalkeepers)	32	53
Yellow Cards	105	62
Red Cards	4	1
Full Internationals	8	7

Age/Height

Charlton Athletic Age	Portsmouth Age
27 yrs, 4 mo	27 yrs
Charlton Athletic Height	Portsmouth Height
6'	5'11"

Match Statistics

League Table after Fixture

	Played	Won	Drawn	Lost	For	Against	Pts
↑ 11 Charlton	35	13	8	14	40	45	47
↓ 12 Everton	35	13	6	16	31	47	45
↑ 13 Middlesbrough	34	12	7	15	47	55	43
↓ 14 Man City	34	12	4	18	40	41	40
● 15 Aston Villa	34	9	12	13	37	47	39
● 16 Fulham	34	11	6	17	43	55	39
● 17 Portsmouth	35	8	8	19	32	57	32
● 18 Birmingham	34	7	8	19	26	48	29
● 19 West Brom	35	7	8	20	29	52	29

Statistics	O Charlton	Portsmouth O
Goals	2	1
Shots on Target	9	5
Shots off Target	7	6
Hit Woodwork	0	0
Possession %	49	51
Corners	6	9
Offsides	2	5
Fouls	10	17
Disciplinary Points	4	4

2-1 Portsmouth ○
Sunderland ○

➡ Sean Davis battles with Dean Whitehead

Event Line

19 ○ ■	Stefanovic
31 ○ ■	Brown
Half time 0-0	
46 ○ ⇄	Nosworthy > Stead
57 ○ ■	Breen
70 ○ ⊕	Miller / RF / OP / 6Y
	Assist: Arca
71 ○ ■	Kyle
73 ○ ⊕	Todorov / RF / OP / IA
	Assist: Priske
75 ○ ■	Hughes
76 ○ ⇄	Routledge > Hughes
88 ○ ⊕	Taylor / LF / P / IA
88 ○ ⇄	Diao > d'Alessandro
90 ○ ⇄	Pamarot > Todorov
Full time 2-1	

Pompey's dramatic season took another giant turn as already relegated Sunderland looked set to thwart their brave attempts of past weeks to achieve Premier League survival.

But another heart-stopping comeback, resulting in an eighty-eighth minute penalty strike from Matt Taylor, turned defeat into victory and left Pompey on the brink of completing an escape that looked impossible just a few weeks previously.

Sunderland, with nothing to play for but pride, had caused Pompey problems and when they took the lead with twenty minutes to go in what was a 'must win' game for the home side, things looked grim. Julio Arca broke clear down the left and his square ball to a free Tommy Miller produced an easy tap in. Birmingham fans celebrated at Everton where they were fighting out a 0-0 stalemate.

But Pompey were level within three minutes when Todorov took the ball past several defenders and shot into Davis' top corner from the edge of the area.

Still Pompey needed victory and with minutes ticking away Kyle inexplicably handled the ball in his own area and Pompey were awarded their first league penalty of the season, Taylor converting to set Fratton Park rocking again.

Player of the Match	Quote	Premiership Milestone
14 Matthew Taylor	🏈 **Harry Redknapp**	▶ **50**

People said to me 'you can improve your goal average on Saturday' as if we were playing some kind of mugs, but I said, 'No, I'll just settle for three points'.

Salif Diao made his 50th Premiership appearance.

Venue:	Fratton Park	Referee:	M.L.Dean - 05/06		Portsmouth
Attendance:	20,078	Matches:	36		Sunderland
		Yellow Cards:	107		
		Red Cards:	9		

Form Coming into Fixture

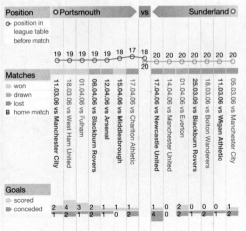

Goal Statistics

○ Portsmouth

by Half		by Situation	
▶ first:	7	▶ set piece:	6
▶ second:	7	▶ open play:	8

○ Sunderland

by Half		by Situation	
▶ first:	3	▶ set piece:	2
▶ second:	1	▶ open play:	2

Goals by Area

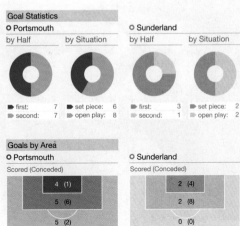

○ Portsmouth — Scored (Conceded)

| 4 (1) |
| 5 (6) |
| 5 (2) |

○ Sunderland — Scored (Conceded)

| 2 (4) |
| 2 (8) |
| 0 (0) |

Team Statistics

Starting Line-Ups

▶ 4 / 4 / 2   ▶ 4 / 4 / 2

Unused Sub: Ashdown, Karadas

Unused Sub: Murphy J, Caldwell, Leadbitter, Woods

Premiership Totals

	○ Portsmouth	Sunderland ○
Premiership Appearances	948	586
Team Appearances	488	399
Goals Scored	39	23
Assists	57	28
Clean Sheets (goalkeepers)	53	4
Yellow Cards	94	82
Red Cards	5	2
Full Internationals	8	4

Age/Height

Portsmouth Age	Sunderland Age
▶ **27 yrs, 8 mo**	▶ **25 yrs, 6 mo**
Portsmouth Height	Sunderland Height
▶ **5'11"**	▶ **6'1"**

Match Statistics

League Table after Fixture

	Played	Won	Drawn	Lost	For	Against	Pts
● 12 Everton	36	13	7	16	31	47	46
● 13 Middlesbrough	34	12	7	15	47	55	43
● 14 Man City	34	12	4	18	40	41	40
● 15 Aston Villa	35	9	12	14	39	50	39
● 16 Fulham	34	11	6	17	43	55	39
↑ 17 Portsmouth	36	9	8	19	34	58	35
↓ 18 Birmingham	36	8	9	19	28	49	33
● 19 West Brom	36	7	8	21	29	55	29
● 20 Sunderland	35	2	6	27	23	63	12

Statistics

	○ Portsmouth	Sunderland ○
Goals	2	1
Shots on Target	17	6
Shots off Target	8	1
Hit Woodwork	0	0
Possession %	52	48
Corners	8	5
Offsides	5	5
Fouls	9	16
Disciplinary Points	8	12

1-2 Wigan Athletic ○
Portsmouth ○

▶ Premiership survival sparks scenes of celebration

Event Line

34 ○ ⊕ Camara / RF / C / 6Y	
Assist: Jackson	
Half time 1-0	
46 ○ ⇄ Pamarot > Davis	
57 ○ ▢ Baines	
63 ○ ⊕ Mwaruwari / H / OP / 6Y	
Assist: Taylor	
68 ○ ⇄ Hughes > Mendes	
70 ○ ▉ Teale	
Handball	
71 ○ ⊕ Taylor / LF / P / IA	
Assist: Mwaruwari	
72 ○ ▢ Henchoz	
72 ○ ⇄ Scharner > Thompson	
80 ○ ⇄ Connolly > Camara	
84 ○ ▢ McCulloch	
84 ○ ⇄ Johansson > Kavanagh	
90 ○ ▢ Hughes	
90 ○ ⇄ Routledge > Todorov	
Full time 1-2	

And so Pompey knew that victory in their first ever visit to Wigan's JJB stadium was essential with a rampant Liverpool to come the following week in the final game.

Quite simply, if Pompey did the business and Birmingham failed to win against Newcastle then the escape would be complete with a game to spare.

The first forty-five minutes belonged to Wigan who went in at half time 1-0 up and very much in the driving seat. They had taken the lead after thirty-three minutes when Camara converted the loose ball from Jackson's header.

The Blues got to grips with the task as the second half got underway. They levelled on sixty three minutes when Benjani finally broke his duck since signing in January, heading home Taylor's shot which had hit the woodwork. Seven minutes later midfielder Teale handled Benjani's header on the line and saw red. For the second week running Taylor showed an ice cool nerve to beat Pollitt from the spot.

Within two minutes of this game ending, news of Birmingham's goalless stalemate was confirmed and Pompey, along with their fans, were free to celebrate a truly remarkable escape from the jaws of relegation.

Player of the Match	Quote	Premiership Milestone
25 B. Mwaruwari	⑥ **Milan Mandaric**	▶ **First Goal**

There are not enough words. I'm just delighted, delighted, delighted. It's been a tough season for tough guys! It's been a very difficult season, but we're delighted with the result and the outcome.

Benjani Mwaruwari netted his first Premiership goal.

Venue:	JJB Stadium	Referee:	M.A.Riley - 05/06		**Wigan Athletic**
Attendance:	21,126	Matches:	37		**Portsmouth**
Capacity:	25,023	Yellow Cards:	122		
		Red Cards:	9		

Form Coming into Fixture

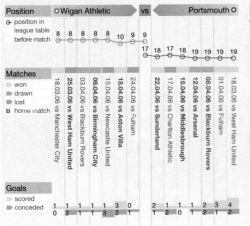

Position
○ Wigan Athletic   vs   Portsmouth ○

○ position in league table before match

8 8 8 8 8 10 9 9
17 18 17 18 19 19 19 19

Matches
▶ won
▶ drawn
▶ lost
B home match

Goals
▶ scored
▶ conceded

1 1 1 1 1 3 0 | 2 1 1 1 2 3 4
0 2 1 1 3 2 1 | 1 2 0 1 2 1 2

Goal Statistics

○ **Wigan Athletic**
by Half   by Situation

▶ first: 3   ▶ set piece: 4
   second: 5   ▶ open play: 4

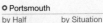

○ **Portsmouth**
by Half   by Situation

▶ first: 7   ▶ set piece: 5
▶ second: 7   ▶ open play: 9

Goals by Area

○ Wigan Athletic
Scored (Conceded)
2 (3)
3 (7)
3 (0)

○ Portsmouth
Scored (Conceded)
4 (1)
7 (6)
3 (2)

Team Statistics

Starting Line-Ups

Baines   McCulloch   O'Neil   Priske

Jackson   Kavanagh/Johansson   Roberts Mwaruwari   Davis/Pamarot   Primus

Pollitt   Kiely

Henchoz   Thompson/Scharner   Camara/Connolly   Todorov/Routledge   Mendes/Hughes   Stefanovic

Chimbonda   Teale   d'Alessandro   Taylor

▶ 4/4/2   ▶ 4/4/2

Unused Sub: Wright, Francis   Unused Sub: Ashdown, Karadas

Premiership Totals	○ Wigan	Portsmouth ○
Premiership Appearances	877	955
Team Appearances	325	504
Goals Scored	65	44
Assists	65	57
Clean Sheets (goalkeepers)	3	53
Yellow Cards	127	96
Red Cards	6	4
Full Internationals	9	8

Age/Height

Wigan Athletic Age
▶ **29 yrs**

Portsmouth Age
▶ **27 yrs, 6 mo**

Wigan Athletic Height
▶ **5'11"**

Portsmouth Height
▶ **5'11"**

Match Statistics

League Table after Fixture

		Played	Won	Drawn	Lost	For	Against	Pts
●	9 Wigan	37	15	6	16	43	48	51
●	10 West Ham	36	14	7	15	49	54	49
↑	11 Everton	37	14	7	16	32	47	49
↓	12 Charlton	37	13	8	16	41	51	47
↑	13 Fulham	36	13	6	17	46	56	45
↓	14 Man City	36	13	4	19	42	43	43
↓	15 Middlesbrough	35	12	7	16	47	56	43
●	16 Aston Villa	37	9	12	16	40	54	39
●	17 Portsmouth	37	10	8	19	36	59	38

Statistics	○ Wigan	Portsmouth ○
Goals	1	2
Shots on Target	7	9
Shots off Target	6	6
Hit Woodwork	0	2
Possession %	44	56
Corners	3	9
Offsides	5	8
Fouls	11	8
Disciplinary Points	24	4

1-3

Portsmouth ○
Liverpool ○

➡ Linvoy Primus challenges Harry Kewell

Event Line

40 ○ ▨	Taylor
41 ○ ⇄	Kromkamp > Alonso
Half time 0-0	
52 ○ ✪	Fowler / LF / OP / IA
	Assist: Morientes
62 ○ ⇄	Koroman > Hughes
67 ○ ⇄	Crouch > Morientes
68 ○ ⇄	Routledge > d'Alessandro
83 ○ ⇄	Cisse > Fowler
84 ○ ✪	Crouch / RF / OP / 6Y
	Assist: Cisse
85 ○ ✪	Koroman / RF / OP / 6Y
	Assist: Routledge
86 ○ ⇄	Pamarot > Primus
89 ○ ✪	Cisse / RF / OP / IA
	Assist: Crouch
Full time 1-3	

This was strictly celebration time with the pressure off for the first time.

Fratton Park was bathed in sunshine and a carnival atmosphere for a game that might have potentially been fraught with anxiety and heartbreak. Pompey's remarkable run with just one defeat in nine games had averted that.

It was very much an even first half and as a spectacle the game only really burst into life in the last ten minutes. Robbie Fowler put Liverpool ahead with a typical effort from just inside the box after fifty-three minutes, but it was only a late spurt which added to the score-line.

Former Pompey striker Peter Crouch made it 2-0 six minutes from time after Kiely had beaten Cissé's shot away into his path, but within a minute Ognjen Koroman converted Routledge's cross at the far post for Pompey.

Three minutes later Crouch turned provider for Cissé to strike Liverpool's third. With the result immaterial the curtain came down on a long, hard, but ultimately rewarding season that had provided the most amazing twist.

Player of the Match	Quote	Premiership Milestone
4 A. d'Alessandro	❝ **Harry Redknapp**	➡ **20,240**
	Overall I thought that we played OK and that 3-1 was a bit flattering for Liverpool, though they are a good side.	The attendance of 20,240 was a Premiership record at Fratton Park.

Venue:	Fratton Park	Referee:	G.Poll - 05/06		Portsmouth
Attendance:	20,240	Matches:	41		Liverpool
		Yellow Cards:	134		
		Red Cards:	6		

Form Coming into Fixture

Position ○ Portsmouth vs Liverpool ○

○ position in league table before match

B home match

Matches
- won
- drawn
- lost
- B home match

Goals
- scored
- conceded

Goal Statistics

○ Portsmouth

by Half   by Situation

- first: 4
- second: 8
- set piece: 5
- open play: 7

○ Liverpool

by Half   by Situation

- first: 9
- second: 6
- set piece: 2
- open play: 12
- own goals: 1

Goals by Area

○ Portsmouth — Scored (Conceded)

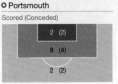

2 (2)
8 (4)
2 (2)

○ Liverpool — Scored (Conceded)

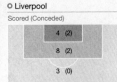

4 (2)
8 (2)
3 (0)

Team Statistics

Starting Line-Ups

Taylor   d'Alessandro (Routledge)   Gerrard   Finnan

Stefanovic   Hughes (Koroman)   Todorov   Fowler (Cisse)   Sissoko   Carragher

Kiely   Dudek

Mwaruwari   Morientes (Crouch)

Primus (Pamarot)   Davis   Alonso (Kromkamp)   Hyypia

Priske   O'Neil   Kewell   Riise

▶ 4/4/2   ▶ 4/4/2

Unused Sub: Ashdown, Pericard   Unused Sub: Reina, Traore

Premiership Totals	○ Portsmouth	Liverpool ○
Premiership Appearances	927	2,118
Team Appearances	506	1,693
Goals Scored	42	343
Assists	58	230
Clean Sheets (goalkeepers)	53	49
Yellow Cards	89	179
Red Cards	4	13
Full Internationals	8	14

Age/Height

Portsmouth Age ▶ **27 yrs, 7 mo**   Liverpool Age ▶ **27 yrs, 8 mo**

Portsmouth Height ▶ **5'11"**   Liverpool Height ▶ **6'1"**

Match Statistics

League Table after Fixture

		Played	Won	Drawn	Lost	For	Against	Pts
●	3 Liverpool	38	25	7	6	57	25	82
...	...	...	...	...	...	...	...	...
↓	14 Middlesbrough	38	12	9	17	48	58	45
●	15 Man City	38	13	4	21	43	48	43
●	16 Aston Villa	38	10	12	16	42	55	42
●	17 Portsmouth	38	10	8	20	37	62	38
●	18 Birmingham	38	8	10	20	28	50	34
●	19 West Brom	38	7	9	22	31	58	30
●	20 Sunderland	38	3	6	29	26	69	15

Statistics	○ Portsmouth	Liverpool ○
Goals	1	3
Shots on Target	4	4
Shots off Target	2	4
Hit Woodwork	0	0
Possession %	49	51
Corners	5	6
Offsides	5	1
Fouls	5	11
Disciplinary Points	4	0

Season Review 2005/06

Pompey's season began with a home loss and ended with one. However, what came between transformed the presented meal set before the fan from a plain offering, to one that titillated the taste buds of even the most fussy supporter during an amazing transformation of flavour and colour in the life and times of this famous old football club.

The opening day defeat against a re-vitalised Spurs, played in torrential August rain to baptise the first game, was in many ways indicative of how Pompey's season would progress up to December. Inventive and pretty football had Tottenham looking vulnerable

at times, but by the final whistle a 2-0 defeat depressingly justified the fact that the North London side took their chances when it mattered.

By the time Liverpool visited on the last day of the season nine months later, a 3-1 defeat was played in a carnival atmosphere of joviality and good humour. Indeed the dark August clouds of the opening encounter and the bright sunny May skies of the closing game epitomise all that came between in Pompey's dramatic season. It was almost as if a message had come from above.

'Fortress Fratton Park' was where Pompey's best chance of taking maximum points lay, but the drawbridge was coming down too easily and when December came without a win at home, despite the vociferous aid of the fanatical support, drastic measures had to be taken. In that period ten man Aston Villa (1-1) and Birmingham (1-1) had survived, despite being handicapped with dismissed players for a large chunk of the game. Newcastle had also held on for a draw (0-0) whilst Charlton (2-1), Wigan (2-0) and predictably Chelsea (2-0) had all come away with three points from what were disappointing encounters. The presentation was pretty enough, but

the end product was wholly bland.

Away from home there had been the odd tasty morsel. Pompey's early season win at Everton, the first for half a century, had temporarily lifted spirits whilst a draw at Middlesbrough (1-1) and four goals away at fellow strugglers Sunderland (4-1) in the club's first ever win at The Stadium of Light suggested an improved appetite. However, once more it was what came in between these tempting crumbs of comfort that set the tone: Defeats at West Brom (2-1), Manchester City (2-1), Bolton (1-0), Liverpool (3-0) and Manchester United (3-0), plus a

● Pedro Mendes scores another cracker in a galvanizing 4-2 win at West Ham ...

catastrophic Carling Cup exit at the first hurdle to League 1 Gillingham (3-2), were the unpalatable offerings of the feast and put together on the banquet table they made for pretty meagre fare.

Alan Perrin's imports such as John Viafara, Zvomimir Vukic, Gregory Vignal and Azar Karadas struggled to make any impact in the world's toughest league. Despite his undoubted class, Laurent Robert's individualistic temperament was hardly suited to what had become an 'all hands to the pump' effort and Sander Westerveld, for all his experience at the top level, showed erratic tendencies.

What all this added up to with Christmas approaching was ten miserly points and no home win in sight which might have delighted Ebenezer Scrooge, but hardly placated the more ravenous at the Christmas table.

The time had come for a few more spices and herbs.

The palate needed stimulating and the hunger of both owner and fans needed to be satisfied. In Gotham City when crisis looms they call for Batman, but here at Fratton Park Milan Mandaric picked up the red phone and called for Harry Redknapp. True, the parting of the ways last time had been hardly mutual and the destination of the recalled manager was undoubtedly highly controversial, but amidst the concerns and the local prejudices this brave returning to the fold was seen by most as the only one possible.

Those who expected a culinary treat were disappointed though. Only one messiah was able to turn water into wine immediately, but for a mere mortal like Redknapp, despite his eventual magic, this was more a grinding process. In his early days an opening defeat at Spurs (3-1), a thrashing at Arsenal (4-0) and a disappointing defeat at Blackburn (2-1) were the orders of the day.

➡ ... and celebrates

But things were slowly moving. Suddenly the first Fratton Park win in his first home game had come against West Brom (1-0) and from the next two home matches a further four points were amassed against West Ham (1-1) and Fulham (1-0). In another mid-season change of direction, a highly significant off the field development occurred as the wealthy young Alexandre Gaydamak became a partner to the revered elder Milan Mandaric. Now this was pure Michelin standard and additions such as Pedro Mendes, Sean Davis, Dean Kiely, Andres d'Alessandro, Noé Pamarot, Wayne Routledge and Benjani Mwaruwari were a combination that equally got the taste buds functioning again. The menu had been transformed.

There was a definite buzz when Pompey took to the field against Everton with this new look, but even now the problem was that the immediate presentation of the fare was better than its consumption. Expectancy levels had gone into overdrive and a 1-0 defeat followed by a catastrophic 5-0 hammering at relegation rivals Birmingham the following week were a shock to the system. Like good cheese or wine, these players needed time to breathe, blend and mature. The trouble was, time was not on their side so the uncorking and unwrapping had to happen now.

A 4th round FA Cup exit to Liverpool (2-1) at Fratton Park was merely a blessing after an earlier 3rd round triumph at Ipswich (1-0.) A late goal from one of the old school, Azar Karadas, against Bolton rescued a home point (1-1), but on the first day of February that was as good as it got amongst a series of tough encounters. The road to March and spring brought a home loss to Manchester United (3-1) and away defeats to Newcastle (2-0) and Chelsea (2-0): Forgivable defeats, but not ones that could be afforded.

▶ LuaLua celebrates as only LuaLua can against Arsenal

► The captain applauds the twelfth man

Things really had to start cooking at a high temperature. With March upon us, Redknapp and his troops were second from bottom, eight points from safety and down to eleven games left. Even Birmingham in the third relegation spot had a healthy five point lead and a game in hand, but a 1-0 defeat at a mediocre Aston Villa hardly produced any crumbs of comfort.

Yet something was stirring. Indeed the wine was maturing. Pedro Mendes uncorked not one, but two delectable strikes that put Manchester City in their place (2-1). His injury time strike after City had the temerity to try and gatecrash the initial offering was of such intoxication that it will live on for many a day. Yet it did something much more profound. Suddenly, to borrow a phrase from a Dickens classic, just like Oliver Twist, the players and supporters 'wanted more'.

Two capital days in London aptly demonstrated this heightened appetite. The fans sang for Harry, the players played for the shirt, the football was irresistible and both West Ham (4-2) and Fulham (3-1) were soundly beaten. In turn only an inferior goal

▶ Defeat against Liverpool on the last day of the season at Fratton Park could not ruin the party atmosphere

difference now separated Pompey from the safety zone and nobody could quite wait for the next serving to see what came up.

There were one or two hiccups only to be expected at such an extraordinarily lavish feast. Consecutive draws in a hectic period against Blackburn (2-2) and Arsenal (1-1) were not too difficult to digest however due to thoroughly creditable results and performances. And by the time hardened opponents Middlesbrough came to town, Pompey's third game in seven days, even the most hearty diner was a little bloated. Nevertheless Pompey scrapped for more tiny morsels and their 1-0 victory finally took them out of a relegation zone which they had occupied for most of the season, but to which they would only temporarily return for three short days.

An Easter Monday defeat at Charlton (2-1) was one that was hard to swallow. Victory, which d'Alessandro's goal had made probable, would have virtually banished relegation fears.

The question now was did Pompey still have the stomach after being left sick? A win by Birmingham forty-eight hours later had posted the Blues back into the relegation zone, but a 2-1 win at home to already relegated Sunderland answered that question emphatically. Trailing 1-0 with twenty minutes remaining this was win or bust quite literally, but the hunger was there for all to see. Todorov had levelled within 3 minutes but the real drama was still to be played out. Pompey had not been awarded a Premier League penalty all season but in the 88th minute, Kyle's inexplicable handball changed that. Step forward Matthew Taylor, who sent the 'keeper the wrong way.

Now the equation was simple. A win at Wigan was vital as Pompey's destiny lay in their own hands. Liverpool were more than capable of gate-crashing the feast in eight days time, but Birmingham could also spoil the party. Redknapp's troops needed one more immense offering and over the ninety minutes, despite a rocky forty-five in which they went a goal behind, this was the new look menu with the hunger and appetite written everywhere. Benjani could not have picked a better time or place to end his goal famine as he picked up Taylor's rebound off the bar to head home and he was there once more to head Todorov's cross goalwards, forcing Teale to handle on the line. Taylor once again showed ice cool composure to hit home the spot kick. Another feast was being witnessed at the JJB stadium whilst over at St Andrews Birmingham's failure to breach Newcastle signalled the beginning of their last supper. Incredibly it was the party of all parties as Pompey had survived with a game to spare.

And so Liverpool came to Fratton Park bathed in metrological and metaphorical sunshine. The rain and clouds that had opened the season against Spurs were but a distant memory. Unlike defeat that day, this 3-1 loss mattered not. For in between the sandwich that had first looked unpalatable, a relish had been added in time to make the 2005/06 season a feast fit for a king.

Premiership Results Table 2005/06

■ Won
■ Drawn
■ Lost
■ Yellow Card
■ Red Card
■ Goal

45 Time of 1st Sub
45 Time of 2nd Sub
45 Time of 3rd Sub
45 Time of Goal
45 Time of Assist

Match: | Players: | Substitutes:

Date	H/A	Opponent	H/T	F/T	Pos	First String
13-08	H	Tottenham	0-1	0-2	20	Westerveld
20-08	A	West Brom	0-1	1-2	19	Westerveld
23-08	A	Aston Villa	1-1	1-1	17	Westerveld
27-08	H	Man City	0-0	0-1	17	Westerveld
10-09	A	Everton	0-0	0-1	15	Ashdown
17-09	H	Birmingham	1-1	1-1	14	Ashdown
24-09	A	Bolton	0-0	0-1	15	Ashdown
01-10	H	Newcastle	0-0	0-0	15	Ashdown
15-10	A	Middlesbrough	0-0	0-1	15	Ashdown
22-10	H	Charlton	0-1	1-1	15	Ashdown
29-10	A	Sunderland	0-1	4-1	14	Ashdown
05-11	H	Wigan	0-0	0-2	15	Ashdown
19-11	A	Liverpool	0-2	0-3	17	Ashdown
26-11	H	Chelsea	0-1	0-2	17	Ashdown
03-12	A	Man Utd	0-1	0-3	18	Ashdown
12-12	A	Tottenham	1-1	1-3	18	Ashdown
17-12	H	West Brom	1-1	1-1	18	Ashdown
26-12	H	West Ham	1-1	1-1	18	Ashdown
28-12	A	Arsenal	0-4	0-4	18	Ashdown
31-12	H	Fulham	1-0	1-0	18	Ashdown
02-01	A	Blackburn	1-2	1-2	18	Westerveld
14-01	H	Everton	0-1	0-1	18	Ashdown
21-01	A	Birmingham	0-2	0-5	19	Ashdown
01-02	H	Bolton	0-0	0-0	19	Kiely
04-02	A	Newcastle	0-1	0-2	19	Kiely
11-02	A	Man Utd	0-3	1-3	19	Kiely
25-02	A	Chelsea	0-0	0-2	19	Kiely
04-03	H	Aston Villa	0-1	0-1	19	Kiely
11-03	H	Man City	0-0	2-1	19	Kiely
18-03	A	West Ham	3-0	4-2	19	Kiely
01-04	H	Fulham	2-1	3-1	18	Kiely
08-04	A	Blackburn	1-1	2-2	18	Kiely
12-04	H	Arsenal	1-1	1-1	18	Kiely
15-04	H	Middlesbrough	0-1	1-0	17	Kiely
17-04	A	Charlton	1-0	1-2	17	Kiely
22-04	A	Sunderland	0-0	2-1	17	Kiely
29-04	H	Wigan	2-1	2-1	17	Kiely
07-05	H	Liverpool	0-0	1-3	17	Kiely

101

33 Dean Kiely
Goalkeeper

Republic of Ireland international who started his career at Coventry City, but made his league debut on loan at York City in 1990.

Dean moved to Bury in 1996 and helped the Shakers to the Division Two Championship, before later achieving hero status, somehow keeping an impressive 19 clean sheets despite relegation in '98/'99.

Charlton then paid £1 million for his services and he kept another 18 clean sheets as the Addicks stormed to the Division One Championship. The 35-year-old played 248 times for Charlton, sitting out just three games between August 2001 and August 2005. He joined Portsmouth in January 2006.

Player Details:

Date of Birth:	10.10.1970
Place of Birth:	Salford
Nationality:	Irish
Height:	6'1"
Weight:	12st 13lb
Foot:	Left

Player Performance 05/06

League Performance

Percentage of total possible time player was on pitch   ⊖ position in league table at end of month

Month:	Aug	Sep	Oct	Nov	Dec	Jan	Feb	Mar	Apr	May	Total
	18	16	14	18	18	19	19	19	17	17	39%
	0%	0%	0%	0%	0%	0%	100%	100%	100%	100%	
Team Pts:	1/12	4/9	5/12	0/9	7/18	0/9	1/12	6/9	14/21	0/3	38/114
Team Gls F:	3	2	6	0	4	1	2	6	12	1	37
Team Gls A:	7	2	4	7	11	8	8	4	8	3	62
Total mins:	0	0	0	0	0	0	360	270	630	90	1,350
Starts (sub):	0	0	0	0	0	0	4	3	7	1	15
Goals:	0	0	0	0	0	0	0	0	0	0	0
Assists:	0	0	0	0	0	0	0	0	0	0	0
Clean sheets:	0	0	0	0	0	0	0	0	1	0	1
Cards (Y/R):	0	0	0	0	0	0	0	0	0	0	0

League Performance Totals

Clean Sheets

- ▶ Kiely: 1
- ▣ Team-mates: 4
- **Total: 5**

Assists

- ▶ Kiely: 0
- ▣ Team-mates: 31
- **Total: 31**

Cards

- ▶ Kiely: 0
- ▣ Team-mates: 54
- **Total: 54**

Cup Games

	Apps	CS	Cards
FA Cup	1	0	0
Carling Cup	0	0	0
Total	**1**	**0**	**0**

Career History

Career Milestones

Club Debut:
vs Liverpool (H), L 1-2, FA Cup

▶ **29.01.06**

Time Spent at the Club:

▶ **0.5 Seasons**

First Goal Scored for the Club:
—

▶ **—**

Full International:

▶ **Rep. Ireland**

Premiership Totals

92-06

Appearances	192
Clean Sheets	53
Assists	3
Yellow Cards	4
Red Cards	1

Clubs

Year	Club	Apps	CS
06-06	Portsmouth	16	1
99-06	Charlton Ath	248	76
96-99	Bury	157	55
90-96	York C.	239	
89-89	Ipswich T.	0	0
87-90	Coventry C.	0	0

Off the Pitch

Age:

- ▶ Kiely: 35 years, 7 months
- ▣ Team: 27 years, 5 months
- ▎ League: 26 years, 11 months

Height:

- ▶ Kiely: 6'1"
- ▣ Team: 5'11"
- ▎ League: 5'11"

Weight:

- ▶ Kiely: 12st 13lb
- ▣ Team: 12st
- ▎ League: 12st

15 Jamie Ashdown
Goalkeeper

OK

OK

Season Review 05/06

Reading born shot-stopper who rose through the ranks with the Royals before gaining first team experience in loan spells with Gravesend, Bournemouth and Rushden & Diamonds. His performances alerted the attention of Premiership clubs and the former England Schoolboy signed for Pompey in June 2004.

Jamie spent much of 2005/06 as Pompey's first choice goalkeeper before the arrival of the experienced Dean Kiely in January saw him back on the bench. However, his confidence and ability have impressed.

Player Details:

Date of Birth:	30.11.1980
Place of Birth:	Reading
Nationality:	English
Height:	6'3"
Weight:	14st 7lb
Foot:	Right

Player Performance 05/06

League Performance

Percentage of total possible time player was on pitch   ⊖ position in league table at end of month

Month:	Aug	Sep	Oct	Nov	Dec	Jan	Feb	Mar	Apr	May	Total
	0%	100%	100%	100%	83%	67%	0%	0%	0%	0%	45%
Team Pts:	1/12	4/9	5/12	0/9	7/18	0/9	1/12	6/9	14/21	0/3	38/114
Team Gls F:	3	2	6	0	4	1	2	6	12	1	37
Team Gls A:	7	2	4	7	11	8	8	4	8	3	62
Total mins:	0	270	360	270	450	180	0	0	0	0	1,530
Starts (sub):	0	3	4	3	5	2	0	0	0	0	17
Goals:	0	0	0	0	0	0	0	0	0	0	0
Assists:	0	0	0	0	0	0	0	0	0	0	0
Clean sheets:	0	1	1	0	1	0	0	0	0	0	3
Cards (Y/R):	0	0	0	0	0	0	0	0	0	0	0

League table positions: 18, 16, 14, 18, 18, 19, 19, 19, 17, 17

League Performance Totals

Clean Sheets

▶ Ashdown:	3
▷ Team-mates:	2
Total:	**5**

Assists

▶ Ashdown:	0
▷ Team-mates:	31
Total:	**31**

Cards

▶ Ashdown:	0
▷ Team-mates:	54
Total:	**54**

Cup Games

	Apps	CS	Cards
FA Cup	0	0	0
Carling Cup	1	0	0
Total	**1**	**0**	**0**

Career History

Career Milestones

Club Debut:
vs Tranmere (A), W 0-1, League Cup

▶ 21.09.04

Time Spent at the Club:

▶ 2 Seasons

First Goal Scored for the Club:
—

▶ —

Full International:

▶ —

Premiership Totals
92-06

Appearances	33
Clean Sheets	5
Assists	0
Yellow Cards	0
Red Cards	0

Clubs

Year	Club	Apps	CS
04-06	Portsmouth	39	8
03-04	Rushden & D's	19	4
02-02	Bournemouth	2	1
01-01	Gravesend		
98-04	Reading	16	4

Off the Pitch

Age:

- ▶ Ashdown: 25 years, 6 months
- ▷ Team: 27 years, 5 months
- | League: 26 years, 11 months

Height:

- ▶ Ashdown: 6'3"
- ▷ Team: 5'11"
- | League: 5'11"

Weight:

- ▶ Ashdown: 14st 7lb
- ▷ Team: 12st
- | League: 12st

OK

1

Sander Westerveld
Goalkeeper

Season Review 05/06

Sander began his career at FC Twente before being poached by Vitesse Arnhem, for whom he made more than 100 appearances between 1996 and 1999 when he was signed by Liverpool for £4 million.

The Dutchman made 103 appearances for the Reds, lifting the UEFA, FA, European Super and League Cups before joining Real Sociedad in 2001.

After breaking a finger in February 2004, he never regained his place and instead moved on loan to Real Mallorca. He joined Portsmouth on a free transfer in July 2005 but struggled to recapture his past form, making just seven appearances before moving on loan to Everton and finally being released in May 2006.

Player Details:

Date of Birth:	23.10.1974
Place of Birth:	Enschede
Nationality:	Dutch
Height:	6'3"
Weight:	13st 8lb
Foot:	Right

Player Performance 05/06

League Performance

Percentage of total possible time player was on pitch   ⦵ position in league table at end of month

Month:	Aug	Sep	Oct	Nov	Dec	Jan	Feb	Mar	Apr	May	Total
	100% 18	16 0%	14 0%	18 0%	18 17%	33% 19	19 0%	19 0%	17 0%	17 0%	16%
Team Pts:	1/12	4/9	5/12	0/9	7/18	0/9	1/12	6/9	14/21	0/3	38/114
Team Gls F:	3	2	6	0	4	1	2	6	12	1	37
Team Gls A:	7	2	4	7	11	8	8	4	8	3	62
Total mins:	360	0	0	0	90	90	0	0	0	0	540
Starts (sub):	4	0	0	0	1	1	0	0	0	0	6
Goals:	0	0	0	0	0	0	0	0	0	0	0
Assists:	0	0	0	0	0	0	0	0	0	0	0
Clean sheets:	0	0	0	0	1	0	0	0	0	0	1
Cards (Y/R):	0	0	0	0	0	0	0	0	0	0	0

League Performance Totals

Clean Sheets
- Westerveld: 1
- Team-mates: 4
- **Total: 5**

Assists
- Westerveld: 0
- Team-mates: 31
- **Total: 31**

Cards
- Westerveld: 0
- Team-mates: 54
- **Total: 54**

Cup Games

	Apps	CS	Cards
FA Cup	1	1	0
Carling Cup	0	0	0
Total	1	1	0

Career History

Career Milestones

Club Debut:
vs Tottenham (H), L 0-2, Premiership
▶ **13.08.05**

First Goal Scored for the Club:
—
▶ **—**

Time Spent at the Club:
▶ **1 Season**

Full International:
▶ **Netherlands**

Premiership Totals

92-06

Appearances	83
Clean Sheets	29
Assists	0
Yellow Cards	1
Red Cards	1

Clubs

Year	Club	Apps	CS
06-06	Everton	2	0
05-06	Portsmouth	7	2
04-05	RCD Mallorca		
01-05	Real Sociedad		
99-01	Liverpool	103	42
	Vitesse Arnhem		
	Twente Enschede		

Off the Pitch

Age:
- Westerveld: 31 years, 7 months
- Team: 27 years, 5 months
- League: 26 years, 11 months

Height:
- Westerveld: 6'3"
- Team: 5'11"
- League: 5'11"

Weight:
- Westerveld: 13st 8lb
- Team: 12st
- League: 12st

3 Dejan Stefanovic
Defence

Club Captain Dejan Stefanovic began his career at Red Star Belgrade before moving to then top-flight Sheffield Wednesday in 1995 for £2 million. Three years in Holland with Vitesse Arnhem followed before making a £1.9 million move to Pompey in July 2003.

A cultured but uncompromising defender, Stefanovic, who operates best on the left side of central defence has been an automatic choice when fit since his arrival at Fratton Park, and was handed the captain's armband at the start of the 2005/06 season, when, despite battling with an ankle injury, he remained one of the club's most consistent players.

Player Details:

Date of Birth:	28.10.1974
Place of Birth:	Belgrade
Nationality:	Serbian
Height:	6'2"
Weight:	12st 2lb
Foot:	Left

Player Performance 05/06

League Performance

Percentage of total possible time player was on pitch   ⊖ position in league table at end of month

Month:	Aug	Sep	Oct	Nov	Dec	Jan	Feb	Mar	Apr	May	Total
	100%	100%	100%	67%	83%	64%			75%	100%	69%
	18	16	14	18	18	19	4% / 19	0% / 19	17	17	
Team Pts:	1/12	4/9	5/12	0/9	7/18	0/9	1/12	6/9	14/21	0/3	38/114
Team Gls F:	3	2	6	0	4	1	2	6	12	1	37
Team Gls A:	7	2	4	7	11	8	8	4	8	3	62
Total mins:	360	270	360	180	450	173	15	0	474	90	2,372
Starts (sub):	4	3	4	2	5	2	1	0	5 (1)	1	27 (1)
Goals:	0	0	0	0	0	0	0	0	0	0	0
Assists:	0	0	0	0	0	0	0	0	0	0	0
Clean sheets:	0	1	1	0	2	0	0	0	1	0	5
Cards (Y/R):	0	1	0	2	0	1	0	0	1	0	5

League Performance Totals

Goals

- ▶ Stefanovic: 0
- ▶ Team-mates: 36

Total: 36

▶ own goals: 1

Assists

- ▶ Stefanovic: 0
- ▶ Team-mates: 31

Total: 31

Cards

- ▶ Stefanovic: 5
- ▶ Team-mates: 49

Total: 54

Cup Games

	Apps	Goals	Cards
FA Cup	2	0	0
Carling Cup	1	0	1
Total	3	0	1

Career History

Career Milestones

Club Debut:

vs Aston Villa (H), W 2-1, Premiership

▶ **16.08.03**

Time Spent at the Club:

▶ **3 Seasons**

First Goal Scored for the Club:

vs Leeds (H), W 6-1, Premiership

▶ **08.11.03**

Full International:

▶ **Serbia**

Premiership Totals

92-06

Appearances	158
Goals	7
Assists	3
Yellow Cards	28
Red Cards	3

Clubs

Year	Club	Apps	Gls
03-06	Portsmouth	105	3
	Vitesse Arnhem		
	OFK Belgrade		
	Perugia		
95-99	Sheff Wed	72	5
	Red Star Belgrade		
	FK Radnicki		

Off the Pitch

Age:

- ▶ Stefanovic: 31 years, 7 months
- ▶ Team: 27 years, 5 months
- | League: 26 years, 11 months

Height:

- ▶ Stefanovic: 6'2"
- ▶ Team: 5'11"
- | League: 5'11"

Weight:

- ▶ Stefanovic: 12st 2lb
- ▶ Team: 12st
- | League: 12st

16 Andrew Griffin
Defence

Season Review 05/06

Right-back who originally began his career at Fratton Park as a 17-year-old Stoke City debutant in October 1996. After representing England at U18 and U21 level Andy was snapped up by Kenny Dalglish's Newcastle for £1.5 million in January 1998 and despite his youth, soon became a first team regular.

However, under Bobby Robson, Griffin drifted in and out of the team; a winning goal against Juventus in the Champions League the high point of a disappointing four years that eventually prompted his free transfer move to Pompey in 2004. He has since proved a worthy acquisition with some impressively feisty displays.

Player Details:

Date of Birth:	07.03.1979
Place of Birth:	Wigan
Nationality:	English
Height:	5'9"
Weight:	10st 10lb
Foot:	Right/Left

Player Performance 05/06

League Performance

Percentage of total possible time player was on pitch   ⊖ position in league table at end of month

Month:	Aug	Sep	Oct	Nov	Dec	Jan	Feb	Mar	Apr	May	Total
%	72%	0%	59%	95%	100%	100%	43%	29%	0%	0%	52%
Position	18	16	14	18	18	19	19	19	17	17	
Team Pts:	1/12	4/9	5/12	0/9	7/18	0/9	1/12	6/9	14/21	0/3	38/114
Team Gls F:	3	2	6	0	4	1	2	6	12	1	37
Team Gls A:	7	2	4	7	11	8	8	4	8	3	62
Total mins:	259	0	212	256	540	270	156	79	0	0	1,772
Starts (sub):	3	0	3	3	6	3	1 (2)	1	0	0	20 (2)
Goals:	0	0	0	0	0	0	0	0	0	0	0
Assists:	0	0	0	0	0	0	0	0	0	0	0
Clean sheets:	0	0	1	0	2	0	0	0	0	0	3
Cards (Y/R):	0	0	1	1	1	2	1	0	0	0	6

League Performance Totals

Goals
- ▶ Griffin: 0
- ▧ Team-mates: 36
- **Total: 36**
- ▶ own goals: 1

Assists
- ▶ Griffin: 0
- ▧ Team-mates: 31
- **Total: 31**

Cards
- ▶ Griffin: 6
- ▧ Team-mates: 48
- **Total: 54**

Cup Games

	Apps	Goals	Cards
FA Cup	0	0	0
Carling Cup	0	0	0
Total	**0**	**0**	**0**

Career History

Career Milestones

Club Debut:
vs Birmingham (H), D 1-1, Premiership
▶ **14.08.04**

Time Spent at the Club:
▶ **2 Seasons**

First Goal Scored for the Club:
—
▶ **—**

Full International:
▶ **—**

Premiership Totals
92-06

Appearances	120
Goals	2
Assists	1
Yellow Cards	23
Red Cards	1

Clubs

Year	Club	Apps	Gls
04-06	Portsmouth	49	0
98-04	Newcastle	103	3
96-98	Stoke	64	2

Off the Pitch

Age:

- ▶ Griffin: 27 years, 2 months
- ▧ Team: 27 years, 5 months
- | League: 26 years, 11 months

Height:
- ▶ Griffin: 5'9"
- ▧ Team: 5'11"
- | League: 5'11"

Weight:
- ▶ Griffin: 10st 10lb
- ▧ Team: 12st
- | League: 12st

5 Andy O'Brien
Defence

Season Review 05/06

Combative central defender who came through the youth ranks at Bradford, making his debut at the tender age of 17. He was soon a first team regular and represented England U18s before choosing to pursue an international career with the Republic of Ireland.

Domestically O'Brien played an important role in Bradford's promotion to the Premier League before being snapped up by Newcastle in 2001. The Ireland international continued in the same vein at St James' Park before moving south in June 2005 and after 32 impressive appearances in his first season, he has proved himself a reliable squad player at Fratton Park.

Player Details:

Date of Birth:	29.06.1979
Place of Birth:	Harrogate
Nationality:	Irish
Height:	5'10"
Weight:	10st 6lb
Foot:	Right

Player Performance 05/06

League Performance

Percentage of total possible time player was on pitch   ⊖ position in league table at end of month

Month:	Aug	Sep	Oct	Nov	Dec	Jan	Feb	Mar	Apr	May	Total
	100%	100%	75%	67%	100%	100%	100%	100%	14%	0%	76%
	18	16	14	18	18	19	19	19	17	17	
Team Pts:	1/12	4/9	5/12	0/9	7/18	0/9	1/12	6/9	14/21	0/3	38/114
Team Gls F:	3	2	6	0	4	1	2	6	12	1	37
Team Gls A:	7	2	4	7	11	8	8	4	8	3	62
Total mins:	360	270	270	180	540	270	360	270	90	0	2,610
Starts (sub):	4	3	3	2	6	3	4	3	1	0	29
Goals:	0	0	0	0	0	0	0	0	0	0	0
Assists:	0	0	1	0	0	0	0	0	0	0	1
Clean sheets:	0	1	1	0	2	0	0	0	0	0	4
Cards (Y/R):	0	0	0	0	0	0	0	0	0	0	0

League Performance Totals

Goals

▶ O'Brien:	0
⬞ Team-mates:	36
Total:	**36**
▶ own goals:	1

Assists

▶ O'Brien:	1
⬞ Team-mates:	30
Total:	**31**

Cards

▶ O'Brien:	0
⬞ Team-mates:	54
Total:	**54**

Cup Games

	Apps	Goals	Cards
FA Cup	2	0	0
Carling Cup	1	0	0
Total	**3**	**0**	**0**

Career History

Career Milestones

Club Debut:

vs Tottenham (H), L 0-2, Premiership

 13.08.05

Time Spent at the Club:

▶ **1 Season**

First Goal Scored for the Club:

—

▶ **—**

Full International:

 Rep. Ireland

Premiership Totals

92-06

Appearances	203
Goals	7
Assists	1
Yellow Cards	12
Red Cards	2

Clubs

Year	Club	Apps	Gls
05-06	Portsmouth	32	0
01-05	Newcastle	172	7
94-01	Bradford	149	3

Off the Pitch

Age:

- ▶ O'Brien: 26 years, 11 months
- ⬞ Team: 27 years, 5 months
- | League: 26 years, 11 months

Height:

- ▶ O'Brien: 5'10"
- ⬞ Team: 5'11"
- | League: 5'11"

Weight:

- ▶ O'Brien: 10st 6lb
- ⬞ Team: 12st
- | League: 12st

6

Brian Priske
Defence

Versatile defender who began his career with Aarhus in Denmark before joining Aalborg Boldspilklub two years later. Priske led AaB to the Danish championship in his first season and was made club captain.

After almost 160 appearances Brian moved to Belgian outfit Genk in 2003, where he established himself in the Danish national side in time for Euro 2004. He has since become an automatic choice for his country and after impressing against England in August 2005, he was snapped up by Portsmouth.

Brian's tall frame makes him a natural central defender, but he has taken exceptionally well to the role of right-back at Fratton Park.

Player Details:

Date of Birth:	14.05.1977
Place of Birth:	Horsens
Nationality:	Danish
Height:	6'2"
Weight:	12st
Foot:	Right

Player Performance 05/06

League Performance

Percentage of total possible time player was on pitch   ⊖ position in league table at end of month

Month:	Aug	Sep	Oct	Nov	Dec	Jan	Feb	Mar	Apr	May	Total
	50%	100%	100%	100%	63%	36%	0%	71%	100%	100%	71%
	18	16	14	18	18	19	19	19	17	17	
Team Pts:	1/12	4/9	5/12	0/9	7/18	0/9	1/12	6/9	14/21	0/3	38/114
Team Gls F:	3	2	6	0	4	1	2	6	12	1	37
Team Gls A:	7	2	4	7	11	8	8	4	8	3	62
Total mins:	180	270	360	270	341	97	0	191	630	90	2,429
Starts (sub):	2	3	4	3	3 (2)	1 (1)	0	2 (1)	7	1	26 (4)
Goals:	0	0	0	0	0	0	0	0	0	0	0
Assists:	0	0	0	0	0	0	0	1	1	0	2
Clean sheets:	0	1	1	0	1	0	0	0	1	0	4
Cards (Y/R):	0	1	0	0	0	0	0	0	0	0	1

League Performance Totals

Goals

▶ Priske: 0
▷ Team-mates: 36
Total: 36
◆ own goals: 1

Assists

▶ Priske: 2
▷ Team-mates: 29
Total: 31

Cards

▶ Priske: 1
▷ Team-mates: 53
Total: 54

Cup Games

	Apps	Goals	Cards
FA Cup	2	0	1
Carling Cup	1	0	0
Total	**3**	**0**	**1**

Career History

Career Milestones

Club Debut:
vs Aston Villa (H), D 1-1, Premiership
▶ **23.08.05**

Time Spent at the Club:
▶ **1 Season**

First Goal Scored for the Club:
—
▶ **—**

Full International:
▶ **Denmark**

Premiership Totals

92-06	
Appearances	30
Goals	0
Assists	2
Yellow Cards	1
Red Cards	0

Clubs

Year	Club	Apps	Gls
05-06	Portsmouth	33	0
	RC Genk		
	Aalborg		
	Aarhus		
	AC Horsens		

Off the Pitch

Age:

▶ Priske: 29 years
▷ Team: 27 years, 5 months
❙ League: 26 years, 11 months

Height:

▶ Priske: 6'2"
▷ Team: 5'11"
❙ League: 5'11"

Weight:

▶ Priske: 12st
▷ Team: 12st
❙ League: 12st

7

Gregory Vignal
Defence

Player Details:

Date of Birth:	19.07.1981
Place of Birth:	Montpellier
Nationality:	French
Height:	5'11"
Weight:	12st 3lb
Foot:	Left

Season Review 05/06

Vignal joined Liverpool from Montpellier in 2000, but despite good performances, his appearances were sporadic and eventually the left-back joined Bastia on loan in January 2003 - the first of four loan spells. A change in manager didn't increase Gregory's chances of action and Rafael Benitez sent him to Glasgow Rangers in August 2004.

He thrived at Ibrox as Rangers wrestled the Scottish Premier League title from Celtic and also won the Scottish League Cup, racking up 42 appearances and three goals before joining Portsmouth last summer. However, following Alain Perrin's departure, he lost his place in the team and was released in May 2006.

Player Performance 05/06

League Performance

Percentage of total possible time player was on pitch   G- position in league table at end of month

Month:	Aug	Sep	Oct	Nov	Dec	Jan	Feb	Mar	Apr	May	Total
	100%	100%	84%	56%							34%
	18	16	14	18	17% / 18	0% / 19	0% / 19	0% / 19	0% / 17	0% / 17	
Team Pts:	1/12	4/9	5/12	0/9	7/18	0/9	1/12	6/9	14/21	0/3	38/114
Team Gls F:	3	2	6	0	4	1	2	6	12	1	37
Team Gls A:	7	2	4	7	11	8	8	4	8	3	62
Total mins:	360	270	302	150	90	0	0	0	0	0	1,172
Starts (sub):	4	3	3 (1)	2	1	0	0	0	0	0	13 (1)
Goals:	0	0	0	0	0	0	0	0	0	0	0
Assists:	0	0	0	0	0	0	0	0	0	0	0
Clean sheets:	0	1	1	0	0	0	0	0	0	0	2
Cards (Y/R):	1	0	2	0	0	0	0	0	0	0	3

League Performance Totals

Goals

- Vignal: 0
- Team-mates: 36

Total: 36

- own goals: 1

Assists

- Vignal: 0
- Team-mates: 31

Total: 31

Cards

- Vignal: 3
- Team-mates: 51

Total: 54

Cup Games

	Apps	Goals	Cards
FA Cup	2	0	0
Carling Cup	1	0	1
Total	**3**	**0**	**1**

Career History

Career Milestones

Club Debut:
vs Tottenham (H), L 0-2, Premiership

 **13.08.05**

Time Spent at the Club:

▶ **1 Season**

First Goal Scored for the Club:
—

▶ —

Full International:

▶ —

Premiership Totals

92-06

Appearances	25
Goals	0
Assists	0
Yellow Cards	7
Red Cards	0

Clubs

Year	Club	Apps	Gls
05-06	Portsmouth	17	0
04-05	Rangers		
04-04	Espanyol		
03-03	Rennes		
03-03	Bastia		
00-05	Liverpool	20	0
	Montpellier		

Off the Pitch

Age:

- Vignal: 24 years, 10 months
- Team: 27 years, 5 months
- League: 26 years, 11 months

Height:

- Vignal: 5'11"
- Team: 5'11"
- League: 5'11"

Weight:

- Vignal: 12st 3lb
- Team: 12st
- League: 12st

2 Linvoy Primus
Defence

Reliable Forest Gate born defender who constantly disproves his critics. Linvoy learned his trade at Charlton Athletic before signing for Barnet in 1994 where he played almost 150 games. He moved to Reading for £250,000 in 1997 and after over 100 appearances, signed for Pompey in July 2000, where he has gone on to become a consistently dependable performer.

After winning countless player of the year awards in 2002/03, Primus' dedication and determination has continued to set a glowing example. The 2005/06 season was no exception, earning him a new contract which will keep him at Fratton Park until 2008.

Player Details:

Date of Birth:	14.09.1973
Place of Birth:	Forest Gate
Nationality:	English
Height:	5'10"
Weight:	13st 7lb
Foot:	Right

Player Performance 05/06

League Performance

Percentage of total possible time player was on pitch   ⊖ position in league table at end of month

Month:	Aug	Sep	Oct	Nov	Dec	Jan	Feb	Mar	Apr	May	Total
	0%	0%	25%	33%	37%	0%	100%	100%	100%	96%	50%
	18	16	14	18	18	19	19	19	17	17	
Team Pts:	1/12	4/9	5/12	0/9	7/18	0/9	1/12	6/9	14/21	0/3	38/114
Team Gls F:	3	2	6	0	4	1	2	6	12	1	37
Team Gls A:	7	2	4	7	11	8	8	4	8	3	62
Total mins:	0	0	90	90	200	0	360	270	630	86	1,726
Starts (sub):	0	0	1	1	3	0	4	3	7	1	20
Goals:	0	0	0	0	0	0	0	0	0	0	0
Assists:	0	0	0	0	0	0	0	0	0	0	0
Clean sheets:	0	0	0	0	1	0	0	0	1	0	2
Cards (Y/R):	0	0	0	0	0	0	0	0	0	0	0

League Performance Totals

Goals

Primus: 0
Team-mates: 36
Total: 36
own goals: 1

Assists

Primus: 0
Team-mates: 31
Total: 31

Cards

Primus: 0
Team-mates: 54
Total: 54

Cup Games

	Apps	Goals	Cards
FA Cup	1	0	0
Carling Cup	0	0	0
Total	**1**	**0**	**0**

Career History

Career Milestones

Club Debut:
vs Sheff Utd (A), L 2-0, Championship
▶ **12.08.00**
Time Spent at the Club:
▶ **6 Seasons**

First Goal Scored for the Club:
vs Bradford (A), L 3-1, Championship
▶ **12.01.02**
Full International:
▶ **—**

Premiership Totals

92-06

Appearances	76
Goals	1
Assists	0
Yellow Cards	2
Red Cards	0

Clubs

Year	Club	Apps	Gls
00-06	Portsmouth	179	4
97-00	Reading	113	1
94-97	Barnet	147	8
92-94	Charlton	6	0

Off the Pitch

Age:

Primus: 32 years, 8 months
Team: 27 years, 5 months
League: 26 years, 11 months

Height:
Primus: 5'10"
Team: 5'11"
League: 5'11"

Weight:
Primus: 13st 7lb
Team: 12st
League: 12st

14 Matthew Taylor
Defence

Player Details:

Date of Birth:	27.11.1981
Place of Birth:	Oxford
Nationality:	English
Height:	5'10"
Weight:	11st 8lb
Foot:	Left/Right

Season Review 05/06

Flying left wing-back who was a steal for Pompey in June 2002 when he signed for £400,000. Taylor began his career at Luton Town, making his league debut as a 17-year-old and appearing almost 150 times for The Hatters. A key member of Pompey's Championship side, Matt's attacking performances earned him an England U21 call up before a troublesome ankle injury interrupted his progress. Since recovering midway through 2003/04 he has been a regular in the first team and achieved hero status when his two penalties against Sunderland and Wigan at the end of last season virtually secured Portsmouth's place in the Premiership.

Player Performance 05/06

League Performance

Percentage of total possible time player was on pitch — position in league table at end of month

Month:	Aug	Sep	Oct	Nov	Dec	Jan	Feb	Mar	Apr	May	Total
	10%	24%	98%	100%	96%	97%	100%	100%	100%	100%	83%
	18	16	14	18	18	19	19	19	17	17	
Team Pts:	1/12	4/9	5/12	0/9	7/18	0/9	1/12	6/9	14/21	0/3	38/114
Team Gls F:	3	2	6	0	4	1	2	6	12	1	37
Team Gls A:	7	2	4	7	11	8	8	4	8	3	62
Total mins:	35	66	351	270	518	262	360	270	630	90	2,852
Starts (sub):	0 (2)	1	4	3	6	3	4	3	7	1	32 (2)
Goals:	0	0	2	0	0	1	1	0	2	0	6
Assists:	0	0	2	0	0	0	0	1	2	0	5
Clean sheets:	0	0	1	0	2	0	0	0	1	0	4
Cards (Y/R):	0	0	0	1	2	0	0	0	0	1	4

League Performance Totals

Goals
- ► Taylor: 6
- ► Team-mates: 30
- **Total: 36**
- ► own goals: 1

Assists
- ► Taylor: 5
- ► Team-mates: 26
- **Total: 31**

Cards
- ► Taylor: 4
- ► Team-mates: 50
- **Total: 54**

Cup Games

	Apps	Goals	Cards
FA Cup	2	0	0
Carling Cup	1	1	0
Total	**3**	**1**	**0**

Career History

Career Milestones

Club Debut:
vs Nottm Forest (H), W 2-0, Champ.
► **10.08.02**
Time Spent at the Club:
► **4 Seasons**

First Goal Scored for the Club:
vs Brighton (H), W 4-2, Champ.
► **31.08.02**
Full International:
► **—**

Premiership Totals
92-06

Appearances	96
Goals	7
Assists	12
Yellow Cards	10
Red Cards	0

Clubs

Year	Club	Apps	Gls
02-06	Portsmouth	149	19
98-02	Luton	146	17

Off the Pitch

Age:

- ► Taylor: 24 years, 6 months
- ► Team: 27 years, 5 months
- | League: 26 years, 11 months

Height:
- ► Taylor: 5'10"
- ► Team: 5'11"
- | League: 5'11"

Weight:
- ► Taylor: 11st 8lb
- ► Team: 12st
- | League: 12st

11

Noé Pamarot
Defence

Defender who first enjoyed a loan spell at Fratton Park in 1999/00. Noé began his career at Paris FC before moving to Nice where he became well known for his strength and pace. But after five years in Ligue 1, the Frenchman's desire to play Premier League football lead to a 2004, £1.7million move to Tottenham.

After a promising start at White Hart Lane, Noé's first team action was curtailed when he tore knee ligaments. He moved to Portsmouth in January 2006 aiming to prove himself in the Premiership and show Pompey fans how far he has come since his days here as a 20-year-old.

Player Details:

Date of Birth:	14.04.1979
Place of Birth:	Fontenay-sous-Bois
Nationality:	French
Height:	6'
Weight:	13st 7lb
Foot:	Right

Player Performance 05/06

League Performance

Percentage of total possible time player was on pitch   position in league table at end of month

Month:	Aug	Sep	Oct	Nov	Dec	Jan	Feb	Mar	Apr	May	Total
Percentage	0%	0%	0%	0%	0%	67%	37%	0%	21%	4%	13%
Position	18	16	14	18	18	19	19	19	17	17	
Team Pts:	1/12	4/9	5/12	0/9	7/18	0/9	1/12	6/9	14/21	0/3	38/114
Team Gls F:	3	2	6	0	4	1	2	6	12	1	37
Team Gls A:	7	2	4	7	11	8	8	4	8	3	62
Total mins:	0	0	0	0	0	180	134	0	134	4	452
Starts (sub):	0	0	0	0	0	2	1 (1)	0	1 (2)	0 (1)	4 (4)
Goals:	0	0	0	0	0	0	0	0	0	0	0
Assists:	0	0	0	0	0	0	0	0	0	0	0
Clean sheets:	0	0	0	0	0	0	0	0	0	0	0
Cards (Y/R):	0	0	0	0	0	0	0	0	0	0	0

League Performance Totals

Goals
- Pamarot: 0
- Team-mates: 36
- **Total: 36**
- own goals: 1

Assists
- Pamarot: 0
- Team-mates: 31
- **Total: 31**

Cards
- Pamarot: 0
- Team-mates: 54
- **Total: 54**

Cup Games

	Apps	Goals	Cards
FA Cup	0	0	0
Carling Cup	0	0	0
Total	**0**	**0**	**0**

Career History

Career Milestones

Club Debut:
vs Blackburn R. (H), L 0-3, Lge Cup

▶ **14.09.99**

Time Spent at the Club:

▶ **1.5 Seasons**

First Goal Scored for the Club:
—

▶ **—**

Full International:

▶ **—**

Premiership Totals

92-06

Appearances	33
Goals	1
Assists	0
Yellow Cards	5
Red Cards	0

Clubs

Year	Club	Apps	Gls
06-06	Portsmouth	8	0
04-06	Tottenham	30	2
99-00	Portsmouth	3	0
98-04	Nice		
	Martigues		
	Paris FC		

Off the Pitch

Age:
- Pamarot: 27 years, 1 month
- Team: 27 years, 5 months
- League: 26 years, 11 months

Height:
- Pamarot: 6'
- Team: 5'11"
- League: 5'11"

Weight:
- Pamarot: 13st 7lb
- Team: 12st
- League: 12st

18 Aliou Cissé
Midfield

Season Review 05/06

Tough-tackling Aliou began his career with Lille before moving to Sedan then Paris Saint-Germain. In 2002 he captained Senegal in the World Cup and to the final of the African Nations.

His international displays attracted Birmingham, who signed the midfielder before Pompey later secured his services in a £300,000 deal in summer 2004.

By January 2005 Aliou finally pinned down a place in the first team, operating in a variety of positions including midfield and full-back. However, injury troubles set 2005/06 off to a bad start and he finished the season with just 3 appearances to his name and was released in May 2006.

Player Details:

Date of Birth:	24.03.1976
Place of Birth:	Zinguinchor
Nationality:	Senegalese
Height:	5'11"
Weight:	12st 8lb
Foot:	Right

Player Performance 05/06

League Performance

Percentage of total possible time player was on pitch   ⊙ position in league table at end of month

Month:	Aug	Sep	Oct	Nov	Dec	Jan	Feb	Mar	Apr	May	Total
	18 0%	16 0%	14 0%	18 0%	18 17%	28% 19	19 0%	19 0%	17 0%	17 0%	5%
Team Pts:	1/12	4/9	5/12	0/9	7/18	0/9	1/12	6/9	14/21	0/3	38/114
Team Gls F:	3	2	6	0	4	1	2	6	12	1	37
Team Gls A:	7	2	4	7	11	8	8	4	8	3	62
Total mins:	0	0	0	0	90	76	0	0	0	0	166
Starts (sub):	0	0	0	0	1 (1)	1	0	0	0	0	2 (1)
Goals:	0	0	0	0	0	0	0	0	0	0	0
Assists:	0	0	0	0	0	0	0	0	0	0	0
Clean sheets:	0	0	0	0	0	0	0	0	0	0	0
Cards (Y/R):	0	0	0	0	0	1	0	0	0	0	1

League Performance Totals

Goals
- Cisse: 0
- Team-mates: 36
- **Total: 36**
- own goals: 1

Assists
- Cisse: 0
- Team-mates: 31
- **Total: 31**

Cards
- Cisse: 1
- Team-mates: 53
- **Total: 54**

Cup Games

	Apps	Goals	Cards
FA Cup	0	0	0
Carling Cup	0	0	0
Total	0	0	0

Career History

Career Milestones

Club Debut:
vs Tranmere (A), W 0-1, League Cup

21.09.04

Time Spent at the Club:

▶ **2 Seasons**

First Goal Scored for the Club:
—

▶ —

Full International:

▶ **Senegal**

Premiership Totals

92-06

Appearances	59
Goals	0
Assists	2
Yellow Cards	17
Red Cards	1

Clubs

Year	Club	Apps	Gls
04-06	Portsmouth	28	0
02-04	Birmingham	38	0
	Montpellier		
	Paris-SG		
	Sedan		
	Lille		

Off the Pitch

Age:

- Cisse: 30 years, 2 months
- Team: 27 years, 5 months
- League: 26 years, 11 months

Height:

- Cisse: 5'11"
- Team: 5'11"
- League: 5'11"

Weight:

- Cisse: 12st 8lb
- Team: 12st
- League: 12st

4

Andres d'Alessandro
Midfield

Left footed playmaker who began his career with River Plate and first grabbed attention at the 2001 World Youth Championship where he inspired Argentina to glory. On the club scene, River won the Clausura in 2002 and 2003 and Andres became a star, prompting Diego Maradona to enthuse, "He is the only Argentine player I would pay to watch". Observers also made natural comparisons between the two small, phenomenally skilful players.

In the summer of 2003 the attacking midfielder made a record £7.5 million move to VFL Wolfsburg, where he continued to shine until his loan move to Portsmouth in January 2006.

Player Details:

Date of Birth:	15.04.1981
Place of Birth:	Buenos Aires
Nationality:	Argentinian
Height:	5'9"
Weight:	10st 10lb
Foot:	Left

Player Performance 05/06

League Performance

Percentage of total possible time player was on pitch   ⊖ position in league table at end of month

Month:	Aug	Sep	Oct	Nov	Dec	Jan	Feb	Mar	Apr	May	Total
							63%	67%	96%	76%	32%
	18	16	14	18	18	19	19	19	17	17	
	0%	0%	0%	0%	0%	0%					
Team Pts:	1/12	4/9	5/12	0/9	7/18	0/9	1/12	6/9	14/21	0/3	38/114
Team Gls F:	3	2	6	0	4	1	2	6	12	1	37
Team Gls A:	7	2	4	7	11	8	8	4	8	3	62
Total mins:	0	0	0	0	0	0	226	180	604	68	1,078
Starts (sub):	0	0	0	0	0	0	3	2	7	1	13
Goals:	0	0	0	0	0	0	0	0	1	0	1
Assists:	0	0	0	0	0	0	0	1	1	0	2
Clean sheets:	0	0	0	0	0	0	0	0	1	0	1
Cards (Y/R):	0	0	0	0	0	0	0	0	0	0	0

League Performance Totals

Goals
- ▶ D'Alessandro: 1
- ▷ Team-mates: 35
- **Total: 36**
- ▶ own goals: 1

Assists
- ▶ D'Alessandro: 2
- ▷ Team-mates: 29
- **Total: 31**

Cards
- ▶ D'Alessandro: 0
- ▷ Team-mates: 54
- **Total: 54**

Cup Games

	Apps	Goals	Cards
FA Cup	0	0	0
Carling Cup	0	0	0
Total	**0**	**0**	**0**

Career History

Career Milestones

Club Debut:
vs Bolton (H), D 1-1, Premiership
▶ **01.02.06**
Time Spent at the Club:
▶ **0.5 Seasons**

First Goal Scored for the Club:
vs Charlton (A), L 2-1, Premiership
▶ **17.04.06**
Full International:
▶ **Argentina**

Premiership Totals
92-06

Appearances	13
Goals	1
Assists	2
Yellow Cards	0
Red Cards	0

Clubs

Year	Club	Apps	Gls
06-06	Portsmouth	13	1
	Wolfsburg		
	River Plate		

Off the Pitch

Age:
- ▶ D'Alessandro: 25 years, 1 month
- ▷ Team: 27 years, 5 months
- | League: 26 years, 11 months

Height:
- ▶ D'Alessandro: 5'9"
- ▷ Team: 5'11"
- | League: 5'11"

Weight:
- ▶ D'Alessandro: 10st 10lb
- ▷ Team: 12st
- | League: 12st

21 Franck Songo'o
Midfield

The son of former Cameroon World Cup star, Jacques Songo'o, Franck joined Portsmouth in August 2005 from Barcelona. The tricky winger came through the youth setup at Camp Nou, learning his trade alongside the likes of Lionel Messi and Francesc Fabregas and earning France U19 caps into the bargain.

A hot prospect for the future, Franck is yet to make his big break into the first team, making just 3 substitute appearances so far, but any fan that has watched the youngster in action for the reserves will be more than aware of his skill and attacking potential down the right side.

Player Details:

Date of Birth:	14.05.1987
Place of Birth:	Yaounde
Nationality:	French
Height:	5'10"
Weight:	12st 2lb
Foot:	Right

Player Performance 05/06

League Performance

Percentage of total possible time player was on pitch   Ⓖ position in league table at end of month

Month:	Aug	Sep	Oct	Nov	Dec	Jan	Feb	Mar	Apr	May	Total
	18	16	14	18	18	19	19	19	17	17	
	0%	6%	4%	0%	0%	0%	0%	0%	0%	0%	1%
Team Pts:	1/12	4/9	5/12	0/9	7/18	0/9	1/12	6/9	14/21	0/3	38/114
Team Gls F:	3	2	6	0	4	1	2	6	12	1	37
Team Gls A:	7	2	4	7	11	8	8	4	8	3	62
Total mins:	0	17	14	0	0	0	0	0	0	0	31
Starts (sub):	0	0 (1)	0 (1)	0	0	0	0	0	0	0	0 (2)
Goals:	0	0	0	0	0	0	0	0	0	0	0
Assists:	0	0	0	0	0	0	0	0	0	0	0
Clean sheets:	0	0	0	0	0	0	0	0	0	0	0
Cards (Y/R):	0	0	0	0	0	0	0	0	0	0	0

League Performance Totals

Goals
- ▶ Songo'o: 0
- ▶ Team-mates: 36
- **Total: 36**
- ▶ own goals: 1

Assists
- ▶ Songo'o: 0
- ▶ Team-mates: 31
- **Total: 31**

Cards
- ▶ Songo'o: 0
- ▶ Team-mates: 54
- **Total: 54**

Cup Games

	Apps	Goals	Cards
FA Cup	0	0	0
Carling Cup	1	0	0
Total	**1**	**0**	**0**

Career History

Career Milestones

Club Debut:
vs Gillingham (A), L 3-2, League Cup

▶ **20.09.05**

Time Spent at the Club:

▶ **1 Season**

First Goal Scored for the Club:
—

▶ **—**

Full International:

▶ **—**

Premiership Totals

92-06

Appearances	2
Goals	0
Assists	0
Yellow Cards	0
Red Cards	0

Clubs

Year	Club	Apps	Gls
05-06	Portsmouth	3	0
	Barcelona		
	Deportivo La Coruna		

Off the Pitch

Age:
- ▶ Songo'o: 19 years
- ▶ Team: 27 years, 5 months
- | League: 26 years, 11 months

Height:
- ▶ Songo'o: 5'10"
- ▶ Team: 5'11"
- | League: 5'11"

Weight:
- ▶ Songo'o: 12st 2lb
- ▶ Team: 12st
- | League: 12st

20 Giannis Skopelitis
Midfield

Bustling Greek midfielder who joined Pompey in January 2005 to add determination and bite to the middle of the park. Signed from Egaleo for £1 million, the 28-year-old soon became a first team regular, making 11 appearances before the end of the campaign.

The 2005/06 season saw Giannis struggle to build on the impressive start to his career in England and just twelve months after his arrival he returned to Egaleo.

Player Details:

Date of Birth:	02.03.1978
Place of Birth:	Athens
Nationality:	Greek
Height:	6'
Weight:	11st 12lb
Foot:	Right/Left

Player Performance 05/06

League Performance

Percentage of total possible time player was on pitch   ⊖ position in league table at end of month

Month:	Aug	Sep	Oct	Nov	Dec	Jan	Feb	Mar	Apr	May	Total
	3%	0%	12%	6%	0%	0%	0%	0%	0%	0%	2%
Position	18	16	14	18	18	19	19	19	17	17	
Team Pts:	1/12	4/9	5/12	0/9	7/18	0/9	1/12	6/9	14/21	0/3	38/114
Team Gls F:	3	2	6	0	4	1	2	6	12	1	37
Team Gls A:	7	2	4	7	11	8	8	4	8	3	62
Total mins:	11	0	44	16	0	0	0	0	0	0	71
Starts (sub):	0 (2)	0	0 (1)	0 (1)	0 (1)	0	0	0	0	0	0 (5)
Goals:	0	0	0	0	0	0	0	0	0	0	0
Assists:	0	0	0	0	0	0	0	0	0	0	0
Clean sheets:	0	0	0	0	0	0	0	0	0	0	0
Cards (Y/R):	0	0	1	0	0	0	0	0	0	0	1

League Performance Totals

Goals
- Skopelitis: 0
- Team-mates: 36
- **Total: 36**
- own goals: 1

Assists
- Skopelitis: 0
- Team-mates: 31
- **Total: 31**

Cards
- Skopelitis: 1
- Team-mates: 53
- **Total: 54**

Cup Games

	Apps	Goals	Cards
FA Cup	0	0	0
Carling Cup	0	0	0
Total	**0**	**0**	**0**

Career History

Career Milestones

Club Debut:
vs Middlesbrough (H), W 2-1, Prem.

▶ **01.02.05**

Time Spent at the Club:

▶ **1 Season**

First Goal Scored for the Club:
—

▶ **—**

Full International:

▶ **—**

Premiership Totals

92-06

Appearances	18
Goals	0
Assists	0
Yellow Cards	3
Red Cards	0

Clubs

Year	Club	Apps	Gls
05-06	Portsmouth	18	0
	Egaleo		

Off the Pitch

Age:
- Skopelitis: 28 years, 2 months
- Team: 27 years, 5 months
- League: 26 years, 11 months

Height:
- Skopelitis: 6'
- Team: 5'11"
- League: 5'11"

Weight:
- Skopelitis: 11st 12lb
- Team: 12st
- League: 12st

4 John Viafara
Midfield

Box-to-box midfielder who joined Pompey in June 2005, becoming the club's third summer signing. A regular Colombian International, Viafara made the switch from Once Caldas, winners of the 2004 Copa Libertadores (South America's Champions League).

A cultured player, one of Viafara's biggest strengths is his commitment and his early season form last term also proved him to be a goalscorer, a towering header against Manchester City his contribution to Pompey's goal tally. However, inconsistency combined with a language barrier led to the midfielder losing his place in the team and embarking on a loan spell with Real Sociedad in January.

Player Details:

Date of Birth:	27.10.1978
Place of Birth:	Robles
Nationality:	Colombian
Height:	6'
Weight:	13st 5lb
Foot:	Right

Player Performance 05/06

League Performance

Percentage of total possible time player was on pitch   ⊖ position in league table at end of month

Month:	Aug	Sep	Oct	Nov	Dec	Jan	Feb	Mar	Apr	May	Total
	90%	16	56% 14	38% 18	51% 18	19	19	19	17	17	27%
	18	7%				0%	0%	0%	0%	0%	
Team Pts:	1/12	4/9	5/12	0/9	7/18	0/9	1/12	6/9	14/21	0/3	38/114
Team Gls F:	3	2	6	0	4	1	2	6	12	1	37
Team Gls A:	7	2	4	7	11	8	8	4	8	3	62
Total mins:	325	20	202	102	274	0	0	0	0	0	923
Starts (sub):	4	0 (1)	2 (1)	1 (1)	3 (1)	0	0	0	0	0	10 (4)
Goals:	1	0	0	0	0	0	0	0	0	0	1
Assists:	0	0	0	0	0	0	0	0	0	0	0
Clean sheets:	0	0	0	0	0	0	0	0	0	0	0
Cards (Y/R):	3	0	0	1	0	0	0	0	0	0	4

League Performance Totals

Goals

- ▶ Viafara: 1
- ▶ Team-mates: 35
- **Total: 36**
- ▶ own goals: 1

Assists

- ▶ Viafara: 0
- ▶ Team-mates: 31
- **Total: 31**

Cards

- ▶ Viafara: 4
- ▶ Team-mates: 50
- **Total: 54**

Cup Games

	Apps	Goals	Cards
FA Cup	0	0	0
Carling Cup	1	0	0
Total	**1**	**0**	**0**

Career History

Career Milestones

Club Debut:
vs Tottenham (H), L 0-2, Premiership

▶ **13.08.05**

Time Spent at the Club:

▶ **1 Season**

First Goal Scored for the Club:
vs Man City (A), L 2-1, Premiership

▶ **27.08.05**

Full International:

▶ **Colombia**

Premiership Totals
92-06

Appearances	14
Goals	1
Assists	0
Yellow Cards	4
Red Cards	0

Clubs

Year	Club	Apps	Gls
06-06	Real Sociedad		
05-06	Portsmouth	15	1
	Once Caldas		

Off the Pitch

Age:

- ▶ Viafara: 27 years, 7 months
- ▶ Team: 27 years, 5 months
- | League: 26 years, 11 months

Height:

- ▶ Viafara: 6'
- ▶ Team: 5'11"
- | League: 5'11"

Weight:

- ▶ Viafara: 13st 5lb
- ▶ Team: 12st
- | League: 12st

11 Laurent Robert
Midfield

Season Review 05/06

Talented French midfielder who was Pompey's highest profile signing of summer 2005.

The mercurial Robert, renowned for his set-piece prowess, first came to the attention of English supporters when he joined Newcastle from Paris St Germain for £9.5m in August 2001.

He went on to make 181 appearances and score 32 goals in a turbulent time at St James' Park, before the French connection with Alain Perrin attracted him to Fratton Park where he quickly became a hit. However, his form dropped as he failed to settle and in January he made the move to Portugal to join Benfica.

Player Details:

Date of Birth:	21.05.1975
Place of Birth:	Saint-Benoit
Nationality:	French
Height:	5'9"
Weight:	10st 13lb
Foot:	Left

Player Performance 05/06

League Performance
Percentage of total possible time player was on pitch   ⊖ position in league table at end of month

Month:	Aug	Sep	Oct	Nov	Dec	Jan	Feb	Mar	Apr	May	Total
	100%	93%	40%	35%	53%						34%
Team Pts:	1/12	4/9	5/12	0/9	7/18	0/9	1/12	6/9	14/21	0/3	38/114
Team Gls F:	3	2	6	0	4	1	2	6	12	1	37
Team Gls A:	7	2	4	7	11	8	8	4	8	3	62
Total mins:	360	252	145	94	286	14	0	0	0	0	1,151
Starts (sub):	4	3	2	1 (1)	3 (2)	0 (1)	0	0	0	0	13 (4)
Goals:	1	0	0	0	0	0	0	0	0	0	1
Assists:	1	2	0	0	1	0	0	0	0	0	4
Clean sheets:	0	0	0	0	2	0	0	0	0	0	2
Cards (Y/R):	0	0	1	0	0/1	0	0	0	0	0	1/1

League Performance Totals

Goals		Assists		Cards			Cup Games	Apps	Goals	Cards
▶ Robert:	1	▶ Robert:	4	▶ Robert:	2		FA Cup	0	0	0
▷ Team-mates:	35	▷ Team-mates: 27		▷ Team-mates:	52		Carling Cup	0	0	0
Total:	**36**	**Total:**	**31**	**Total:**	**54**		**Total**	**0**	**0**	**0**
◆ own goals:	1									

Career History

Career Milestones

Club Debut:
vs Tottenham (H), L 0-2, Premiership

▶ **13.08.05**

Time Spent at the Club:

▶ **0.5 Seasons**

First Goal Scored for the Club:
vs West Brom (A), L 2-1, Premiership

▶ **20.08.05**

Full International:

▶ **France**

Premiership Totals

92-06	
Appearances	146
Goals	23
Assists	49
Yellow Cards	15
Red Cards	3

Clubs

Year	Club	Apps	Gls
06-06	SL Benfica		
05-06	Portsmouth	17	1
01-06	Newcastle	181	32
	Paris-SG		
	Montpellier		

Off the Pitch

Age:

▶ Robert: 31 years
▷ Team: 27 years, 5 months
▌ League: 26 years, 11 months

Height:

▶ Robert: 5'9"
▷ Team: 5'11"
▌ League: 5'11"

Weight:

▶ Robert: 10st 13lb
▷ Team: 12st
▌ League: 12st

26 Gary O'Neil
Midfield

London born Pompey youth product who made his Pompey debut aged just 16 in January 2000. Considered lightweight for a number of years, over the past season and a half Gary has come into his own, holding down the regular first team place that his status as England U21 captain suggested he deserved.

He regularly grabbed headlines last term with consistently impressive performances, not to mention seven goals, all of which contributed to him deputising as skipper in the absence of Dejan Stefanovic, and being named Supporters Player of the Year for 2005/06.

Player Details:

Date of Birth:	18.05.1983
Place of Birth:	Beckenham
Nationality:	English
Height:	5'8"
Weight:	11st
Foot:	Right/Left

Player Performance 05/06

League Performance

Percentage of total possible time player was on pitch   ⊙ position in league table at end of month

Month:	Aug	Sep	Oct	Nov	Dec	Jan	Feb	Mar	Apr	May	Total
	62%	94%	100%	100%	83%	100%	88%	100%	100%	100%	92%
position	18	16	14	18	18	19	19	19	17	17	
Team Pts:	1/12	4/9	5/12	0/9	7/18	0/9	1/12	6/9	14/21	0/3	38/114
Team Gls F:	3	2	6	0	4	1	2	6	12	1	37
Team Gls A:	7	2	4	7	11	8	8	4	8	3	62
Total mins:	222	253	360	270	450	270	316	270	630	90	3,131
Starts (sub):	3	3	4	3	5	3	4	3	7	1	36
Goals:	0	0	1	0	2	0	0	0	3	0	6
Assists:	1	0	0	0	1	0	0	0	0	0	2
Clean sheets:	0	1	1	0	2	0	0	0	1	0	5
Cards (Y/R):	0	0	1	0	0	0	0	0	1	0	2

League Performance Totals

Goals

▶ O'Neil:	6
▧ Team-mates:	30
Total:	**36**
▶ own goals:	1

Assists

▶ O'Neil:	2
▧ Team-mates:	29
Total:	**31**

Cards

▶ O'Neil:	2
▧ Team-mates:	52
Total:	**54**

Cup Games

	Apps	Goals	Cards
FA Cup	2	0	0
Carling Cup	1	1	0
Total	**3**	**1**	**0**

Career History

Career Milestones

Club Debut:
vs Barnsley (H), W 3-0, Championship

 29.01.00

Time Spent at the Club:

▶ **7 Seasons**

First Goal Scored for the Club:
vs Barnsley (H), W 3-0, Championship

 06.05.01

Full International:

▶ **—**

Premiership Totals

92-06

Appearances	63
Goals	10
Assists	5
Yellow Cards	5
Red Cards	0

Clubs

Year	Club	Apps	Gls
04-04	Cardiff	9	1
03-03	Walsall	7	0
99-06	Portsmouth	152	16

Off the Pitch

Age:

| ▶ O'Neil: 23 years
| ▧ Team: 27 years, 5 months
| League: 26 years, 11 months

Height:

| ▶ O'Neil: 5'8"
| ▧ Team: 5'11"
| League: 5'11"

Weight:

| ▶ O'Neil: 11st
| ▧ Team: 12st
| League: 12st

20 Ognjen Koroman
Midfield

27-year-old Ognjen Koroman joined Portsmouth on loan in January 2006 from Russian side Terek Grozny. The Serbian international, was involved in eight out of his country's ten World Cup qualifiers, comfortably granting him a work permit for his move to England, not to mention a trip to the World Cup finals.

A versatile dual footer, Koroman can be deployed in the back four, but his favoured position is on the wing where his pace can terrify defences. Although he made only a handful of appearances for Pompey, he impressed with a goal in the last game of the season against Liverpool.

Player Details:

Date of Birth:	19.09.1978
Place of Birth:	Sarajevo
Nationality:	Serbian
Height:	5'9"
Weight:	11st
Foot:	Left/Right

Player Performance 05/06

League Performance

Percentage of total possible time player was on pitch   G- position in league table at end of month

Month:	Aug	Sep	Oct	Nov	Dec	Jan	Feb	Mar	Apr	May	Total
	0%	0%	0%	0%	0%	0%	19%	8%	0%	31%	3%
Team Pts:	1/12	4/9	5/12	0/9	7/18	0/9	1/12	6/9	14/21	0/3	38/114
Team Gls F:	3	2	6	0	4	1	2	6	12	1	37
Team Gls A:	7	2	4	7	11	8	8	4	8	3	62
Total mins:	0	0	0	0	0	0	68	22	0	28	118
Starts (sub):	0	0	0	0	0	0	1	0 (1)	0	0 (1)	1 (2)
Goals:	0	0	0	0	0	0	0	0	0	1	1
Assists:	0	0	0	0	0	0	0	0	0	0	0
Clean sheets:	0	0	0	0	0	0	0	0	0	0	0
Cards (Y/R):	0	0	0	0	0	0	0	0	0	0	0

(Chart positions: 18, 16, 14, 18, 18, 19, 19, 19, 17, 17)

League Performance Totals

Goals

- Koroman: 1
- Team-mates: 35

Total: 36

- own goals: 1

Assists

- Koroman: 0
- Team-mates: 31

Total: 31

Cards

- Koroman: 0
- Team-mates: 54

Total: 54

Cup Games

	Apps	Goals	Cards
FA Cup	0	0	0
Carling Cup	0	0	0
Total	**0**	**0**	**0**

Career History

Career Milestones

Club Debut:
vs Chelsea (A), L 2-0, Premiership

▶ **25.02.06**

Time Spent at the Club:

▶ **0.5 Seasons**

First Goal Scored for the Club:
vs Liverpool (H), L 1-3, Premiership

▶ **07.05.06**

Full International:

▶ **Serbia**

Premiership Totals

92-06

Appearances	3
Goals	1
Assists	0
Yellow Cards	0
Red Cards	0

Clubs

Year	Club	Apps	Gls
06-06	Portsmouth	3	1
	Terek Grozny		
	KS Samara		
	Dynamo Moscow		
	OFK Belgrade		
	FK Radnicki		

Off the Pitch

Age:

- Koroman: 27 years, 8 months
- Team: 27 years, 5 months
- League: 26 years, 11 months

Height:

- Koroman: 5'9"
- Team: 5'11"
- League: 5'11"

Weight:

- Koroman: 11st
- Team: 12st
- League: 12st

22

Richard Hughes
Midfield

Cultured Scot who was born in Glasgow but moved to Milan whilst still a child. Hughes learned his trade at Atalanta before being snapped up by Arsenal at 18. After a year in the Gunners' reserves he moved to Bournemouth where he was a hit, making over 150 appearances and prompting Harry Redknapp to sign him in 2002.

The combative midfielder began his Portsmouth career well, but lost his place after injury and ended the season on loan at Grimsby. Since then Richard has learned that patience gets its reward and has held down a regular place in the Pompey midfield and become a full Scottish international.

Player Details:

Date of Birth:	25.06.1979
Place of Birth:	Glasgow
Nationality:	Scottish
Height:	6'
Weight:	12st
Foot:	Left

Player Performance 05/06

League Performance

Percentage of total possible time player was on pitch   position in league table at end of month

Month:	Aug	Sep	Oct	Nov	Dec	Jan	Feb	Mar	Apr	May	Total
	100%	91%		90%	83%					69%	53%
	18	16	14 / 32%	18	18	23% 19	20% 19	19 0%	34% 17	17	
Team Pts:	1/12	4/9	5/12	0/9	7/18	0/9	1/12	6/9	14/21	0/3	38/114
Team Gls F:	3	2	6	0	4	1	2	6	12	1	37
Team Gls A:	7	2	4	7	11	8	8	4	8	3	62
Total mins:	360	245	114	242	450	61	72	0	215	62	1,821
Starts (sub):	4	3	1 (2)	3	5	1	1	0	2 (3)	1	21 (5)
Goals:	0	0	0	0	0	0	0	0	0	0	0
Assists:	0	0	0	0	0	0	0	0	0	0	0
Clean sheets:	0	1	0	0	2	0	0	0	0	0	3
Cards (Y/R):	2	1	0	1	2	0	0	0	2	0	8

League Performance Totals

Goals

- Hughes: 0
- Team-mates: 36
- **Total: 36**
- own goals: 1

Assists

- Hughes: 0
- Team-mates: 31
- **Total: 31**

Cards

- Hughes: 8
- Team-mates: 46
- **Total: 54**

Cup Games

	Apps	Goals	Cards
FA Cup	2	0	1
Carling Cup	1	0	0
Total	**3**	**0**	**1**

Career History

Career Milestones

Club Debut:
vs Sheff Utd (A), D 1-1, Championship

▶ **13.08.02**

Time Spent at the Club:

▶ **4 Seasons**

First Goal Scored for the Club:
vs Liverpool (H), W 1-0, FA Cup

▶ **22.02.04**

Full International:

▶ **Scotland**

Premiership Totals

92-06

Appearances	54
Goals	0
Assists	0
Yellow Cards	13
Red Cards	0

Clubs

Year	Club	Apps	Gls
03-03	Grimsby	12	1
02-06	Portsmouth	71	1
98-02	Bournemouth	154	16
97-98	Arsenal	0	0
	Atalanta		

Off the Pitch

Age:

- Hughes: 26 years, 11 months
- Team: 27 years, 5 months
- League: 26 years, 11 months

Height:

- Hughes: 6'
- Team: 5'11"
- League: 5'11"

Weight:

- Hughes: 12st
- Team: 12st
- League: 12st

40 Salif Diao
Midfield

Season Review 05/06

Senegalese International who moved to Liverpool after impressing at the 2002 World Cup.

The 29-year-old ball winner began his career with Epinal before being snapped up by Monaco. He then transferred to Sedan and became the star player, prompting his £5 million move to Anfield in August 2002. Competing for places with Steven Gerrard and Dietmarr Hamann, Salif found himself short on first team action and in 2004/05 spent four months on loan at Birmingham. He returned to Anfield in the summer, but was given the opportunity of another loan, this time at Portsmouth. However, numerous injuries prevented him from establishing himself in the side.

Player Details:

Date of Birth:	10.02.1977
Place of Birth:	Kedougou
Nationality:	Senegalese
Height:	6'
Weight:	11st 7lb
Foot:	Right

Player Performance 05/06

League Performance

Percentage of total possible time player was on pitch   ⊖ position in league table at end of month

Month:	Aug	Sep	Oct	Nov	Dec	Jan	Feb	Mar	Apr	May	Total
	0%	100% 18	14 19%	39% 18 17%	18	40% 19	19 4%	19 0%	17 0%	17 0%	19%
		16									
Team Pts:	1/12	4/9	5/12	0/9	7/18	0/9	1/12	6/9	14/21	0/3	38/114
Team Gls F:	3	2	6	0	4	1	2	6	12	1	37
Team Gls A:	7	2	4	7	11	8	8	4	8	3	62
Total mins:	0	270	69	104	90	107	14	0	2	0	656
Starts (sub):	0	3	1	1 (1)	1	1 (1)	0 (1)	0	0 (1)	0	7 (4)
Goals:	0	0	0	0	0	0	0	0	0	0	0
Assists:	0	0	0	0	0	0	0	0	0	0	0
Clean sheets:	0	1	0	0	0	0	0	0	0	0	1
Cards (Y/R):	0	1	0	1	0	1	0	0	0	0	3

League Performance Totals

Goals

▶ Diao: 0
▶ Team-mates: 36
Total: 36
▶ own goals: 1

Assists

▶ Diao: 0
▶ Team-mates: 31
Total: 31

Cards

▶ Diao: 3
▶ Team-mates: 51
Total: 54

Cup Games

	Apps	Goals	Cards
FA Cup	1	0	0
Carling Cup	1	0	0
Total	**2**	**0**	**0**

Career History

Career Milestones

Club Debut:

vs Everton (A), W 0-1, Premiership

▶ **10.09.05**

Time Spent at the Club:

▶ **1 Season**

First Goal Scored for the Club:

—

▶ **—**

Full International:

▶ **Senegal**

Premiership Totals

92-06

Appearances	50
Goals	1
Assists	2
Yellow Cards	8
Red Cards	1

Clubs

Year	Club	Apps	Gls
05-06	Portsmouth	13	0
05-05	Birmingham	2	0
02-06	Liverpool	61	3
	Sedan		
	AS Monaco		

Off the Pitch

Age:

▶ Diao: 29 years, 3 months
▶ Team: 27 years, 5 months
| League: 26 years, 11 months

Height:

▶ Diao: 6'
▶ Team: 5'11"
| League: 5'11"

Weight:

▶ Diao: 11st 7lb
▶ Team: 12st
| League: 12st

28 Sean Davis
Midfield

Season Review 05/06

After shining for Fulham at youth level, Sean's debut was eagerly anticipated when he made it in 1996, aged barely 17. His vision and commitment earned many admirers and he was soon England U21 captain. As his star continued to rise, Sean won a call up to the senior England squad and in July 2004 made the move across the capital to join Tottenham Hotspur. Injury restricted Sean's impact at White Hart Lane though and when fit again, he found himself surplus to requirements, prompting his transfer to Portsmouth in January 2006.

Player Details:

Date of Birth:	20.09.1979
Place of Birth:	Lambeth
Nationality:	English
Height:	5'9"
Weight:	12st 9lb
Foot:	Right

Player Performance 05/06

League Performance

Percentage of total possible time player was on pitch · position in league table at end of month

Month:	Aug	Sep	Oct	Nov	Dec	Jan	Feb	Mar	Apr	May	Total
	0%	0%	0%	0%	0%	66%	66%	91%	77%	100%	36%
Team Pts:	1/12	4/9	5/12	0/9	7/18	0/9	1/12	6/9	14/21	0/3	38/114
Team Gls F:	3	2	6	0	4	1	2	6	12	1	37
Team Gls A:	7	2	4	7	11	8	8	4	8	3	62
Total mins:	0	0	0	0	0	177	239	246	487	90	1,239
Starts (sub):	0	0	0	0	0	2	3 (1)	3	7	1	16 (1)
Goals:	0	0	0	0	0	0	0	1	0	0	1
Assists:	0	0	0	0	0	0	0	0	0	0	0
Clean sheets:	0	0	0	0	0	0	0	0	0	0	0
Cards (Y/R):	0	0	0	0	0	1	0	0	0	0	1

Table positions: 18, 16, 14, 18, 18, 19, 19, 19, 17, 17

League Performance Totals

Goals
- Davis: 1
- Team-mates: 35
- **Total: 36**
- own goals: 1

Assists
- Davis: 0
- Team-mates: 31
- **Total: 31**

Cards
- Davis: 1
- Team-mates: 53
- **Total: 54**

Cup Games

	Apps	Goals	Cards
FA Cup	1	1	1
Carling Cup	0	0	0
Total	1	1	1

Career History

Career Milestones

Club Debut:
vs Everton (H), L 0-1, Premiership

 14.01.06

Time Spent at the Club:

 0.5 Seasons

First Goal Scored for the Club:
vs Liverpool (H), L 1-2, FA Cup

 29.01.06

Full International:

 —

Premiership Totals

92-06

Appearances	114
Goals	9
Assists	11
Yellow Cards	17
Red Cards	0

Clubs

Year	Club	Apps	Gls
06-06	Portsmouth	18	2
04-06	Tottenham	17	0
96-04	Fulham	198	20

Off the Pitch

Age:
- Davis: 26 years, 8 months
- Team: 27 years, 5 months
- League: 26 years, 11 months

Height:
- Davis: 5'9"
- Team: 5'11"
- League: 5'11"

Weight:
- Davis: 12st 9lb
- Team: 12st
- League: 12st

30 Pedro Mendes
Midfield

Pass master who began his career with FC Felgueira before joining Vitoria Guimaraes in 1999/2000. In 2002/03 Pedro helped Vitoria to the Portuguese Super Cup and was called up to the National squad.

Pedro was snapped up by José Mourinho for FC Porto in July 2003, and he played a key role in attaining the Portuguese title, Cup and UEFA Champions League. A £2million move to Spurs followed in July 2004, where he perhaps became most famous for scoring the spectacular 'goal that wasn't' against Manchester United. After arriving at Portsmouth in January 2006, Pedro again proved himself adept at shooting from range with memorable and crucial strikes against Manchester City and West Ham.

Player Details:

Date of Birth:	26.02.1979
Place of Birth:	Guimaraes
Nationality:	Portuguese
Height:	5'10"
Weight:	12st 1lb
Foot:	Right

Player Performance 05/06

League Performance

Percentage of total possible time player was on pitch   ⊖ position in league table at end of month

Month:	Aug	Sep	Oct	Nov	Dec	Jan	Feb	Mar	Apr	May	Total
Percentage	0%	0%	0%	0%	0%	60%	100%	100%	68%	0%	36%
Position	18	16	14	18	18	19	19	19	17	17	
Team Pts:	1/12	4/9	5/12	0/9	7/18	0/9	1/12	6/9	14/21	0/3	38/114
Team Gls F:	3	2	6	0	4	1	2	6	12	1	37
Team Gls A:	7	2	4	7	11	8	8	4	8	3	62
Total mins:	0	0	0	0	0	163	360	270	428	0	1,221
Starts (sub):	0	0	0	0	0	2	4	3	5	0	14
Goals:	0	0	0	0	0	0	0	3	0	0	3
Assists:	0	0	0	0	0	0	0	0	0	0	0
Clean sheets:	0	0	0	0	0	0	0	0	1	0	1
Cards (Y/R):	0	0	0	0	0	1	0	1	2	0	4

League Performance Totals

Goals
- Mendes: 3
- Team-mates: 33
- **Total: 36**
- own goals: 1

Assists
- Mendes: 0
- Team-mates: 31
- **Total: 31**

Cards
- Mendes: 4
- Team-mates: 50
- **Total: 54**

Cup Games

	Apps	Goals	Cards
FA Cup	1	0	0
Carling Cup	0	0	0
Total	**1**	**0**	**0**

Career History

Career Milestones

Club Debut:
vs Everton (H), L 0-1, Premiership

 **14.01.06**

Time Spent at the Club:

▶ **0.5 Seasons**

First Goal Scored for the Club:
vs Man City (H), W 2-1, Premiership

 11.03.06

Full International:

▶ **Portugal**

Premiership Totals

92-06

Appearances	44
Goals	4
Assists	1
Yellow Cards	8
Red Cards	0

Clubs

Year	Club	Apps	Gls
06-06	Portsmouth	15	3
04-06	Tottenham	36	1
	FC Porto		
	Vitoria Guimaraes		

Off the Pitch

Age:
- Mendes: 27 years, 3 months
- Team: 27 years, 5 months
- League: 26 years, 11 months

Height:
- Mendes: 5'10"
- Team: 5'11"
- League: 5'11"

Weight:
- Mendes: 12st 1lb
- Team: 12st
- League: 12st

24 Wayne Routledge
Midfield

Lightning quick winger who scored in the first minute of his full Crystal Palace league debut, aged just 17. A product of the Palace Academy, Wayne made 123 appearances for the Eagles before moving to Tottenham in July 2005.

After an impressive pre-season, the 21-year-old broke a bone in his foot in Spurs' first game of the season and never found his way back into Martin Jol's side, prompting his January 2006 loan move to Fratton Park.

Routledge has represented England at Under 17, 18, 19, 20 and 21 levels, helping his country to third place in the prestigious Toulon U20 Tournament in 2005.

Player Details:

Date of Birth:	07.01.1985
Place of Birth:	Eltham
Nationality:	English
Height:	5'6"
Weight:	10st 7lb
Foot:	Right/Left

Player Performance 05/06

League Performance

Percentage of total possible time player was on pitch   ⊖ position in league table at end of month

Month:	Aug	Sep	Oct	Nov	Dec	Jan	Feb	Mar	Apr	May	Total
	0%	0%	0%	0%	0%	0%	56%	34%	19%	24%	13%
	18	16	14	18	18	19	19	19	17	17	
Team Pts:	1/12	4/9	5/12	0/9	7/18	0/9	1/12	6/9	14/21	0/3	38/114
Team Gls F:	3	2	6	0	4	1	2	6	12	1	37
Team Gls A:	7	2	4	7	11	8	8	4	8	3	62
Total mins:	0	0	0	0	0	0	202	92	119	22	435
Starts (sub):	0	0	0	0	0	0	2 (2)	1 (1)	0 (6)	0 (1)	3 (10)
Goals:	0	0	0	0	0	0	0	0	0	0	0
Assists:	0	0	0	0	0	0	2	0	0	1	3
Clean sheets:	0	0	0	0	0	0	0	0	0	0	0
Cards (Y/R):	0	0	0	0	0	0	0	0	0	0	0

League Performance Totals

Goals

- ▶ Routledge: 0
- ▶ Team-mates: 36
- **Total: 36**
- ▶ own goals: 1

Assists

- ▶ Routledge: 3
- ▶ Team-mates: 28
- **Total: 31**

Cards

- ▶ Routledge: 0
- ▶ Team-mates: 54
- **Total: 54**

Cup Games

	Apps	Goals	Cards
FA Cup	0	0	0
Carling Cup	0	0	0
Total	**0**	**0**	**0**

Career History

Career Milestones

Club Debut:
vs Bolton (H), D 1-1, Premiership

▶ **01.02.06**

Time Spent at the Club:

▶ **0.5 Seasons**

First Goal Scored for the Club:
—

▶ **—**

Full International:

▶ **—**

Premiership Totals
92-06

Appearances	54
Goals	0
Assists	14
Yellow Cards	1
Red Cards	0

Clubs

Year	Club	Apps	Gls
06-06	Portsmouth	13	0
05-06	Tottenham	3	0
01-05	Crystal Palace	123	11

Off the Pitch

Age:

- ▶ Routledge: 21 years, 4 months
- ▶ Team: 27 years, 5 months
- | League: 26 years, 11 months

Height:

- ▶ Routledge: 5'6"
- ▶ Team: 5'11"
- | League: 5'11"

Weight:

- ▶ Routledge: 10st 7lb
- ▶ Team: 12st
- | League: 12st

38 Zvonimir Vukic
Midfield

Skilful attacking midfielder who joined Portsmouth in August 2005 from Shakhtar Donetsk. Born in Zrenjanin, Serbia, Vukic made his name with Partizan Belgrade, scoring 53 goals in 4 seasons before being lured by Champions League football with Shakhtar. He also earned regular call ups to the Serbian National side and played an instrumental role in his country's first ever World Cup qualification.

Highly rated due to his ability to create and score goals, Zvonimir grabbed his only Portsmouth strike in a 4-1 win over Sunderland in October 2005, but was allowed to leave the club in April having struggled to impress Harry Redknapp.

Player Details:

Date of Birth:	19.07.1979
Place of Birth:	Zrenjanin
Nationality:	Serbian
Height:	6'
Weight:	11st 5lb
Foot:	Right/Left

Player Performance 05/06

League Performance

Percentage of total possible time player was on pitch   Ⓖ position in league table at end of month

Month:	Aug	Sep	Oct	Nov	Dec	Jan	Feb	Mar	Apr	May	Total
	0%	16%	93%	35%	9%	0%	0%	0%	0%	0%	15%
	18	16	14	18	18	19	19	19	17	17	
Team Pts:	1/12	4/9	5/12	0/9	7/18	0/9	1/12	6/9	14/21	0/3	38/114
Team Gls F:	3	2	6	0	4	1	2	6	12	1	37
Team Gls A:	7	2	4	7	11	8	8	4	8	3	62
Total mins:	0	43	336	94	46	0	0	0	0	0	519
Starts (sub):	0	0 (2)	4	1 (1)	1	0	0	0	0	0	6 (3)
Goals:	0	0	1	0	0	0	0	0	0	0	1
Assists:	0	0	2	0	0	0	0	0	0	0	2
Clean sheets:	0	0	1	0	0	0	0	0	0	0	1
Cards (Y/R):	0	0	1	0	0	0	0	0	0	0	1

League Performance Totals

Goals
- ▶ Vukic: 1
- ■ Team-mates: 35
- **Total: 36**
- ▶ own goals: 1

Assists
- ▶ Vukic: 2
- ■ Team-mates: 29
- **Total: 31**

Cards
- ▶ Vukic: 1
- ■ Team-mates: 53
- **Total: 54**

Cup Games

	Apps	Goals	Cards
FA Cup	0	0	0
Carling Cup	0	0	0
Total	**0**	**0**	**0**

Career History

Career Milestones

Club Debut:
vs Everton (A), W 0-1, Premiership
▶ **10.09.05**

Time Spent at the Club:
▶ **0.5 Seasons**

First Goal Scored for the Club:
vs Sunderland (A), W 1-4, Premiership
▶ **29.10.05**

Full International:
▶ **Serbia**

Premiership Totals

92-06

Appearances	9
Goals	1
Assists	2
Yellow Cards	1
Red Cards	0

Clubs

Year	Club	Apps	Gls
06-06	Partizan Belgrade		
05-06	Portsmouth	9	1
	Shakhtar Donetsk		
	Partizan Belgrade		
	Atletico Madrid		
	Proleter Zrenjanin		
	Begej Zitiste		

Off the Pitch

Age:
- ▶ Vukic: 26 years, 10 months
- ■ Team: 27 years, 5 months
- | League: 26 years, 11 months

Height:
- ▶ Vukic: 6'
- ■ Team: 5'11"
- | League: 5'11"

Weight:
- ▶ Vukic: 11st 5lb
- ■ Team: 12st
- | League: 12st

8

Azar Karadas
Forward

Season Review 05/06

Azar joined Pompey in July 2005 on a season long loan from Benfica. The striker began his career with SK Brann before moving to Rosenborg, where he gained Champions League experience and call ups to the Norway squad before being enticed to the Lisbon club in 2004. Karadas is an English-style targetman and made an immediate impression with some solid pre-season performances.

Although his appearances for Pompey were limited to predominately substitute outings, Azar did much to demonstrate his potential with a stunning volleyed goal against Bolton. He also proved his versatility by filling in gaps in defence when needed.

Player Details:

Date of Birth:	09.08.1981
Place of Birth:	Nordfjordeid
Nationality:	Norwegian
Height:	6'3"
Weight:	13st 8lb
Foot:	Right

Player Performance 05/06

League Performance

Percentage of total possible time player was on pitch   position in league table at end of month

Month:	Aug	Sep	Oct	Nov	Dec	Jan	Feb	Mar	Apr	May	Total
	70% 18	16 18%	14 0%	0% 18	1% 18	4% 19	28% 19	13% 19	17 6%	17 0%	14%
Team Pts:	1/12	4/9	5/12	0/9	7/18	0/9	1/12	6/9	14/21	0/3	38/114
Team Gls F:	3	2	6	0	4	1	2	6	12	1	37
Team Gls A:	7	2	4	7	11	8	8	4	8	3	62
Total mins:	252	49	0	0	4	11	99	35	36	0	486
Starts (sub):	3 (1)	0 (3)	0	0	0 (1)	0 (3)	1 (1)	0 (1)	0 (3)	0	4 (13)
Goals:	0	0	0	0	0	0	1	0	0	0	1
Assists:	1	0	0	0	0	0	0	0	0	0	1
Clean sheets:	0	0	0	0	0	0	0	0	0	0	0
Cards (Y/R):	1	0	0	0	1	0	0	1	1	0	4

League Performance Totals

Goals

- Karadas: 1
- Team-mates: 35

Total: 36

- own goals: 1

Assists

- Karadas: 1
- Team-mates: 30

Total: 31

Cards

- Karadas: 4
- Team-mates: 50

Total: 54

Cup Games

	Apps	Goals	Cards
FA Cup	2	0	0
Carling Cup	1	0	0
Total	**3**	**0**	**0**

Career History

Career Milestones

Club Debut:
vs Tottenham (H), L 0-2, Premiership

13.08.05

Time Spent at the Club:

1 Season

First Goal Scored for the Club:
vs Bolton (H), D 1-1, Premiership

01.02.06

Full International:

Norway

Premiership Totals

92-06

Appearances	17
Goals	1
Assists	1
Yellow Cards	4
Red Cards	0

Clubs

Year	Club	Apps	Gls
05-06	Portsmouth	20	1
	SL Benfica		
	Rosenborg BK		
	SK Brann		

Off the Pitch

Age:

- Karadas: 24 years, 9 months
- Team: 27 years, 5 months
- League: 26 years, 11 months

Height:
- Karadas: 6'3"
- Team: 5'11"
- League: 5'11"

Weight:
- Karadas: 13st 8lb
- Team: 12st
- League: 12st

19 Collins Mbesuma
Forward

Season Review 05/06

Rated as one of the hottest properties in African football, Collins Mbesuma quickly became a huge star in his native country as a result of his goal-scoring antics in South Africa, where he netted 34 goals for the Kaiser Chiefs in 2004/05 to help them lift their league championship title for a second successive season.

He joined Portsmouth in the summer of 2005 although, sadly, his fitness has prevented him from making as big an impact as first hoped and Collins' talents have mostly been restricted to reserve team football.

Player Details:

Date of Birth:	03.03.1984
Place of Birth:	Luanshya
Nationality:	Zambian
Height:	6'
Weight:	12st 5lb
Foot:	Left

Player Performance 05/06

League Performance

Percentage of total possible time player was on pitch   ⊖ position in league table at end of month

Month:	Aug	Sep	Oct	Nov	Dec	Jan	Feb	Mar	Apr	May	Total
	4%	0%	4%	7%	0%	0%	0%	0%	0%	0%	1%
Team Pts:	1/12	4/9	5/12	0/9	7/18	0/9	1/12	6/9	14/21	0/3	38/114
Team Gls F:	3	2	6	0	4	1	2	6	12	1	37
Team Gls A:	7	2	4	7	11	8	8	4	8	3	62
Total mins:	16	0	15	20	0	0	0	0	0	0	51
Starts (sub):	0 (1)	0	0 (2)	0 (1)	0	0	0	0	0	0	0 (4)
Goals:	0	0	0	0	0	0	0	0	0	0	0
Assists:	0	0	0	0	0	0	0	0	0	0	0
Clean sheets:	0	0	0	0	0	0	0	0	0	0	0
Cards (Y/R):	0	0	0	0	0	0	0	0	0	0	0

(Position in league table: Aug 18, Sep 16, Oct 14, Nov 18, Dec 18, Jan 19, Feb 19, Mar 19, Apr 17, May 17)

League Performance Totals

Goals
- Mbesuma: 0
- Team-mates: 36
- **Total: 36**
- own goals: 1

Assists
- Mbesuma: 0
- Team-mates: 31
- **Total: 31**

Cards
- Mbesuma: 0
- Team-mates: 54
- **Total: 54**

Cup Games

	Apps	Goals	Cards
FA Cup	0	0	0
Carling Cup	0	0	0
Total	**0**	**0**	**0**

Career History

Career Milestones

Club Debut:
vs Tottenham (H), L 0-2, Premiership

 13.08.05

Time Spent at the Club:
▶ **1 Season**

First Goal Scored for the Club:
—

▶ —

Full International:
▶ **Zambia**

Premiership Totals

92-06

Appearances	4
Goals	0
Assists	0
Yellow Cards	0
Red Cards	0

Clubs

Year	Club	Apps	Gls
05-06	Portsmouth	4	0
	Kaiser Chiefs		
	Roan United		
	Luanshya Mine		

Off the Pitch

Age:

- Mbesuma: 22 years, 2 months
- Team: 27 years, 5 months
- League: 26 years, 11 months

Height:
- Mbesuma: 6'
- Team: 5'11"
- League: 5'11"

Weight:
- Mbesuma: 12st 5lb
- Team: 12st
- League: 12st

25 Benjani Mwaruwari
Forward

Club record signing who was voted South African Player of the Year in 2001 whilst playing for Jomo Cosmos, earning a move to Grasshoppers Zurich.

After just a season Benjani was snapped up by AJ Auxerre whom he helped to French Cup glory in 2003 and 2004. However, the 27-year-old never really settled in France and he jumped at the chance to prove himself in the Premiership with Portsmouth in January 2006.

Benjani scored his first goal for the club in the penultimate game of last season at Wigan; a crucial strike as the 2-1 win secured Portsmouth's survival in the Premiership.

Player Details:

Date of Birth:	13.08.1978
Place of Birth:	Harare
Nationality:	Zimbabwean
Height:	6'2"
Weight:	12st 3lb
Foot:	Right

Player Performance 05/06

League Performance

Percentage of total possible time player was on pitch   ⊙ position in league table at end of month

Month:	Aug	Sep	Oct	Nov	Dec	Jan	Feb	Mar	Apr	May	Total
% on pitch	0%	0%	0%	0%	0%	67%	98%	44%	86%	100%	37%
Position	18	16	14	18	18	19	19	19	17	17	
Team Pts:	1/12	4/9	5/12	0/9	7/18	0/9	1/12	6/9	14/21	0/3	38/114
Team Gls F:	3	2	6	0	4	1	2	6	12	1	37
Team Gls A:	7	2	4	7	11	8	8	4	8	3	62
Total mins:	0	0	0	0	0	180	351	120	540	90	1,281
Starts (sub):	0	0	0	0	0	2	4	2	7	1	16
Goals:	0	0	0	0	0	0	0	0	1	0	1
Assists:	0	0	0	0	0	0	0	0	4	0	4
Clean sheets:	0	0	0	0	0	0	0	0	0	0	0
Cards (Y/R):	0	0	0	0	0	0	0	0	1	0	1

League Performance Totals

Goals
- Mwaruwari: 1
- Team-mates: 35
- **Total: 36**
- own goals: 1

Assists
- Mwaruwari: 4
- Team-mates: 27
- **Total: 31**

Cards
- Mwaruwari: 1
- Team-mates: 53
- **Total: 54**

Cup Games

	Apps	Goals	Cards
FA Cup	0	0	0
Carling Cup	0	0	0
Total	0	0	0

Career History

Career Milestones

Club Debut:
vs Everton (H), L 0-1, Premiership
▶ 14.01.06

Time Spent at the Club:
▶ 0.5 Seasons

First Goal Scored for the Club:
vs Wigan (A), W 1-2, Premiership
▶ 29.04.06

Full International:
▶ Zimbabwe

Premiership Totals

92-06	
Appearances	16
Goals	1
Assists	4
Yellow Cards	1
Red Cards	0

Clubs

Year	Club	Apps	Gls
06-06	Portsmouth	16	1
	AJ Auxerre		
	Grasshopper-Club		
	Jomo Cosmos		

Off the Pitch

Age:
- Mwaruwari: 27 years, 9 months
- Team: 27 years, 5 months
- League: 26 years, 11 months

Height:
- Mwaruwari: 6'2"
- Team: 5'11"
- League: 5'11"

Weight:
- Mwaruwari: 12st 3lb
- Team: 12st
- League: 12st

31 Dario Silva
Forward

Iconic Uruguay striker who moved to Portsmouth in August 2005 after 5 years playing in La Liga with Malaga and Sevilla. Silva, whose stereotypical South American tricks coupled with his bustling power, make him a handful for any defence, was his country's first choice striker for a whole decade, before temporarily retiring from international football after a falling out with his national coach.

He later made his Uruguayan comeback and played a part in the climax to his country's unsuccessful World Cup Qualifying campaign. Dario opened his Pompey goal account with two stunning strikes in October, but was allowed to leave in February 2006.

Player Details:

Date of Birth:	02.11.1972
Place of Birth:	Treinta y Tres
Nationality:	Uruguayan
Height:	5'10"
Weight:	11st 7lb
Foot:	Right/Left

Player Performance 05/06

League Performance

Percentage of total possible time player was on pitch   position in league table at end of month

Month:	Aug	Sep	Oct	Nov	Dec	Jan	Feb	Mar	Apr	May	Total
	0%	91%	84%	57%	43%	17%	0%	0%	0%	0%	29%
	18	16	14	18	18	19	19	19	17	17	
Team Pts:	1/12	4/9	5/12	0/9	7/18	0/9	1/12	6/9	14/21	0/3	38/114
Team Gls F:	3	2	6	0	4	1	2	6	12	1	37
Team Gls A:	7	2	4	7	11	8	8	4	8	3	62
Total mins:	0	245	303	153	231	46	0	0	0	0	978
Starts (sub):	0	3	4	2	3	1	0	0	0	0	13
Goals:	0	0	2	0	0	0	0	0	0	0	2
Assists:	0	0	1	0	1	0	0	0	0	0	2
Clean sheets:	0	0	1	0	1	0	0	0	0	0	2
Cards (Y/R):	0	1	0	0	0	0	0	0	0	0	1

League Performance Totals

Goals

- Silva: 2
- Team-mates: 34

Total: 36

- own goals: 1

Assists

- Silva: 2
- Team-mates: 29

Total: 31

Cards

- Silva: 1
- Team-mates: 53

Total: 54

Cup Games

	Apps	Goals	Cards
FA Cup	1	1	1
Carling Cup	1	0	0
Total	2	1	1

Career History

Career Milestones

Club Debut:
vs Everton (A), W 0-1, Premiership

► **10.09.05**

Time Spent at the Club:

► **0.5 Seasons**

First Goal Scored for the Club:
vs Charlton (H), L 1-2, Premiership

► **22.10.05**

Full International:

► **Uruguay**

Premiership Totals

92-06

Appearances	13
Goals	2
Assists	2
Yellow Cards	1
Red Cards	0

Clubs

Year	Club	Apps	Gls
05-06	Portsmouth	15	3
	Sevilla		
	Malaga		
	Espanyol		
	Cagliari		
	Penarol		
	Defensor SC		
	Yerbalense		

Off the Pitch

Age:
- Silva: 33 years, 6 months
- Team: 27 years, 5 months
- League: 26 years, 11 months

Height:
- Silva: 5'10"
- Team: 5'11"
- League: 5'11"

Weight:
- Silva: 11st 7lb
- Team: 12st
- League: 12st

23 Emmanuel Olisadebe
Forward

Season Review 05/06

Nigerian-born Polish international who joined Portsmouth from Panathinaikos in January 2006, but was unable to make his mark because impressive performances from his teammates prevented him breaking into the squad.

Emmanuel has caught the eye with his pace, strength and energy ever since moving to Europe in 1997, attracting the attention of KP Polonia Warsaw of Poland who eagerly snapped up the promising striker. He helped Polonia to a domestic double in 1999/00 and was awarded Polish citizenship by presidential decree in 2000, making his international debut against Romania a month later and marking the occasion with a debut goal.

Player Details:

Date of Birth:	22.12.1978
Place of Birth:	Waria
Nationality:	Polish
Height:	6'
Weight:	11st
Foot:	Right/Left

Player Performance 05/06

League Performance

Percentage of total possible time player was on pitch   ⊙ position in league table at end of month

Month:	Aug	Sep	Oct	Nov	Dec	Jan	Feb	Mar	Apr	May	Total
	0% 18	0% 16	0% 14	0% 18	0% 18	24% 19	0% 19	0% 19	0% 17	0% 17	2%
Team Pts:	1/12	4/9	5/12	0/9	7/18	0/9	1/12	6/9	14/21	0/3	38/114
Team Gls F:	3	2	6	0	4	1	2	6	12	1	37
Team Gls A:	7	2	4	7	11	8	8	4	8	3	62
Total mins:	0	0	0	0	0	66	0	0	0	0	66
Starts (sub):	0	0	0	0	0	0 (2)	0	0	0	0	0 (2)
Goals:	0	0	0	0	0	0	0	0	0	0	0
Assists:	0	0	0	0	0	0	0	0	0	0	0
Clean sheets:	0	0	0	0	0	0	0	0	0	0	0
Cards (Y/R):	0	0	0	0	0	0	0	0	0	0	0

League Performance Totals

Goals

▶ Olisadebe:	0
▶ Team-mates:	36
Total:	**36**
▶ own goals:	1

Assists

▶ Olisadebe:	0
▶ Team-mates:	31
Total:	**31**

Cards

▶ Olisadebe:	0
▶ Team-mates:	54
Total:	**54**

Cup Games

	Apps	Goals	Cards
FA Cup	0	0	0
Carling Cup	0	0	0
Total	**0**	**0**	**0**

Career History

Career Milestones

Club Debut:
vs Everton (H), L 0-1, Premiership

 14.01.06

Time Spent at the Club:

▶ **0.5 Seasons**

First Goal Scored for the Club:
—

▶ —

Full International:

 Poland

Premiership Totals

92-06

Appearances	2
Goals	0
Assists	0
Yellow Cards	0
Red Cards	0

Clubs

Year	Club	Apps	Gls
06-06	Portsmouth	2	0
	Panathinaikos		
	Polonia Warsaw		
	Jasper United		

Off the Pitch

Age:

- ▶ Olisadebe: 27 years, 5 months
- ▶ Team: 27 years, 5 months
- | League: 26 years, 11 months

Height:

- ▶ Olisadebe: 6'
- ▶ Team: 5'11"
- | League: 5'11"

Weight:

- ▶ Olisadebe: 11st
- ▶ Team: 12st
- | League: 12st

10 Ivica Mornar
Forward

Powerful forward who joined Pompey from Anderlecht in January 2004 to add muscle to Harry Redknapp's strikeforce. However, the Croat failed to make much of an impression and after representing his country at Euro 2004, was loaned to Rennes for the whole of season 2004/05.

The appointment of Alain Perrin gave Mornar a fresh chance to impress and the towering striker looked set to play a significant part in last season's plans (albeit in the strange position of right midfield) before picking up an injury in the first game of the season.

Player Details:

Date of Birth:	12.01.1974
Place of Birth:	Split
Nationality:	Croatian
Height:	6'
Weight:	12st 4lb
Foot:	Right/Left

Player Performance 05/06

League Performance

Percentage of total possible time player was on pitch   ○ position in league table at end of month

Month:	Aug	Sep	Oct	Nov	Dec	Jan	Feb	Mar	Apr	May	Total
	13%	18 / 0%	16 / 0%	14 / 0%	18 / 1%	18 / 0%	19 / 0%	19 / 0%	19 / 0%	17 / 0%	17 / 2%
Team Pts:	1/12	4/9	5/12	0/9	7/18	0/9	1/12	6/9	14/21	0/3	38/114
Team Gls F:	3	2	6	0	4	1	2	6	12	1	37
Team Gls A:	7	2	4	7	11	8	8	4	8	3	62
Total mins:	46	0	0	0	7	0	0	0	0	0	53
Starts (sub):	1	0	0	0	0 (1)	0	0	0	0	0	1 (1)
Goals:	0	0	0	0	0	0	0	0	0	0	0
Assists:	0	0	0	0	0	0	0	0	0	0	0
Clean sheets:	0	0	0	0	0	0	0	0	0	0	0
Cards (Y/R):	0	0	0	0	0	0	0	0	0	0	0

League Performance Totals

Goals
- Mornar: 0
- Team-mates: 36
- **Total: 36**
- own goals: 1

Assists
- Mornar: 0
- Team-mates: 31
- **Total: 31**

Cards
- Mornar: 0
- Team-mates: 54
- **Total: 54**

Cup Games

	Apps	Goals	Cards
FA Cup	0	0	0
Carling Cup	0	0	0
Total	**0**	**0**	**0**

Career History

Career Milestones

Club Debut:
vs Wolverhampton (H), D 0-0, Prem.

► **31.01.04**

Time Spent at the Club:
► **2.5 Seasons**

First Goal Scored for the Club:
vs Tottenham (A), L 4-3, Prem.
► **07.02.04**

Full International:
► **Croatia**

Premiership Totals

92-06	
Appearances	10
Goals	1
Assists	0
Yellow Cards	0
Red Cards	0

Clubs

Year	Club	Apps	Gls
04-04	Rennes		
04-06	Portsmouth	12	1
	RSC Anderlecht		
	Standard Liege		
	Ourense		
	Sevilla		
	Eintracht Frankfurt		
	Hajduk Split		

Off the Pitch

Age:
- Mornar: 32 years, 4 months
- Team: 27 years, 5 months
- League: 26 years, 11 months

Height:
- Mornar: 6'
- Team: 5'11"
- League: 5'11"

Weight:
- Mornar: 12st 4lb
- Team: 12st
- League: 12st

34 James Keene
Forward

Season Review 05/06

20-year-old striker who was discovered by former Pompey defender Paul Hardyman and immediately signed up to the club's youth development scheme. In 2004/05 James grabbed attention with a prolific goalscoring rate for both the U18s and Reserves, earning him a pro-contract and promotion to the first team squad. A loan spell at Kidderminster followed before he returned to Fratton Park to make his Premiership debut against Bolton in May 2005.

Last season Keene enjoyed successful loan spells at Bournemouth and Boston United, before being sent to spend a season in the Swedish top-flight with G.A.I.S. in March 2006. There he has held down a first team place and continued his goalscoring.

Player Details:

Date of Birth:	26.12.1985
Place of Birth:	Wells
Nationality:	English
Height:	5'11"
Weight:	11st 8lb
Foot:	Right

Player Performance 05/06

League Performance

Percentage of total possible time player was on pitch   ⊖ position in league table at end of month

Month:	Aug	Sep	Oct	Nov	Dec	Jan	Feb	Mar	Apr	May	Total
	0%	0%	0%	0%	0%	0%	0%	0%	0%	0%	0%
Team Pts:	1/12	4/9	5/12	0/9	7/18	0/9	1/12	6/9	14/21	0/3	38/114
Team Gls F:	3	2	6	0	4	1	2	6	12	1	37
Team Gls A:	7	2	4	7	11	8	8	4	8	3	62
Total mins:	0	0	0	0	0	0	0	0	0	0	0
Starts (sub):	0	0	0	0	0	0	0	0	0	0	0
Goals:	0	0	0	0	0	0	0	0	0	0	0
Assists:	0	0	0	0	0	0	0	0	0	0	0
Clean sheets:	0	0	0	0	0	0	0	0	0	0	0
Cards (Y/R):	0	0	0	0	0	0	0	0	0	0	0

Line graph positions: Aug 18, Sep 16, Oct 14, Nov 18, Dec 18, Jan 19, Feb 19, Mar 19, Apr 17, May 17

League Performance Totals

Goals
- Keene: 0
- Team-mates: 36
- **Total: 36**
- own goals: 1

Assists
- Keene: 0
- Team-mates: 31
- **Total: 31**

Cards
- Keene: 0
- Team-mates: 54
- **Total: 54**

Cup Games

	Apps	Goals	Cards
FA Cup	0	0	0
Carling Cup	0	0	0
Total	**0**	**0**	**0**

Career History

Career Milestones

Club Debut:
vs Bolton W. (H), D 1-1, Premiership
▶ 07.05.05

First Goal Scored for the Club:
—
▶ —

Time Spent at the Club:
▶ 2 Seasons

Full International:
▶ —

Premiership Totals

92-06

Appearances	2
Goals	0
Assists	0
Yellow Cards	0
Red Cards	0

Clubs

Year	Club	Apps	Gls
06-06	GAIS		
06-06	Boston Utd	6	1
05-05	Bournemouth	14	4
04-04	Kidderminster H.	6	0
04-06	Portsmouth	2	0

Off the Pitch

Age:
- Keene: 20 years, 5 months
- Team: 27 years, 5 months
- League: 26 years, 11 months

Height:
- Keene: 5'11"
- Team: 5'11"
- League: 5'11"

Weight:
- Keene: 11st 8lb
- Team: 12st
- League: 12st

32 Lomana Tresor LuaLua
Forward

Season Review 05/06

Speedy frontman with amazing natural flair who first proved his worth on loan at Fratton Park in February 2004. LuaLua began his career at Colchester where he attracted the attention of Newcastle whom he joined in September 2000. Used primarily as a substitute, Lua became frustrated and fell out of favour, resulting in his move to Pompey.

2005/06 presented Lua with the toughest of tests. He first overcame a life-threatening bout of malaria, to play a starring role in the African Nations Cup, before later having to deal with the death of his son. It is testament to his strength of character that despite this he continued to shine as one of Pompey's stars.

Player Details:

Date of Birth:	28.12.1980
Place of Birth:	Kinshasa
Nationality:	Congolese
Height:	5'10"
Weight:	10st
Foot:	Right/Left

Player Performance 05/06

League Performance

Percentage of total possible time player was on pitch    position in league table at end of month

Month:	Aug	Sep	Oct	Nov	Dec	Jan	Feb	Mar	Apr	May	Total
	100%	57%	14	67%	99%	67%	50%	100%	39% 17	17	62%
	18	16	0%	18	18	19	19	19		0%	
Team Pts:	1/12	4/9	5/12	0/9	7/18	0/9	1/12	6/9	14/21	0/3	38/114
Team Gls F:	3	2	6	0	4	1	2	6	12	1	37
Team Gls A:	7	2	4	7	11	8	8	4	8	3	62
Total mins:	360	155	0	182	533	180	180	270	248	0	2,108
Starts (sub):	4	2	0	2 (1)	6	2	2	3	3	0	24 (1)
Goals:	1	1	0	0	1	0	0	1	3	0	7
Assists:	0	0	0	0	1	0	0	1	1	0	3
Clean sheets:	0	1	0	0	2	0	0	0	0	0	3
Cards (Y/R):	1	0	0	0	0	0	1	0	0	0	2

League Performance Totals

Goals

- Lua Lua: 7
- Team-mates: 29
- **Total: 36**
- own goals: 1

Assists

- Lua Lua: 3
- Team-mates: 28
- **Total: 31**

Cards

- Lua Lua: 2
- Team-mates: 52
- **Total: 54**

Cup Games

	Apps	Goals	Cards
FA Cup	1	0	0
Carling Cup	0	0	0
Total	**1**	**0**	**0**

Career History

Career Milestones

Club Debut:
vs Tottenham (A), L 4-3, Premiership

▶ 07.02.04

Time Spent at the Club:

▶ 2.5 Seasons

First Goal Scored for the Club:
vs Tottenham (A), L 4-3, Premiership

▶ 07.02.04

Full International:

▶ Congo DR

Premiership Totals

92-06

Appearances	124
Goals	22
Assists	13
Yellow Cards	8
Red Cards	1

Clubs

Year	Club	Apps	Gls
04-06	Portsmouth	67	17
00-04	Newcastle	88	9
98-00	Colchester	68	21

Off the Pitch

Age:

- Lua Lua: 25 years, 5 months
- Team: 27 years, 5 months
- League: 26 years, 11 months

Height:

- Lua Lua: 5'10"
- Team: 5'11"
- League: 5'11"

Weight:

- Lua Lua: 10st
- Team: 12st
- League: 12st

9
Svetoslav Todorov
Forward

Season Review 05/06

Bulgarian International striker who was Harry Redknapp's first Portsmouth acquisition when he signed for £750,000 in 2002. 27 goals in Pompey's Championship season won 'Toddy' the Division One Golden Boot, but torn medial ligaments and subsequent complications resulted in a two year lay-off.

He returned in 2005 and after scoring twice for Bulgaria in a 6-2 win over Georgia he followed up with the winner as Pompey beat West Bromwich Albion at Fratton Park. Three more crucial goals towards the end of the campaign then showed signs that the fan favourite is set to return to his best.

Player Details:

Date of Birth:	30.08.1978
Place of Birth:	Dobrich
Nationality:	Bulgarian
Height:	5'11"
Weight:	11st 11lb
Foot:	Right/Left

Player Performance 05/06

League Performance

Percentage of total possible time player was on pitch   position in league table at end of month

Month:	Aug	Sep	Oct	Nov	Dec	Jan	Feb	Mar	Apr	May	Total
	9%	2%	15%	10%	29%	16%	24%	43%	64%	100%	30%
	18	16	14	18	18	19	19	19	17	17	
Team Pts:	1/12	4/9	5/12	0/9	7/18	0/9	1/12	6/9	14/21	0/3	38/114
Team Gls F:	3	2	6	0	4	1	2	6	12	1	37
Team Gls A:	7	2	4	7	11	8	8	4	8	3	62
Total mins:	34	5	53	27	159	44	88	115	403	90	1,018
Starts (sub):	0 (2)	0 (1)	0 (3)	0 (1)	0 (3)	0 (1)	0 (2)	1 (2)	4 (3)	1	6 (18)
Goals:	0	0	0	0	1	0	0	1	2	0	4
Assists:	0	0	0	0	0	0	0	0	0	0	0
Clean sheets:	0	0	0	0	1	0	0	0	1	0	2
Cards (Y/R):	0	0	0	0	0	0	0	0	0	0	0

League Performance Totals

Goals

- Todorov: 4
- Team-mates: 32

Total: 36

- own goals: 1

Assists

- Todorov: 0
- Team-mates: 31

Total: 31

Cards

- Todorov: 0
- Team-mates: 54

Total: 54

Cup Games

	Apps	Goals	Cards
FA Cup	2	0	0
Carling Cup	1	0	0
Total	**3**	**0**	**0**

Career History

Career Milestones

Club Debut:
vs Sheff Wed (H), D 0-0, Championship
▶ 23.03.02

Time Spent at the Club:
▶ 4.5 Seasons

First Goal Scored for the Club:
vs Burnley (H), D 1-1, Championship
▶ 01.04.02

Full International:
▶ Bulgaria

Premiership Totals

92-06

Appearances	39
Goals	5
Assists	3
Yellow Cards	3
Red Cards	0

Clubs

Year	Club	Apps	Gls
02-06	Portsmouth	79	31
01-02	West Ham	17	2
	PFC Litex Lovech		
	Dobrudzha Dobrich		

Off the Pitch

Age:

- Todorov: 27 years, 9 months
- Team: 27 years, 5 months
- League: 26 years, 11 months

Height:

- Todorov: 5'11"
- Team: 5'11"
- League: 5'11"

Weight:

- Todorov: 11st 11lb
- Team: 12st
- League: 12st

17 Vincent Pericard
Forward

French U21 International striker of Cameroonian descent, who impressed at Fratton Park in a season-long loan from Juventus in 2002/03. However, Vincent endured a frustrating 03/04, struggling with his fitness after tearing a thigh muscle. He made a brief return to reserve football in 04/05, but tragically damaged knee ligaments almost immediately.

A loan spell with Sheffield United was his fate in 2005/06 before he was recalled to Pompey by Harry Redknapp. However, another untimely injury ended his big chance after just two appearances and after January signings pushed him down the pecking order, he embarked on a fruitful loan spell at Plymouth before being released in May 2006.

Player Details:

Date of Birth:	03.10.1982
Place of Birth:	Efok
Nationality:	French
Height:	6'1"
Weight:	13st 8lb
Foot:	Right

Player Performance 05/06

League Performance

Percentage of total possible time player was on pitch   ○ position in league table at end of month

Month:	Aug	Sep	Oct	Nov	Dec	Jan	Feb	Mar	Apr	May	Total
	17%	0%	0%	0%	18%	20%	0%	0%	0%	0%	6%
	18	16	14	18	18	19	19	19	17	17	
Team Pts:	1/12	4/9	5/12	0/9	7/18	0/9	1/12	6/9	14/21	0/3	38/114
Team Gls F:	3	2	6	0	4	1	2	6	12	1	37
Team Gls A:	7	2	4	7	11	8	8	4	8	3	62
Total mins:	60	0	0	0	96	53	0	0	0	0	209
Starts (sub):	0 (3)	0	0	0	2	1	0	0	0	0	3 (3)
Goals:	0	0	0	0	0	0	0	0	0	0	0
Assists:	0	0	0	0	0	0	0	0	0	0	0
Clean sheets:	0	0	0	0	0	0	0	0	0	0	0
Cards (Y/R):	0	0	0	0	0	0	0	0	0	0	0

League Performance Totals

Goals
- ► Pericard: 0
- ► Team-mates: 36
- **Total: 36**
- ► own goals: 1

Assists
- ► Pericard: 0
- ► Team-mates: 31
- **Total: 31**

Cards
- ► Pericard: 0
- ► Team-mates: 54
- **Total: 54**

Cup Games

	Apps	Goals	Cards
FA Cup	1	0	1
Carling Cup	0	0	0
Total	**1**	**0**	**1**

Career History

Career Milestones

Club Debut:
vs Nottm Forest (H), W 2-0, Champ.

► **10.08.02**

Time Spent at the Club:

► **4 Seasons**

First Goal Scored for the Club:
vs Nottm Forest (H), W 2-0, Champ.

► **10.08.02**

Full International:

► **—**

Premiership Totals
92-06

Appearances	12
Goals	0
Assists	1
Yellow Cards	1
Red Cards	0

Clubs

Year	Club	Apps	Gls
06-06	Plymouth	15	4
05-05	Sheff Utd	11	2
02-06	Portsmouth	49	10
	Juventus		
	St Etienne		

Off the Pitch

Age:
- ► Pericard: 23 years, 7 months
- ► Team: 27 years, 5 months
- | League: 26 years, 11 months

Height:
- ► Pericard: 6'1"
- ► Team: 5'11"
- | League: 5'11"

Weight:
- ► Pericard: 13st 8lb
- ► Team: 12st
- | League: 12st

Reserves

▶ Daryl Fordyce blocks Andy Reid of Spurs in the Reserves

Pompey's Reserve team experienced a mixed season in the Barclays Premier League South Division, but given the youth and inexperience of the players who were mainly used, the achievement of finishing off the bottom was a worthy one in itself.

Indeed there were highlights to the campaign, none more so than when new Arsenal 'wonder kid' Theo Walcott was upstaged on his debut by one of our own when Marc Wilson's two goals gave Pompey a deserved 3-2 victory. There was also a 6-1 opening day hammering of Leicester at Westleigh Park in which young players such as Liam Horsted, James Keene and Daryl Fordyce all got on the score sheet.

The players also had to adapt to the style of a new manager when Brett Angell joined the club during the season, and they did so well. Obviously first team professionals also played in matches throughout and the likes of Svetoslav Todorov, Vincent Pericard and Jamie Ashdown can only have inspired the younger charges.

There were some poignant moments too, for example when goalkeeper Nick Jordan, 15, was given permission to miss school for the afternoon to play against Watford. In goal for the opposition that evening was veteran 'keeper Alex Chamberlain who has played for a host of professional clubs and in major FA Cup finals over two decades, but who complimented the youngster on his performance that evening. Reserve performances are not based on results as much as they are individuals' progress and with moments such as these who can measure how much Pompey's youth can benefit?

Reserve Fixtures and Results 2005/06

Wed Aug 10th	**Leicester (H)**	**6-1**	**Wed Dec 14th**	**Ipswich (H)**	**4-3**	
Mon Aug 15th	Ipswich (A)	1-2	**Wed Jan 11th**	**Coventry (H)**	**0-1**	
Wed Aug 31st	**West Ham (H)**	**1-3**	Tues Jan 17th	West Ham (A)	1-1	
Tue Sep 6th	Coventry (A)	1-0	Wed Feb 1st	Leicester (A)	4-4	
Wed Sep 21st	Arsenal (A)	3-5	**Wed Feb 8th**	**Arsenal (H)**	**3-2**	
Wed Sep 28th	**Crystal Palace (H)**	**1-2**	**Tue Feb 14th**	**Southampton (H)**	**1-2**	
Tues Oct 4th	Southampton (A)	2-4	Mon Feb 27th	Norwich (A)	3-2	
Wed Oct 12th	**Norwich (H)**	**1-0**	Mon Mar 13th	Tottenham (A)	0-2	
Wed Oct 19th	Charlton (A)	1-3	**Wed Mar 22nd**	**Watford (H)**	**1-3**	
Mon Nov 7th	Watford (A)	0-1	Mon Mar 27th	Fulham (A)	0-1	
Wed Nov 16th	**Fulham (H)**	**0-3**	**Wed Apr 5th**	**Chelsea (H)**	**0-0**	
Mon Nov 21st	Chelsea (A)	0-1	**Mon Apr 24th**	**Charlton (H)**	**0-0**	
Tues Nov 29th	**Tottenham (H)**	**0-3**	Mon May 1st	Crystal Palace (A)	1-5	

Reserve Appearances and Goals 2005/06

Name	Pos	DOB	Apps	Gls	Name	Pos	DOB	Apps	Gls
Jamie Ashdown	GK	30.11.80	5		TJ McClory-Cuthbertson	M	18.06.89	3(2)	1
Louis Bell	F	21.12.88	(3)		Ivica Mornar	F	12.01.74	8	3
Joe Bye	M	29.01.88	4(3)		Emmanuel Olisadebe	F	22.12.78	2	
Joe Carter-Harris	F	07.10.87	2(3)		Noé Pamarot	D	14.04.79	1	
Aliou Cisse	D	24.03.76	7	2	Jason Pearce	D	06.12.87	13(1)	1
Jack Compton	F	02.09.88	3(1)		Vincent Pericard	F	03.10.82	5	2
Phil Cousins	M	29.12.87	9(5)		Jack Plummer	M	31.01.89	(1)	
Matthew Day	D	24.03.87	17(2)		Linvoy Primus	D	14.09.73	4	
Salif Diao	M	10.02.77	4		Brian Priske	D	14.05.77	4	
Harry Donaghey	D	14.10.87	14(3)		Tom Roberts	D	23.09.88	5(4)	
James Eyles	D	02.11.87	9(1)		Ray Rogers	D	05.01.89	3(1)	
Daryl Fordyce	M	31.12.87	11(2)	1	Tom Settle	D	29.10.87	5 (2)	
Andy Griffin	D	17.03.79	2		Gary Silk	D	13.09.84	14	
Andrea Guatelli	GK	05.05.84	10		Dario Silva	F	02.11.72	1	1
Dean Harris	GK	27.12.87	(1)		Giannis Skopelitis	M	02.03.78	5	
Scott Harris	M	24.07.85	3(1)		Franck Songo'o	M	14.05.87	16	2
Matthew Hartmann	M	19.08.89	1(3)		Kyle Swayne	F	21.11.86	9(5)	1
Liam Horsted	M	28.10.85	3	3	Matthew Taylor	D	27.11.81	2	
Richard Hughes	M	25.06.79	2		Svetoslav Todorov	F	30.08.78	7	3
Nick Jordan	GK	13.11.89	4		Giovanni Torre	F	15.11.88	1(5)	2
Azar Karadas	F	09.08.81	8(1)		John Viafara	M	27.10.78	3	1
James Keene	F	26.12.85	4(2)	4	Gregory Vignal	D	19.07.81	6	
Ognjen Koroman	M	19.09.78	3		Sander Westerveld	G	23.10.74	6	
Collins Mbesuma	F	03.02.84	10	4	Marc Wilson	M	17.08.87	16	3

Centre of Excellence

▶ Ex-youth team graduate Gary O'Neil is now an integral member of the first team

The Portsmouth FC Youth Development Department also experienced an unsettled season as the club bid farewell to long-serving U18s coach, Mark O'Connor who took up the role of First Team Coach at Plymouth Argyle. In his place, Brett Angell and Shaun North oversaw what was, in terms of results, a mixed bag of a season.

The U16s enjoyed convincing wins against Gillingham on the opening day (5-1), Southend (4-1) and Swindon (4-2), but suffered disappointing defeats at Bournemouth (1-3) and Oxford (1-5), whilst the U18s may have struggled to find consistency, but managed creditable wins against Brentford in the Youth Alliance Cup (5-1) and Northampton on the final day (3-1).

Of course, like Reserve team football, success isn't so much measured in score lines as it is long-term results and in that sense it has been a particularly

good year for the PFC youth department's recent graduates. Gary O'Neil stepped up to the mantle of first team captain on several occasions, whilst Marc Wilson and Daryl Fordyce received regular International call ups, the latter finishing as top scorer in May's European U19 Championship with five goals for Northern Ireland. Both Marc and Daryl also joined the likes of James Keene and Liam Horsted on the list of those who enjoyed spells away from Fratton Park on loan at other Football League clubs.

An impressive seven of this season's U16s were offered apprenticeships for next term and the majority of the U18s and a significant number of U16s have already experienced Reserve Team football, making it a very rewarding year in terms of player progression.

2005/06 also marked Youth Development Officer, Dave Hurst's 25th year at the club.

● James Keene making his way up through the ranks

U18 Team Fixtures and Results 2005/06

13.08.05	Gillingham (A)	0-3		17.12.05	Luton (A)	1-3
20.08.05	**Cambridge Utd (H)**	**2-0**		**07.01.06**	**Wycombe W (H)**	**1-1**
03.09.05	Leyton Orient (A)	1-1		**14.01.06**	**QPR (H)**	**2-2**
10.09.05	Northampton (A)	2-1		21.01.06	Brentford (A)	2-3
01.10.05	**Yeovil (YA Cup) (H)**	**2-1**		**04.02.06**	**Colchester (H)**	**2-1**
08.10.05	QPR (A)	0-2		11.02.06	Brighton (A)	0-2
15.10.05	**Brentford (H)**	**1-4**		**18.02.06**	**Southend (H)**	**0-2**
29.10.05	**Brentford (YA Cup) (H)**	**5-1**		25.02.06	Rushden & Diamonds (A)	0-1
19.11.05	Colchester (A)	0-4		**04.03.06**	**Luton (H)**	**1-2**
26.11.05	**Brighton (H)**	**0-2**		11.03.06	Wycombe Wand.	0-2
03.12.05	Southend (A)	1-1		**18.03.06**	**Gillingham (H)**	**1-4**
07.12.05	**Millwall (FAY Cup) (H)**	**0-2**		**01.04.06**	**Leyton Orient (H)**	**2-2**
10.12.05	**Rushden & Diamonds (H)**	**1-3**		08.04.06	Northampton (A)	3-1

U16 Team Fixtures and Results 2005/06

10.09.05	Gillingham (A)	5-1		**21.01.06**	**Leyton Orient (H)**	**3-0**
17.09.05	**QPR (H)**	**2-4**		28.01.06	Northampton (A)	2-1
01.10.05	**Brentford (H)**	**2-1**		04.02.06	QPR (A)	2-3
08.10.05	Southend (A)	3-1		**11.02.06**	**Brentford (H)**	**3-2**
22.10.05	**Oxford (H)**	**2-2**		**15.02.06**	**Bristol Rovers (H)**	**0-0**
05.11.05	Leyton Orient (A)	3-2		18.02.06	Southend (A)	0-1
12.11.05	**Gillingham (H)**	**2-0**		25.02.06	Oxford (A)	1-5
19.11.05	**Wycombe W (H)**	**1-0**		04.03.06	Wycombe W (A)	2-2
26.11.05	Brentford (A)	3-2		**11.03.06**	**Brighton (H)**	**0-2**
03.12.05	**Southend (H)**	**4-1**		18.03.06	Bournemouth (A)	1-0
17.12.05	**Bournemouth (H)**	**1-3**		25.03.06	Reading (A)	3-1
07.01.06	Brighton (A)	2-2		**08.04.06**	**QPR (H)**	**1-3**
14.01.06	**Swindon (H)**	**4-2**				

Arsenal

Nickname: The Gunners
Manager: Arsène Wenger
Chairman: Peter Hill-Wood
Website: www.arsenal.com

Telephone: 020 7704 4000
Ticket Office: 020 7704 4040
Club Shop: 020 7704 4120

Season Review 05/06

It was a season of mixed fortunes for an Arsenal side that grew up enormously over the course of the campaign.

Reaching the Champions League Final was a terrific achievement, with defeat to Barcelona tempered by Thierry Henry's decision to stay at the club. Prior to that, the Gunners said goodbye to Highbury by clinching fourth place at the expense of Tottenham.

Points / Position

won drawn lost H home A away

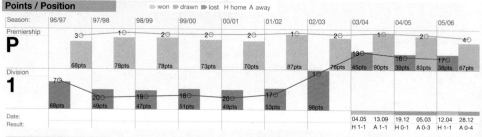

Season:	96/97	97/98	98/99	99/00	00/01	01/02	02/03	03/04	04/05	05/06
Premiership **P**	3	1	2	2	2	1	2	1	2	4
	68pts	78pts	78pts	73pts	70pts	87pts	78pts / 45pts	90pts	83pts	67pts
Division **1**	7	20	19	18	20	17	1	13	16	17
	68pts	49pts	47pts	51pts	49pts	53pts	98pts	39pts	38pts	

Date:	04.05	13.09	19.12	05.03	12.04	28.12
Result:	H 1-1	A 1-1	H 0-1	A 0-3	H 1-1	A 0-4

Recent Meetings

19.12.04	05.03.05	28.12.05	12.04.06
0-1 Attendance: 20,170	**3-0** Attendance: 38,079	**4-0** Attendance: 38,223	**1-1** Attendance: 20,230
Referee: H.M.Webb	Referee: C.J.Foy	Referee: M.Clattenburg	Referee: U.D.Rennie
○ 75 Campbell	○ 39 Henry	○ 7 Bergkamp	○ 66 Lua Lua ○ 36 Henry
	○ 53 Henry	○ 13 Reyes	
	○ 85 Henry	○ 37 Henry	
		○ 43 Henry	

Prem. Head-to-Head

Facts	○ Portsmouth	Arsenal ○
Games		
Points	3	12
Won	0	3
Drawn	3	3
Goals		
For	3	11
Clean Sheets	0	3
Shots on Target	21	29
Disciplinary		
Fouls	89	68
Yellow Cards	7	6
Red Cards	0	0

Goals by Area
○ Portsmouth   ○ Arsenal

Goals by Position
○ Portsmouth   ○ Arsenal

► forward:	3		► forward:	10
► midfield:	0		► midfield:	0
► defence:	0		► defence:	0

Goals Scored by Period

	0	2	0	0	1	0
	0	15	30	45	60	75	90
	2	0	5	2	1	1

Average Attendance
► **20,180**
► **38,118**

All-Time Records

Total Premiership Record	○ Portsmouth	Arsenal ○
Played	114	544
Points	122	1,013
Won	32	289
Drawn	26	146
Lost	56	109
For	127	911
Against	175	481
Players Used	64	113

All-Time Record vs Portsmouth

Competition	Played	Won	Drawn	Lost	For	Against
League	58	24	20	14	107	71
FA Cup	4	3	1	0	11	4
League Cup	0	0	0	0	0	0
Other	0	0	0	0	0	0
Total	**62**	**27**	**21**	**14**	**118**	**75**

Emirates Stadium

Stadium History

The new 60,000-capacity Emirates Stadium has been designed to take Arsenal to a new level both on and off the pitch. Built at an entire cost of £390 million, the state-of-the-art facility is located within walking distance of Highbury.

Though everything has been constructed on a grander scale, it is the increased dimensions of the playing surface that will perhaps take most getting used to. Players will now run out onto a pitch measuring 113m by 76m.

Seating Plan

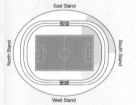

Capacity
60,000

- family area
- away fans
  disabled

Stadium Statistics 05/06

Highest attendance (Highbury)
38,359 vs Wigan Athletic 07.05.06

Lowest attendance (Highbury)
37,867 vs Fulham 24.08.05

Average attendance (Highbury)
38,184

How to Get There

Travel Information

Car parking
Parking near the ground is difficult; it is advised to park further away and get the Tube in.

Train & Tube
Arsenal (Piccadilly Line) is the nearest tube station, around 3 minutes walk from the ground. Finsbury Park (Victoria & Piccadilly Lines and GN rail) and Highbury & Islington (Victoria Line, North London Line and Great Northern Line) stations are around a 10 minute walk. King's Cross is the main connecting station for overgound rail and many underground lines. From here you can travel to the ground via the Piccadilly Line (to Arsenal) or the Victoria Line (to Highbury & Islington). Alternatively, a short overground rail journey of one stop will take you to Finsbury Park station.

Area Map

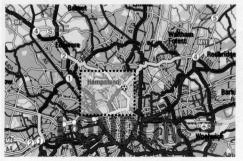

Local Map

Aston Villa °

Nickname: The Villans
Manager: David O'Leary
Chairman: Doug Ellis
Website: www.avfc.co.uk

Telephone: 0121 327 2299
Ticket Office: 0121 327 5353
Club Shop: 0121 326 1559

Season Review 05/06

It was a season of frustration at Villa Park, with many disillusioned fans calling for the heads of Manager David O'Leary and Chairman Doug Ellis.

A 3-0 Carling Cup hammering at League One side Doncaster was the low point of a campaign in which Villa finished just eight points and two places away from relegation to the Championship.

Points / Position

won ▶ drawn ▶ lost H home A away

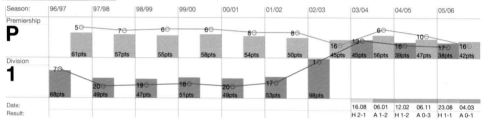

Season:	96/97	97/98	98/99	99/00	00/01	01/02	02/03	03/04	04/05	05/06
Premiership **P**	5○ 61pts	7○ 57pts	6○ 55pts	6○ 58pts	8○ 54pts	8○ 50pts	16○ 45pts	13○ 56pts / 6○ 45pts	10○ 47pts / 16○ 38pts	16○ 42pts
Division **1**	7○ 68pts	20○ 49pts	19○ 47pts	18○ 51pts	20○ 49pts	17○ 53pts	1○ 98pts			

Date:								16.08	06.01	12.02	06.11	23.08	04.03
Result:								H 2-1	A 1-2	H 1-2	A 0-3	H 1-1	A 0-1

Recent Meetings

06.11.04
○○3-0 Attendance: 32,633
Referee: M.R.Halsey
○ 18 Whittingham
○ 25 Angel
○ 40 Solano

12.02.05
○○1-2 Attendance: 20,160
Referee: D.J.Gallagher
○ 24 Yakubu ○ 17 De Zeeuw
○ 73 Hitzlsperger

23.08.05
○○1-1 Attendance: 19,778
Referee: G.Poll
○ 42 Lua Lua ○ 11 Hughes (o.g.)

04.03.06
○○1-0 Attendance: 30,194
Referee: M.L.Dean
○ 36 Baros

Prem. Head-to-Head

Facts	○ Portsmouth	Aston Villa ○
Games		
Points	4	13
Won	1	4
Drawn	1	1
Goals		
For	5	10
Clean Sheets	0	2
Shots on Target	31	35
Disciplinary		
Fouls	89	98
Yellow Cards	9	6
Red Cards	0	2

Goals by Area
○ Portsmouth ○ Aston Villa

	1	4	
3			5
1			1

Goals Scored by Period

0	1	2	1	1	0
0	15	30	45	60	75	90
1	4	2	0	1	2

Goals by Position
○ Portsmouth ○ Aston Villa

▶ forward: 4   ▶ forward: 4
▶ midfield: 1   ▶ midfield: 4
▶ defence: 0   ▶ defence: 0
                ● own goals: 2

Average Attendance
▶ **20,013**
▶ **30,484**

All-Time Records

Total Premiership Record	○ Portsmouth	Aston Villa
Played	114	544
Points	122	767
Won	32	203
Drawn	26	158
Lost	56	183
For	127	668
Against	175	632
Players Used	64	120

All-Time Record vs Portsmouth

Competition	Played	Won	Drawn	Lost	For	Against
League	66	31	15	20	125	109
FA Cup	8	3	3	2	13	10
League Cup	2	1	1	0	5	4
Other	0	0	0	0	0	0
Total	76	35	19	22	143	123

Aston Villa

Villa Park

Stadium History

Opened in 1897, Villa Park has become an important venue for English football. The ground was used during Euro '96, and has hosted more FA Cup Semi-Finals than any other stadium.

The club recorded its highest Premiership attendance in the final game of the 1993/94 season against Liverpool. The Villa fans turned out to see the terracing in the Holte End for the last time, before it was replaced with seating. More recently, the Trinity Road stand has been redeveloped.

Seating Plan

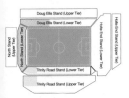

Capacity
42,573

family area
away fans
disabled

Stadium Statistics 05/06

Highest attendance
42,551 vs Liverpool 05.11.05

Lowest attendance
26,422 vs Manchester City 25.04.06

Average attendance
34,111

How to Get There

Travel Information

Car parking
Use local car parks – Aston Villa Events Centre Car Park or at the Aston Hall Road. You are advised not to park in the streets surrounding Villa Park.

Train
New Street Station, Birmingham City Centre – Take taxi to Villa Park (15 minutes away). Or from Birmingham New Street Station change for Aston or Witton.

Bus
From Birmingham City Centre: Catch West Midlands Travel Bus No.7 to Witton.

Area Map

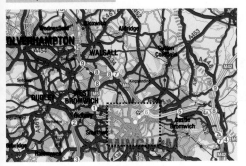

Local Map

Blackburn Rovers °

Nickname: Rovers
Manager: Mark Hughes
Chairman: John Williams
Website: www.rovers.co.uk

Telephone: 08701 113 232
Ticket Office: 08701 123 456
Club Shop: 0870 042 3875

Season Review 05/06

Mark Hughes guided Blackburn to sixth place and UEFA Cup qualification in his first full season in charge. Despite operating with a relatively small squad, the Ewood Park outfit also reached the last four in the Carling Cup.

Craig Bellamy proved to be a shrewd acquisition, whilst the likes of Steven Reid and Morten Gamst Pedersen really shone.

Points / Position

▶ won ▶ drawn ▶ lost H home A away

Season:	96/97	97/98	98/99	99/00	00/01	01/02	02/03	03/04	04/05	05/06
Premiership **P**		13○ 42pts	6○ 58pts	19○ 35pts			10○ 46pts	6○ 60pts	13○ 45pts	15○ 44pts	16○ 39pts	15○ 42pts	17○ 38pts	6○ 63pts
Division **1**	7○ 68pts	20○ 49pts	19○ 47pts	18○ 51pts	11○ 62pts	20○ 49pts	2○ 91pts	17○ 53pts	1○ 98pts			
Date:				28.12	15.04	11.11	29.04			20.09	27.03	15.01	18.09	08.04	02.01
Result:				H 1-2	A 1-1	H 2-2	A 1-3			H 1-2	A 2-1	H 0-1	A 0-1	H 2-2	A 1-2

Recent Meetings

○○○ 1-0 18.09.04 Attendance: 20,647
Referee: M.Clattenburg
○ 75 Jansen

○○○ 0-1 15.01.05 Attendance: 19,904
Referee: A.P.D'Urso
○ 55 Pedersen

○○ 2-1 02.01.06 Attendance: 19,521
Referee: M.L.Dean
○ 9 Pedersen ○ 3 Taylor
○ 39 Dickov

○○ 2-2 08.04.06 Attendance: 20,048
Referee: S.G.Bennett
○ 41 Lua Lua ○ 32 Bellamy
○ 78 Todorov ○ 62 Bellamy

Prem. Head-to-Head

Facts	○ Portsmouth	Blackburn ○
Games		
Points	4	13
Won	1	4
Drawn	1	1
Goals		
For	6	9
Clean Sheets	0	2
Shots on Target	26	28
Disciplinary		
Fouls	82	87
Yellow Cards	11	13
Red Cards	2	0

Goals by Area
○ Portsmouth ○ Blackburn

	1	2
2		6
3		1

Goals Scored by Period

○ Portsmouth
1	1	1	1	0	2
0	15	30	45	60	75	90
○ Blackburn
| 1 | 0 | 5 | 1 | 2 | 0 |

Goals by Position
○ Portsmouth ○ Blackburn

forward: 4   forward: 5
midfield: 1   midfield: 2
defence: 1   defence: 1
              own goals: 1

Average Attendance

▶ **19,992**

▶ **21,008**

All-Time Records

Total Premiership Record	○ Portsmouth	Blackburn ○
Played	114	468
Points	122	695
Won	32	190
Drawn	26	125
Lost	56	153
For	127	650
Against	175	553
Players Used	64	124

All-Time Record vs Portsmouth

Competition	Played	Won	Drawn	Lost	For	Against
League	62	25	16	21	92	93
FA Cup	13	5	6	2	20	10
League Cup	4	3	1	0	11	2
Other	0	0	0	0	0	0
Total	**79**	**33**	**23**	**23**	**123**	**105**

Blackburn Rovers

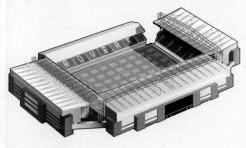

Stadium History

After occupying five different grounds in 15 years, Blackburn finally settled at Ewood Park in 1890. Laurence Cotton took over as chairman in 1905, and by 1913 he had spent thousands of pounds on completely redeveloping the stadium.

Sir Jack Walker followed in his footsteps towards the end of the century, providing the steel needed to build the 'Walkersteel Stand' in 1987, and then taking over as chairman in 1991. Investment followed both on and off the pitch, giving the town a facility to be proud of.

Seating Plan

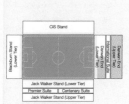

Stadium Statistics 05/06

Capacity	**Highest attendance**
31,367	29,142 vs Liverpool 16.04.06
family area	**Lowest attendance**
away fans	16,953 vs Fulham 20.08.05
disabled	
	Average attendance
	21,015

How to Get There

Travel Information

Car parking
Street parking close to Ewood Park is restricted, please use the car parks provided.

Train
Blackburn station is approximately a mile and a half from Ewood Park. Mill Hill station is approximately one mile away from the ground.

Bus
Services 3, 3A, 3B, 46, 346 all go from Blackburn to Darwen, Ewood Park is about a mile and a half along the journey.

Area Map

Local Map

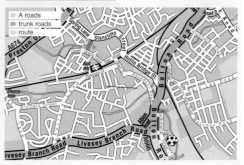

Bolton Wanderers

Nickname: **The Trotters**
Manager: **Sam Allardyce**
Chairman: **Phil Gartside**
Website: **www.bwfc.co.uk**

Telephone: **01204 673 673**
Ticket Office: **0871 871 2932**
Club Shop: **01204 673 650**

Season Review 05/06

It was another encouraging season for Bolton, with a top-half finish and European adventure to boot. Games against the likes of eventual winners Sevilla in the UEFA Cup only served to raise the profile of the club.

A disappointing end to the campaign was attributed in many quarters to the incessant speculation linking boss Sam Allardyce to the England job.

Points / Position

won drawn lost H home A away

Season:	96/97	97/98	98/99	99/00	00/01	01/02	02/03	03/04	04/05	05/06
Premiership **P**						16⊖ 40pts	17⊖ 44pts	13⊖ 45pts	8⊖ 8⊖ 6⊖ 16⊖ 53pts 39pts	17⊖ 8⊖ 58pts 38pts	56pts
Division **1**	7⊖ 68pts	1⊖ 98pts	20⊖ 19⊖ 49pts 47pts	6⊖ 18⊖ 76pts 51pts	6⊖ 20⊖ 76pts 49pts	3⊖ 87pts	1⊖ 53pts	98pts			
Date:	11.01	14.09	09.05 19.12	27.11 22.02	13.02 16.09			26.08 17.01	07.05 27.11	01.02 24.09
Result:	H 0-3	A 0-2	H 0-2 A 1-3	H 0-0 A 0-3	H 1-2 A 0-2			H 4-0 A 0-1	H 1-1 A 1-0	H 1-1 A 0-1

Recent Meetings

27.11.04	07.05.05	24.09.05	01.02.06
OO 0-1 Attendance: 25,008	**OO 1-1** Attendance: 20,188	**OO 1-0** Attendance: 23,134	**OO 1-1** Attendance: 19,128
Referee: S.W.Dunn	Referee: M.D.Messias	Referee: M.Clattenburg	Referee: D.J.Gallagher
O 45 De Zeeuw	O 72 Yakubu O 11 Diouf	O 25 Nolan	O 85 Karadas O 69 Fadiga

Prem. Head-to-Head

Facts	O Portsmouth	Bolton O
Games		
Points	8	8
Won	2	2
Drawn	2	2
Goals		
For	7	4
Clean Sheets	2	2
Shots on Target	28	27
Disciplinary		
Fouls	71	78
Yellow Cards	6	9
Red Cards	1	0

Goals by Area
O Portsmouth   O Bolton

2	0
5	3
0	1

Goals Scored by Period

	0	0	1	2	1	3
	0	15	30	45	60	75	90
	1	1	0	1	1	0

Goals by Position
O Portsmouth   O Bolton

▶ forward:	5	▶ forward:	2
▶ midfield:	1	▶ midfield:	2
▶ defence:	1	▶ defence:	0

Average Attendance

▶ **19,810**

▶ **24,900**

All-Time Records

Total Premiership Record	O Portsmouth	Bolton O
Played	114	266
Points	122	320
Won	32	81
Drawn	26	77
Lost	56	108
For	127	311
Against	175	386
Players Used	64	109

All-Time Record vs Portsmouth

Competition	Played	Won	Drawn	Lost	For	Against
League	84	36	20	28	132	103
FA Cup	5	2	1	2	5	7
League Cup	0	0	0	0	0	0
Other	0	0	0	0	0	0
Total	**89**	**38**	**21**	**30**	**137**	**110**

Bolton Wanderers

Stadium History

Though leaving Burnden Park at the end of the 1996–97 season was a wrench for Bolton fans, they were delighted to move into the purpose-built £35m Reebok Stadium. The first competitive match at their new home was a 0-0 draw against Everton on September 1st 1997.

Playing in such impressive surroundings has helped attract high-profile stars such as Jay-Jay Okocha and Fernando Hierro to the club, resulting in the ground playing host to European football for the first time in 2005/06.

Seating Plan

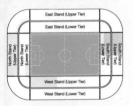

Capacity
28,723

▪ family area
▪ away fans
▪ disabled

Stadium Statistics 05/06

Highest attendance
27,718 vs Manchester United 01.04.06

Lowest attendance
22,733 vs Middlesbrough 03.05.06

Average attendance
25,265

How to Get There

Travel Information

Car parking
2,800 spaces at the ground – costs £5. In the surrounding industrial estate cheaper parking options available.

Train
Horwich Parkway railway station serves the stadium, with regular trains from Bolton's main station. Horwich Parkway is only a few minutes walk from the stadium.

Area Map

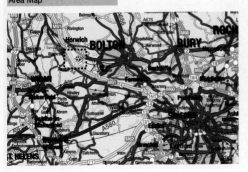

Local Map

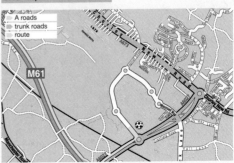

A roads
trunk roads
route

Charlton Athletic

Nickname: The Addicks
Manager: Iain Dowie
Chairman: Richard Murray
Website: www.cafc.co.uk

Telephone: 020 8333 4000
Ticket Office: 020 8333 4010
Club Shop: 020 8333 4035

Season Review 05/06

The 2005/06 season will be remembered at Charlton as the last in Alan Curbishley's 15-year reign. A great start saw the Addicks win five of their first six league games, but they ultimately slipped to a respectable 13th place.

Darren Bent arrived from Ipswich with a bang, firing in 18 goals to finish as the leading English marksman in the Premiership.

Points / Position

won drawn lost H home A away

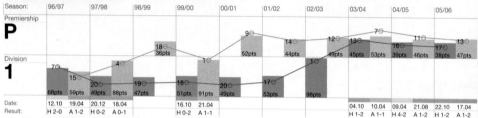

Season:	96/97	97/98	98/99	99/00	00/01	01/02	02/03	03/04	04/05	05/06
Premiership P			18○ 36pts		9○ 52pts	14○ 44pts	12○ 49pts 45pts	7○ 53pts	11○ 39pts 46pts	16○ 17○ 13○ 38pts 47pts
Division 1	7○ 68pts	15○ 59pts	20○ 49pts	19○ 88pts	18○ 47pts	20○ 51pts 91pts	17○ 49pts 53pts	1○ 98pts		
Date:	12.10	19.04	20.12	18.04	16.10	21.04			04.10	10.04	09.04	21.08	22.10	17.04
Result:	H 2-0	A 1-2	H 0-2	A 0-1	H 0-2	A 1-1			H 1-2	A 1-1	H 4-2	A 1-2	H 1-2	A 1-2

Recent Meetings

21.08.04	09.04.05	22.10.05	17.04.06
○○ 2-1 Attendance: 25,204	○○ 4-2 Attendance: 20,108	○○ 1-2 Attendance: 19,030	○○ 2-1 Attendance: 25,419
Referee: A.G.Wiley	Referee: G.Poll	Referee: H.M.Webb	Referee: H.M.Webb
○ 23 Euell ○ 53 Berger	○ 3 Yakubu ○ 22 Fortune	○ 14 Silva ○ 61 Ambrose	○ 76 Hughes ○ 40 D'Alessandro
○ 87 Unsworth (o.g.)	○ 20 Stone ○ 45 Murphy	○ 77 Rommedahl	○ 83 Bent D
	○ 83 Kamara		
	○ 90 Lua Lua		

Prem. Head-to-Head

Facts	○ Portsmouth	Charlton ○
Games		
Points	4	13
Won	1	4
Drawn	1	1
Goals		
For	9	11
Clean Sheets	0	0
Shots on Target	35	41
Disciplinary		
Fouls	79	78
Yellow Cards	9	10
Red Cards	0	0

Goals by Area

○ Portsmouth ○ Charlton

	2	2
6		8
1		1

Goals by Position

○ Portsmouth ○ Charlton

■ forward: 6
■ midfield: 3
■ defence: 0

■ forward: 4
■ midfield: 4
■ defence: 2
● own goals: 1

Goals Scored by Period

2	1	2	1	1	2
0	15	30	45	60	75	90
1	2	1	0	1	6

Average Attendance

▶ 19,748

▶ 25,669

All-Time Records

Total Premiership Record	○ Portsmouth	Charlton ○
Played	114	266
Points	122	327
Won	32	85
Drawn	26	72
Lost	56	109
For	127	308
Against	175	382
Players Used	64	74

All-Time Record vs Portsmouth

Competition	Played	Won	Drawn	Lost	For	Against
League	94	31	25	38	132	150
FA Cup	5	1	2	2	10	9
League Cup	0	0	0	0	0	0
Other	0	0	0	0	0	0
Total	99	32	27	40	142	159

Charlton Athletic

The Valley

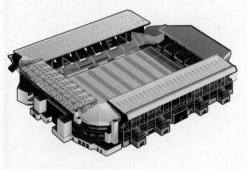

Stadium History

After years of ground sharing and financial problems, Charlton returned to The Valley on December 5th 1992. The move back home owed much to a crusade by supporters, who in 1989 undertook a massive clean-up operation to prepare the ground for redevelopment. It was another two years before planning permission was granted to build on the site, but things have gone from strength to strength since then. Work on the East Stand will raise the capacity to 30,900, with future redevelopment of the South Stand also a possibility.

Seating Plan

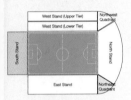

Capacity
27,111

- family area
- away fans
- disabled

Stadium Statistics 05/06

Highest attendance
27,111 vs Chelsea 17.09.05

Lowest attendance
23,453 vs Wigan Athletic 20.08.05

Average attendance
26,195

How to Get There

Travel Information

Car parking
Parking around the ground is limited to 2 hours only.

Train
Connex runs train services to Charlton railway station, which is about a two minute walk from the stadium.

Bus
Extensive network. Routes include the 177, 180, 472, 161, 53 and 54. The M1 service provides an overland link to Charlton train station from the North Greenwich Tube station.

Area Map

Local Map

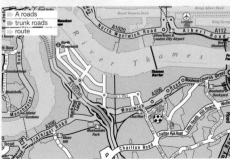

Chelsea ○

Nickname: The Blues
Manager: José Mourinho
Chairman: Bruce Buck
Website: www.chelseafc.com

Telephone: 0870 300 2322
Ticket Office: 0870 300 2322
Club Shop: 0870 300 1212

Season Review 05/06

Chelsea dominated the league season from start to finish, though they were less successful in cup competitions. Barcelona, Liverpool and Charlton ensured that José Mourinho had to be content with the Premiership and Community Shield.

John Terry and Frank Lampard were once again star performers, whilst Joe Cole found the consistency to match his abundance of skill.

Points / Position

▶ won ▶ drawn ▶ lost H home A away

Season:	96/97	97/98	98/99	99/00	00/01	01/02	02/03	03/04	04/05	05/06
Premiership	6⊖	4⊖	3⊖	5⊖	6⊖	6⊖	4⊖	2⊖	1⊖	1⊖
P	59pts	63pts	75pts	65pts	61pts	64pts	67pts	13⊖ 45pts	16⊖ 79pts 39pts 95pts	17⊖ 38pts 91pts
Division	7⊖						1⊖			
1	68pts	20⊖ 49pts	19⊖ 47pts	18⊖ 51pts	20⊖ 49pts	17⊖ 53pts	98pts			

Date:								11.02	28.12	28.12	22.01	26.11	25.02
Result:								H 0-2	A 0-3	H 0-2	A 0-3	H 0-2	A 0-2

Recent Meetings

28.12.04		22.01.05		26.11.05		25.02.06	
○○**0-2**	Attendance: 20,210	○○**3-0**	Attendance: 42,267	○○**0-2**	Attendance: 20,182	○○**2-0**	Attendance: 42,254
Referee: A.G.Wiley		Referee: M.A.Riley		Referee: P.Dowd		Referee: M.A.Riley	
○ 79 Robben		○ 15 Drogba		○ 27 Crespo		○ 65 Lampard	
○ 90 Cole J		○ 21 Robben		○ 67 Lampard		○ 78 Robben	
		○ 39 Drogba					

Prem. Head-to-Head

Facts	○ Portsmouth	Chelsea ○
Games		
Points	0	18
Won	0	6
Drawn	0	0
Goals		
For	0	14
Clean Sheets	0	6
Shots on Target	16	40
Disciplinary		
Fouls	84	55
Yellow Cards	8	6
Red Cards	0	0

Goals by Area

○ Portsmouth ○ Chelsea

0	2
0	8

0 | 4

Goals Scored by Period

0	0	0	0	0	0
0	15	30	45	60	75	90
1	3	1	0	4	5

Goals by Position

○ Portsmouth ○ Chelsea

	▶ forward:	0	▶ forward:	4
	▶ midfield:	0	▶ midfield:	9
	▶ defence:	0	▶ defence:	1

Average Attendance

▶ **20,177**

▶ **42,024**

All-Time Records

Total Premiership Record	○ Portsmouth	Chelsea ○
Played	114	544
Points	122	930
Won	32	261
Drawn	26	147
Lost	56	136
For	127	848
Against	175	556
Players Used	64	135

All-Time Record vs Portsmouth

Competition	Played	Won	Drawn	Lost	For	Against
League	66	26	21	19	117	102
FA Cup	3	1	1	1	5	3
League Cup	3	1	1	1	3	3
Other	0	0	0	0	0	0
Total	**72**	**28**	**23**	**21**	**125**	**108**

Chelsea

Stamford Bridge

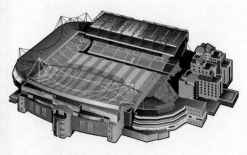

Stadium History

Stamford Bridge is more than just a football stadium. Alongside it stands 'Chelsea Village', a complex housing, amongst other things, two hotels, five restaurants and a health club.

The ground was initially offered to Fulham, but their decision not to play there led to the formation of Chelsea in 1905. After years of uncertainty, chairman Ken Bates secured the future of the venue in 1992. Since then wholesale changes have taken place, with completion of the West Stand in 2001 resulting in a spectacular facility.

Seating Plan

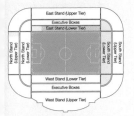

Capacity
42,449

family area
away fans
disabled

Stadium Statistics 05/06

Highest attendance
42,321 vs Manchester City 25.03.06

Lowest attendance
40,652 vs Birmingham City 31.12.05

Average attendance
41,901

How to Get There

Travel Information

Train
West Brompton is a new station accessible from Clapham Junction.

Tube
The nearest tube station is Fulham Broadway on the District Line.

Bus
Bus numbers 14, 211, 11, 28, 295 and C4.

Area Map

Local Map

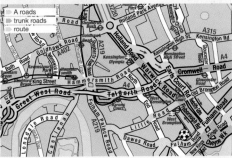

Everton °

Everton

Nickname: The Toffees
Manager: David Moyes
Chairman: Bill Kenwright
Website: www.evertonfc.com

Telephone: 0870 442 1878
Ticket Office: 0870 442 1878
Club Shop: 0870 442 1878

Season Review 05/06

Everton followed up the amazing form of their previous campaign with a mid-table finish. A return to European football brought only heartbreak, as the Toffees fell early in both the Champions League and UEFA Cup.

Nigel Martyn continued to defy his advancing years in goal, whilst James Beattie began to show what he could do at the other end.

Points / Position

● won ● drawn ● lost H home A away

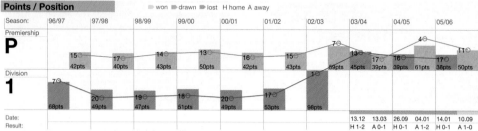

Season:	96/97	97/98	98/99	99/00	00/01	01/02	02/03	03/04	04/05	05/06

Premiership

P

15● 42pts | 17● 40pts | 14● 43pts | 13● 50pts | 16● 42pts | 15● 43pts | 7● / 45pts | 13● 39pts 17● | 4● / 16● 39pts 61pts | 17● 38pts | 11● 50pts

Division

1

7● 68pts | 20● 49pts | 19● 47pts | 18● 51pts | 20● 49pts | 17● 53pts | 1● 98pts |

| Date: | | | | | | | | 13.12 | 13.03 | 26.09 | 04.01 | 14.01 | 10.09 |
| Result: | | | | | | | | H 1-2 | A 0-1 | H 0-1 | A 1-2 | H 0-1 | A 1-0 |

Recent Meetings

26.09.04
○○ **0-1** Attendance: 20,125
Referee: D.J Gallagher
○ 80 Cahill

04.01.05
○○ **2-1** Attendance: 35,480
Referee: P.Walton
○ 29 Stubbs   ○ 31 Yakubu
○ 90 Osman

10.09.05
○○ **0-1** Attendance: 36,831
Referee: M.Atkinson
○ 60 Ferguson

14.01.06
○○ **0-1** Attendance: 20,094
Referee: A.Marriner
○ 31 O'Brien

Prem. Head-to-Head

Facts	○ Portsmouth	Everton ○
Games		
Points	3	15
Won	1	5
Drawn	0	0
Goals		
For	3	7
Clean Sheets	1	3
Shots on Target	35	23
Disciplinary		
Fouls	80	68
Yellow Cards	7	6
Red Cards	0	0

Goals by Area
○ Portsmouth   ○ Everton

	1	1	
2			6
0			0

Goals Scored by Period

1	0	1	1	0	0
0	15	30	45	60	75	90
	0	2	2	0	0	3

Goals by Position
○ Portsmouth   ○ Everton

● forward: 2   ● forward: 2
● midfield: 0   ● midfield: 3
● defence: 0   ● defence: 1
● own goals: 1 ● own goals: 1

Average Attendance

▶ **20,107**

▶ **37,472**

All-Time Records

Total Premiership Record	○ Portsmouth	Everton ○
Played	114	544
Points	122	677
Won	32	177
Drawn	26	146
Lost	56	221
For	127	651
Against	175	739
Players Used	64	132

All-Time Record vs Portsmouth						
Competition	Played	Won	Drawn	Lost	For	Against
League	50	21	8	21	78	92
FA Cup	1	1	0	0	5	0
League Cup	2	0	1	1	3	4
Other	0	0	0	0	0	0
Total	53	22	9	22	86	96

Everton

Goodison Park

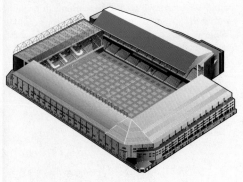

Stadium History

Opened in 1892, Goodison Park achieved the highest average gate during each of the Football League's first 10 seasons. Completion of the Gwladys Street End in 1938 meant that the stadium was the first to house double-decker stands on all four sides.

The Main Stand was replaced in 1970, and Everton were also one of the first clubs to introduce seating in all parts of the ground. Official website users voted a win against Bayern Munich in 1985 as the greatest ever game at the venue.

Seating Plan

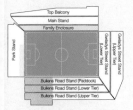

Capacity
40,569

family area
away fans
disabled

Stadium Statistics 05/06

Highest attendance
40,158 vs Liverpool 28.12.05

Lowest attendance
34,333 vs Charlton Athletic 02.01.06

Average attendance
36,860

How to Get There

Travel Information

Train

Lime Street railway station is in the city centre, a couple of miles from Goodison Park. Kirkdale Railway Station is 30 minutes walk from the ground.

Bus

Buses from the city centre 19, 20, F1, F9, F2 and 30.

Area Map

Local Map

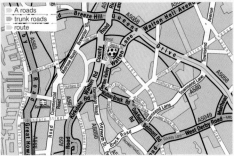

Fulham

Nickname:	The Cottagers	Telephone:	0870 442 1222
Manager:	Chris Coleman	Ticket Office:	0870 442 1234
Chairman:	Mohamed Al Fayed	Club Shop:	0870 442 1223
Website:	www.fulhamfc.com		

Season Review 05/06

Fulham experienced a real Jekyll and Hyde campaign, with an abysmal away record undoing much of their good work at Craven Cottage. It took Chris Coleman's team until April to win on the road, whilst they claimed 13 Premiership victories on home soil.

Luis Boa Morte excelled in his role as captain, notably scoring the only goal in a memorable win against local rivals Chelsea.

Points / Position

won | drawn | lost H home A away

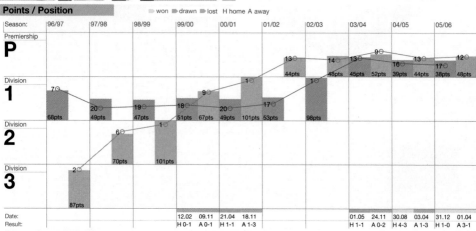

Season:	96/97	97/98	98/99	99/00	00/01	01/02	02/03	03/04	04/05	05/06

Premiership P

Division 1

Division 2

Division 3

| Date: | | | | 12.02 | 09.11 | 21.04 | 18.11 | | | 01.05 | 24.11 | 30.08 | 03.04 | 31.12 | 01.04 |
| Result: | | | | H 0-1 | A 0-1 | H 1-1 | A 1-3 | | | H 1-1 | A 0-2 | H 4-3 | A 1-3 | H 1-0 | A 3-3 |

Prem. Head-to-Head

Facts	Portsmouth	Fulham
Games		
Points	10	7
Won	3	2
Drawn	1	1
Goals		
For	10	10
Clean Sheets	1	1
Shots on Target	39	31
Disciplinary		
Fouls	84	69
Yellow Cards	10	13
Red Cards	1	1

Goals by Area

Portsmouth   Fulham

1	2
7	6
2	2

Goals by Position

Portsmouth   Fulham

	forward:	6		forward:	6
	midfield:	4		midfield:	3
	defence:	0		defence:	1

Goals Scored by Period

1	4	2	0	2	1
0	15	30	45	60	75	90
1	1	3	0	2	3

Average Attendance

▶ 19,631
▶ 19,483

All-Time Records

Total Premiership Record	Portsmouth	Fulham
Played	114	190
Points	122	236
Won	32	63
Drawn	26	47
Lost	56	80
For	127	229
Against	175	258
Players Used	64	60

All-Time Record vs Portsmouth

Competition	Played	Won	Drawn	Lost	For	Against
League	44	10	14	20	50	70
FA Cup	3	0	1	2	0	3
League Cup	0	0	0	0	0	0
Other	0	0	0	0	0	0
Total	47	10	15	22	50	73

Craven Cottage

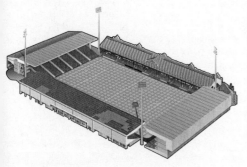

Stadium History

A 0-0 draw with Leicester on April 27th 2002 appeared to mark the end of Craven Cottage. Fulham had plans to build a new stadium, and were forced into a temporary move to Loftus Road in order to comply with the Taylor report on ground safety. Strong opposition from residents led to the abandonment of plans for a new home, however, and it was decided that refurbishing Craven Cottage at a cost of £8m was the way forward. The work was completed in time for the 2004/05 season.

Seating Plan

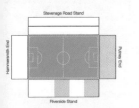

Capacity
22,646

▪ family area
▪ away fans
  disabled

Stadium Statistics 05/06

Highest attendance
22,486 vs Chelsea 19.03.06

Lowest attendance
16,550 vs Birmingham City 13.08.05

Average attendance
20,654

How to Get There

Travel Information

Car parking
It is possible in the streets around the ground but there are council parking meters so bring change (£1 per hour).

Tube
Putney Bridge on the District Line is 15 minutes away. Turn left out of the station and then follow other supporters. Walk through Bishops Park along the riverbank to the ground (note that the park is closed after evening games).

Bus
Numbers 74 & 220.

Area Map

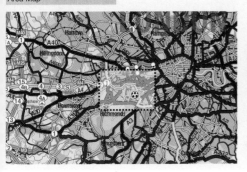

Local Map

▪ A roads
▪ trunk roads
▪ route

Liverpool °

Nickname:	The Reds	Telephone:	0151 263 2361
Manager:	Rafael Benítez	Ticket Office:	0870 444 4949
Chairman:	David Moores	Club Shop:	0870 066 7036
Website:	www.liverpoolfc.tv		

Season Review 05/06

Liverpool added both the UEFA Super Cup and FA Cup to their trophy collection, with captain Steven Gerrard winning the PFA Player of the Year award.

A clear improvement was also evident in the league, as Rafael Benítez's team finished 24 points better off than 12 months previously. In fact, only Champions Chelsea could boast a better defensive record than the Merseysiders.

Points / Position

won drawn lost H home A away

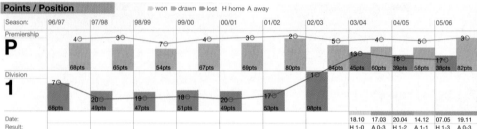

Season:	96/97	97/98	98/99	99/00	00/01	01/02	02/03	03/04	04/05	05/06
Premiership P	4⊖ 68pts	3⊖ 65pts	7⊖ 54pts	4⊖ 67pts	3⊖ 69pts	2⊖ 80pts	5⊖ 64pts	4⊖ 13⊖ 45pts	5⊖ 16⊖ 60pts 39pts	3⊖ 17⊖ 58pts 38pts 82pts
Division 1	7⊖ 68pts	20⊖ 49pts	19⊖ 47pts	18⊖ 51pts	20⊖ 49pts	17⊖ 53pts	1⊖ 98pts			

Date:	18.10	17.03	20.04	14.12	07.05	19.11
Result:	H 1-0	A 0-3	H 1-2	A 1-1	H 1-3	A 0-3

Recent Meetings

14.12.04
○○ 1-1 Attendance: 35,064
Referee: M.Clattenburg
○ 70 Gerrard   ○ 90 Lua Lua

20.04.05
○○ 1-2 Attendance: 20,205
Referee: H.M.Webb
○ 34 Kamara   ○ 4 Morientes
              ○ 45 Garcia

19.11.05
○○ 3-0 Attendance: 44,394
Referee: P.Walton
○ 23 Zenden
○ 39 Cisse
○ 80 Morientes

07.05.06
○○ 1-3 Attendance: 20,240
Referee: G.Poll
○ 85 Koroman   ○ 52 Fowler
               ○ 84 Crouch
               ○ 89 Cisse

Prem. Head-to-Head

Facts	○ Portsmouth	Liverpool ○
Games		
Points	4	13
Won	1	4
Drawn	1	1
Goals		
For	4	12
Clean Sheets	1	2
Shots on Target	28	54
Disciplinary		
Fouls	71	49
Yellow Cards	6	3
Red Cards	0	0

Goals by Area
○ Portsmouth   ○ Liverpool

3	3
1	6
0	3

Goals by Position
○ Portsmouth   ○ Liverpool

Portsmouth:
- forward: 2
- midfield: 2
- defence: 0

Liverpool:
- forward: 8
- midfield: 4
- defence: 0

Goals Scored by Period

	0-15	15-30	30-45	45-60	60-75	75-90
	1	0	1	0	0	2
	2	2	2	2	1	3

Average Attendance
▶ **20,189**
▶ **38,040**

All-Time Records

Total Premiership Record	○ Portsmouth	Liverpool ○
Played	114	544
Points	122	931
Won	32	265
Drawn	26	136
Lost	56	143
For	127	868
Against	175	552
Players Used	64	108

All-Time Record vs Portsmouth

Competition	Played	Won	Drawn	Lost	For	Against
League	52	21	13	18	93	82
FA Cup	5	1	3	1	4	4
League Cup	1	1	0	0	4	1
Other	0	0	0	0	0	0
Total	**58**	**23**	**16**	**19**	**101**	**87**

Anfield

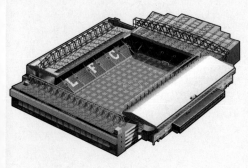

Stadium History

Anfield has been around longer than Liverpool Football Club, originally playing host to Everton. A dispute over rent saw the Toffees move out in 1892, leading to the formation of Liverpool. By 1906 the ground had taken shape, with stands on either side of the pitch and terracing at both ends.

Success on the pitch was matched by improvements to the stadium, which was made all-seater in 1994. To this day, 'The Kop' remains one of the best known places in world football.

Seating Plan

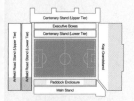

Capacity
45,362

- family area
- away fans
- disabled

Stadium Statistics 05/06

Highest attendance
44,983 vs Tottenham Hotspur 14.01.06

Lowest attendance
42,293 vs Fulham 15.03.06

Average attendance
44,236

How to Get There

Travel Information

Car parking
Limited parking. Only a small number of privately operated car parks are available in the area. Coaches should contact Merseyside Police. Contact Ian Kidd on 0151 777 4766.

Train
Lime Street railway station is in the city centre, two miles from Anfield. Kirkdale Railway Station is 30 minutes walk from the ground.

Area Map

Local Map

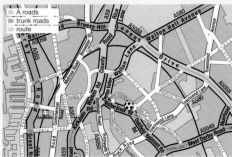

Manchester City

★★★

Nickname: The Citizens
Manager: Stuart Pearce
Chairman: John Wardle
Website: www.mcfc.co.uk

Telephone: 0870 062 1894
Ticket Office: 0870 062 1894
Club Shop: 0870 062 1894

Season Review 05/06

It was largely a season of disappointment for the blue half of Manchester. Stuart Pearce's team made an encouraging start to the campaign, but lost nine of their final 10 games to slide down the table.

There was still reason for optimism, however, with the continued emergence of talented youngsters such as Micah Richards and Stephen Ireland.

Points / Position

▶ won ▶ drawn ▶ lost H home A away

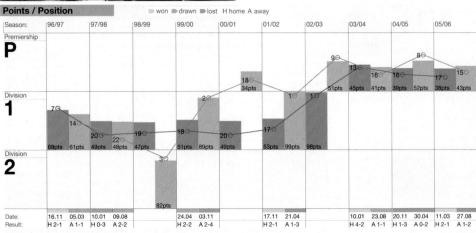

Season:	96/97	97/98	98/99	99/00	00/01	01/02	02/03	03/04	04/05	05/06

Premiership **P**

Division **1**

Division **2**

Date:	16.11	05.03	10.01	09.08		24.04	03.11		17.11	21.04		10.01	23.08	20.11	30.04	11.03	27.08
Result:	H 2-1	A 1-1	H 0-3	A 2-2		H 2-2	A 2-4		H 2-1	A 1-3		H 4-2	A 1-1	H 1-3	A 0-2	H 2-1	A 1-2

Prem. Head-to-Head

Facts	O Portsmouth	Man City O
Games		
Points	7	10
Won	2	3
Drawn	1	1
Goals		
For	9	11
Clean Sheets	0	1
Shots on Target	28	42
Disciplinary		
Fouls	71	70
Yellow Cards	9	5
Red Cards	0	0

Goals by Area

O Portsmouth   O Man City

```
      3    |    2
   3          8
3             1
```

Goals Scored by Period

```
   1   2   0   4   0   2
   0  15  30  45  60  75  90
   2   2   1   0   2   4
```

Goals by Position

O Portsmouth   O Man City

▶ forward:	4		▶ forward:	3
▶ midfield:	4		▶ midfield:	5
▶ defence:	1		▶ defence:	3

Average Attendance

▶ **19,926**

▶ **44,588**

All-Time Records

Total Premiership Record	O Portsmouth	Man City O
Played	114	354
Points	122	410
Won	32	103
Drawn	26	101
Lost	56	150
For	127	413
Against	175	482
Players Used	64	126

All-Time Record vs Portsmouth

Competition	Played	Won	Drawn	Lost	For	Against
League	70	33	15	22	129	104
FA Cup	2	2	0	0	5	2
League Cup	1	0	0	1	0	2
Other	0	0	0	0	0	0
Total	73	35	15	23	134	108

Manchester City

City of Manchester Stadium

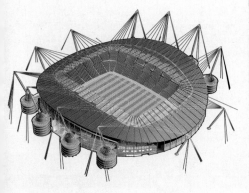

Stadium History

Built to host the 2002 Commonwealth Games, the City of Manchester Stadium was quickly transformed into the home of Manchester City. Having removed the athletics track, the pitch was lowered to make room for an extra tier of seating, while a permanent North Stand was also constructed. A crowd of 46,287 witnessed the first competitive game at the new venue, a 1-1 draw with Portsmouth on August 23rd 2003.

The site also offers 2,000 parking spaces, as well as several restaurants and function rooms.

Seating Plan

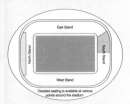

Disabled seating is available at various points around the stadium

Capacity
48,000

▶ family area
▶ away fans
  disabled

Stadium Statistics 05/06

Highest attendance
47,192 vs Manchester United 14.01.06

Lowest attendance
40,256 vs Middlesbrough 02.04.06

Average attendance
42,856

How to Get There

Travel Information

Train

Manchester Piccadilly Railway Station is about a mile away from the stadium, which is about a 20 minute walk away. There is currently no Metrolink service to the stadium, so either jump in a taxi or take a bus (numbers 53, 54, 185, 186, 216, 217, 230, 231, 232, 233, 234, 235, 236, 237, X36 and X37 go to Sportcity) from Piccadilly Gardens (which is a five minute walk from the railway station going straight down the approach from it, look for bus stops situated near to the 'Moon Under Water' pub).

Area Map

Local Map

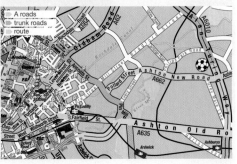

Manchester United

Nickname:	The Red Devils	Telephone:	0870 442 1994
Manager:	Sir Alex Ferguson	Ticket Office:	0870 442 1994
Owner:	Malcolm Glazer	Club Shop:	0870 111 8107
Website:	www.manutd.com		

Season Review 05/06

A Carling Cup triumph and second place in the Premiership would be seen as success at most clubs, but not at Manchester United. In fact, Sir Alex Ferguson's charges never genuinely threatened Chelsea's grip on the title.

The performances of Wayne Rooney continued to win him admirers across the globe, with Edwin van der Sar providing calm assurance in goal.

Points / Position

won   drawn   lost   H home A away

Season:	96/97	97/98	98/99	99/00	00/01	01/02	02/03	03/04	04/05	05/06
Premiership **P**	1	2	1	1	1	3	1	3	3	2
	75pts	77pts	79pts	91pts	80pts	77pts	83pts	13→45pts / 75pts	16→39pts / 77pts	17→38pts / 83pts
Division **1**	7	20	19	18	20	17	1			
	68pts	49pts	47pts	51pts	49pts	53pts	98pts			

Date:								17.04	01.11	30.10	26.02	11.02	03.12
Result:								H 1-0	A 0-3	H 2-0	A 1-2	H 1-3	A 0-3

Recent Meetings

30.10.04 ○○ **2-0** Attendance: 20,190
Referee: N.S.Barry
○ 53 Unsworth
○ 72 Yakubu

26.02.05 ○○ **2-1** Attendance: 67,989
Referee: M.R.Halsey
○ 8 Rooney   ○ 47 O'Neil
○ 81 Rooney

03.12.05 ○○ **3-0** Attendance: 67,684
Referee: C.J.Foy
○ 20 Scholes
○ 80 Rooney
○ 84 van Nistelrooy

11.02.06 ○○ **1-3** Attendance: 20,206
Referee: U.D.Rennie
○ 87 Taylor   ○ 18 van Nistelrooy
○ 38 Ronaldo
○ 45 Ronaldo

Prem. Head-to-Head

Facts	○ Portsmouth	Man Utd ○
Games		
Points	6	12
Won	2	4
Drawn	0	0
Goals		
For	5	11
Clean Sheets	2	2
Shots on Target	27	41
Disciplinary		
Fouls	92	72
Yellow Cards	8	4
Red Cards	0	0

Goals by Area
○ Portsmouth   ○ Man Utd

	2	1	
2			8
1			2

Goals by Position
○ Portsmouth   ○ Man Utd

	Portsmouth		Man Utd
forward:	1	forward:	6
midfield:	3	midfield:	5
defence:	1	defence:	1

Goals Scored by Period

	0	0	1	2	1	1
	0	15	30	45	60	75	90
	1	2	3	0	0	5

Average Attendance
▶ **20,179**
▶ **67,771**

All-Time Records

Total Premiership Record	○ Portsmouth	Man Utd
Played	114	544
Points	122	1,143
Won	32	339
Drawn	26	126
Lost	56	79
For	127	1,057
Against	175	489
Players Used	64	99

All-Time Record vs Portsmouth

Competition	Played	Won	Drawn	Lost	For	Against
League	50	22	12	16	72	56
FA Cup	7	2	3	2	15	14
League Cup	6	4	2	0	10	5
Other	0	0	0	0	0	0
Total	**63**	**28**	**17**	**18**	**97**	**75**

Manchester United

Old Trafford

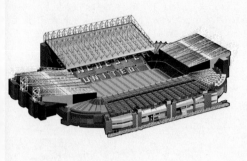

Stadium History

Currently the biggest stadium in English football, Old Trafford has grown in tandem with the success achieved on the pitch by Manchester United. Work to raise the capacity to 45,000 was completed in 1994, but it soon became apparent that more seating was required.

Since then the club has gone from strength to strength, attracting supporters from all over the world. In order to cope with an ever-increasing demand for tickets, the capacity was raised to just in excess of 73,000 during the 2005/06 season.

Seating Plan

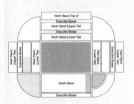

Capacity
76,000

▪ family area
▪ away fans
▪ disabled

Stadium Statistics 05/06

Highest attendance
73,006 vs Charlton Athletic 07.05.06

Lowest attendance
67,684 vs Portsmouth 03.12.05

Average attendance
68,764

How to Get There

Travel Information

Car parking
No on street parking allowed, residential parking permits only.

Train
Train service from Piccadilly/Oxford Road Stations to the ground.

Metrolink
Nearest Metrolink stations are Old Trafford and Trafford Bar.

Bus
Regular service from Manchester Chorlton Street Station.

Area Map

Local Map

Middlesbrough

Nickname: Boro
Manager: Gareth Southgate
Chairman: Steve Gibson
Website: www.mfc.co.uk

Telephone: 0870 421 1986
Ticket Office: 0870 421 1986
Club Shop: 0870 421 1986

Season Review 05/06

An unforgettable season at the Riverside saw Boro struggle in the league but thrive in cup competitions. Victories against FC Basle and Steaua Bucharest resulted in a UEFA Cup Final appearance, whilst an FA Cup Semi-Final was also reached.

Following weeks of intense speculation, manager Steve McClaren was finally unveiled as the successor to Sven-Goran Eriksson as England boss in May.

Points / Position

won drawn lost H home A away

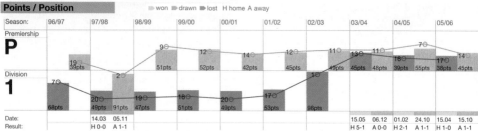

Season:	96/97	97/98	98/99	99/00	00/01	01/02	02/03	03/04	04/05	05/06
Premiership		19○ 39pts	9○	12○ 51pts	14○ 52pts	12○ 42pts	11○ 45pts	13○ 49pts	16○ 45pts 48pts	7○ 17○ 39pts 55pts	14○ 38pts 45pts
Division 1	7○ 68pts	20○ 49pts	2○ 91pts	19○ 47pts	18○ 51pts	20○ 49pts	17○ 53pts	1○ 98pts			

Date:	14.03	05.11						15.05	06.12	01.02	24.10	15.04	15.10
Result:	H 0-0	A 1-1						H 5-1	A 0-0	H 2-1	A 1-1	H 1-0	A 1-1

Recent Meetings

24.10.04 — ○○ 1-1 — Attendance: 30,964
Referee: M.Atkinson
○ 74 Downing ○ 5 Kamara

01.02.05 — ○○ 2-1 — Attendance: 19,620
Referee: P.Crossley
○ 40 Taylor ○ 35 Christie
○ 58 Yakubu

15.10.05 — ○○ 1-1 — Attendance: 26,551
Referee: C.J.Foy
○ 54 Yakubu ○ 46 O'Neil

15.04.06 — ○○ 1-0 — Attendance: 20,204
Referee: A.Marriner
○ 54 O'Neil

Prem. Head-to-Head

Facts	○ Portsmouth	Boro ○
Games		
Points	12	3
Won	3	0
Drawn	3	3
Goals		
For	10	4
Clean Sheets	2	1
Shots on Target	31	34
Disciplinary		
Fouls	68	68
Yellow Cards	8	6
Red Cards	1	0

Goals by Area

○ Portsmouth ○ Middlesbrough

2	1
7	2
1	1

Goals Scored by Period

3	0	2	3	0	2
0	15	30	45	60	75	90
0	1	1	1	1	0

Goals by Position

○ Portsmouth   ○ Middlesbrough

	Portsmouth	Middlesbrough
forward:	7	2
midfield:	3	2
defence:	0	0

Average Attendance

▶ 19,986
▶ 28,515

All-Time Records

Total Premiership Record	○ Portsmouth	Boro ○
Played	114	422
Points	122	516
Won	32	131
Drawn	26	123
Lost	56	168
For	127	506
Against	175	582
Players Used	64	132

All-Time Record vs Portsmouth

Competition	Played	Won	Drawn	Lost	For	Against
League	94	37	23	34	153	134
FA Cup	6	1	3	2	8	10
League Cup	0	0	0	0	0	0
Other	0	0	0	0	0	0
Total	100	38	26	36	161	144

Middlesbrough

Riverside Stadium

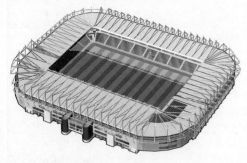

Stadium History

Constructed in just 32 weeks, the Riverside Stadium breathed new life into Middlesbrough. Chelsea were beaten 2-0 on August 26th 1995 in the first competitive match at the new ground, following the move from Ayresome Park.

The fans had been responsible for naming their new home, and saw the capacity increase by 5,000 in the summer of 1998. When it was opened, the stadium was the first in the country to be built in line with the safety requirements set out in the Taylor report.

Seating Plan

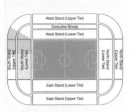

Capacity
35,100

⯈ family area
⯈ away fans
   disabled

Stadium Statistics 05/06

Highest attendance
31,908 vs Liverpool 13.08.05

Lowest attendance
25,971 vs Bolton Wanderers 26.03.06

Average attendance
28,463

How to Get There

Travel Information

Train
Middlesbrough station is located on Albert Road, ten minutes walk from the ground.

Bus
From town centre.

Area Map

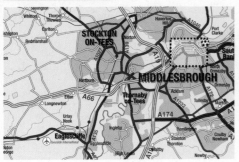

Local Map

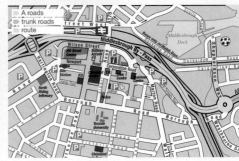

Newcastle United

Nickname: **The Magpies**
Manager: **Glenn Roeder**
Chairman: **Freddy Shepherd**
Website: **www.nufc.co.uk**

Telephone: **0191 201 8400**
Ticket Office: **0191 261 1571**
Club Shop: **0191 201 8426**

Season Review 05/06

Glenn Roeder was the toast of Tyneside as he led Newcastle from a position of adversity to InterToto Cup qualification. The team collected 32 points from 15 games under the former West Ham boss, thus earning him the job on a permanent basis.

Alan Shearer finally hung up his boots, bowing out of competitive action with a goal in the 4-1 triumph at arch-rivals Sunderland.

Points / Position

● won ● drawn ● lost H home A away

Season:	96/97	97/98	98/99	99/00	00/01	01/02	02/03	03/04	04/05	05/06
Premiership	2	13	13	11	11	4	3	5		7
P	68pts	44pts	46pts	52pts	51pts	71pts	69pts	45pts	56pts 16 / 14 / 17 39pts 44pts 38pts	58pts
Division 1	7	20	19	18	20	17	1			
	68pts	49pts	47pts	51pts	49pts	53pts	98pts			

Date:								29.02	25.10	19.03	11.12	01.10	04.02
Result:								H 1-1	A 0-3	H 1-1	A 1-1	H 0-0	A 0-2

Recent Meetings

	11.12.04			19.03.05			01.10.05			04.02.06
○○ **1-1**	Attendance: 51,480		○○ **1-1**	Attendance: 20,165		○○ **0-0**	Attendance: 20,220		○○ **2-0**	Attendance: 51,627
Referee: M.A.Riley			Referee: M.D.Messias			Referee: S.G.Bennett			Referee: M.R.Halsey	
○ 3 Bowyer	○ 30 Stone		○ 45 Stone	○ 43 Dyer					○ 41 N'Zogbia	
									○ 64 Shearer	

Prem. Head-to-Head

Facts	○ Portsmouth	Newcastle ○
Games		
Points	4	10
Won	0	2
Drawn	4	4
Goals		
For	3	8
Clean Sheets	1	3
Shots on Target	25	29
Disciplinary		
Fouls	75	74
Yellow Cards	12	9
Red Cards	0	0

Goals by Area
○ Portsmouth   ○ Newcastle

	1	1
1		5
1		2

Goals by Position
○ Portsmouth   ○ Newcastle

	Portsmouth	Newcastle
● forward:	1	● forward: 4
● midfield:	2	● midfield: 4
● defence:	0	● defence: 0

Goals Scored by Period

	0	1	1	0	0	1
	15	30	45	60	75	90
	1	2	3	0	2	0

Average Attendance

▶ **20,175**

▶ **51,756**

All-Time Records

Total Premiership Record	○ Portsmouth	Newcastle ○
Played	114	502
Points	122	786
Won	32	218
Drawn	26	132
Lost	56	152
For	127	761
Against	175	606
Players Used	64	125

All-Time Record vs Portsmouth

Competition	Played	Won	Drawn	Lost	For	Against
League	60	25	16	19	85	89
FA Cup	2	2	0	0	8	4
League Cup	0	0	0	0	0	0
Other	0	0	0	0	0	0
Total	**62**	**27**	**16**	**19**	**93**	**93**

Newcastle United

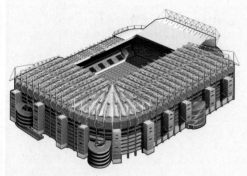

Stadium History

The oldest stadium in the North East, St James' Park houses some of the most devoted supporters in the country. A capacity in excess of 50,000 is still not enough to meet the demand for tickets.

The 1990s saw plans for a new £65m stadium shelved, as the club opted instead to spend £40m on upgrading the Sir John Hall and Milburn stands. The work was completed in August 2000, leaving Newcastle with a fantastic arena and visiting fans reaching for their binoculars.

Seating Plan

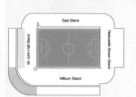

Capacity
52,327

➤ family area
➤ away fans
disabled

Stadium Statistics 05/06

Highest attendance
52,327 vs Manchester United 28.08.05

Lowest attendance
50,451 vs Charlton Athletic 22.02.06

Average attendance
52,032

How to Get There

Travel Information

Train
Newcastle is on the East Coast Main Line route, served by GNR and Virgin railways.

Metro
St James Metro is adjacent to the ground. Haymarket, Monument and Central Station are all a very short walk from

St James' Park.

Bus
Gallowgate or Haymarket bus stations.

Area Map

Local Map

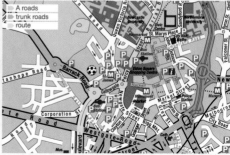

Reading

Nickname:	The Royals	Telephone:	0118 968 1100
Manager:	Steve Coppell	Ticket Office:	0870 999 1871
Chairman:	John Madejski	Club Shop:	0118 968 1234
Website:	www.readingfc.co.uk		

Season Review 05/06

Reading were an unstoppable force as they blazed a trail towards promotion to the top-flight. The 106 points amassed by the Royals were a record for the second-tier of English football, whilst 99 goals were also scored along the way.

Manager Steve Coppell engendered a real spirit of togetherness amongst his troops, with no one player more important than the team.

Points / Position

won drawn lost   H home A away

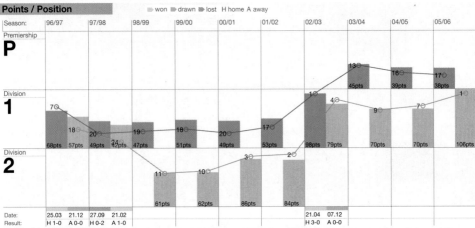

Season:	96/97	97/98	98/99	99/00	00/01	01/02	02/03	03/04	04/05	05/06

Premiership — **P**

Division **1**: 7 (68pts) | 18 (57pts) | 20 24 (49pts 42pts) | 19 (47pts) | 18 (51pts) | 20 (49pts) | 17 (53pts) | 1 (98pts) 79pts | 4 9 (70pts) | 7 (70pts) | 1 (106pts) | 13 (45pts) | 16 (39pts) | 17 (38pts)

Division **2**: 11 (61pts) | 10 (62pts) | 3 (86pts) | 2 (84pts)

Date:	25.03	21.12	27.09	21.02			21.04	07.12		
Result:	H 1-0	A 0-0	H 0-2	A 1-0			H 3-0	A 0-0		

Prem. Head-to-Head

Facts	Portsmouth	Reading
Games		
Points	0	0
Won	0	0
Drawn	0	0
Goals		
For	0	0
Clean Sheets	0	0
Shots on Target	0	0
Disciplinary		
Fouls	0	0
Yellow Cards	0	0
Red Cards	0	0

Goals by Area

Portsmouth   Reading

0   0

0   0

0   0

Goals by Position

Portsmouth   Reading

	forward:	0	forward:	0
	midfield:	0	midfield:	0
	defence:	0	defence:	0

Goals Scored by Period

	0	0	0	0	0	0	
0	15	30	45	60	75	90	
	0	0	0	0	0	0	

Average Attendance

—

—

All-Time Records

Total Premiership Record	Portsmouth	Reading
Played	114	0
Points	122	0
Won	32	0
Drawn	26	0
Lost	56	0
For	127	0
Against	175	0
Players Used	64	0

All-Time Record vs Portsmouth						
Competition	Played	Won	Drawn	Lost	For	Against
League	34	7	12	15	25	45
FA Cup	4	2	0	2	4	5
League Cup	0	0	0	0	0	0
Other	0	0	0	0	0	0
Total	38	9	12	17	29	50

Madejski Stadium

Stadium History

Built at a cost of more than £50m on the site of a former household waste dump, the Madejski Stadium is an impressive modern facility. The complex also plays host to an indoor training centre and both the Royal Berkshire Conference Centre and Millennium Madejski Hotel.

The ground opened its doors in 1998, and has since played host to several Under-21 internationals. Top-class Rugby Union is also on offer, with London Irish playing their home matches at the stadium.

Seating Plan

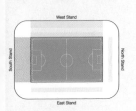

Capacity
24,200

▧ family area
▧ away fans
▧ disabled

Stadium Statistics 05/06

Highest attendance
23,845 vs Southampton 10.02.06

Lowest attendance
14,027 vs Burnley 29.08.05

Average attendance
20,207

How to Get There

Travel Information

Car parking
There are spaces at Shinfield Park, HP Invent and the nearby Greyhound Stadium.

Train
Reading Station is a bus ride away from the ground.

Bus
Number 79 'Football Special' bus runs from near the railway station at a cost of £2.50 return.

Area Map

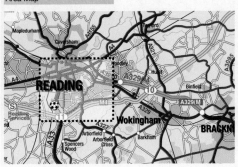

Local Map

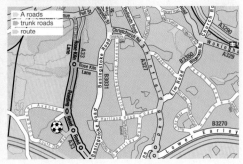

Sheffield United

Nickname: The Blades
Manager: Neil Warnock
Chairman: Derek Dooley
Website: www.sufc.co.uk

Telephone: 0870 787 1960
Ticket Office: 0870 787 1799
Club Shop: 0870 442 8705

SHEFFIELD UNITED F.C.
RUNNERS UP 2006

Season Review 05/06

Having been in the top-two for most of the season, few could argue that Sheffield United deserved to win promotion. Ten wins from the opening 11 games of the campaign laid the foundations for success.

Manager Neil Warnock continued to court controversy on the touchline, getting into a war of words with Norwich's Nigel Worthington and being sent to the stands against Leeds.

Points / Position

■ won ■ drawn ■ lost   H home A away

Season:	96/97	97/98	98/99	99/00	00/01	01/02	02/03	03/04	04/05	05/06
Premiership								13○ 45pts	16○ 39pts	17○ 38pts
Division 1	7○ 68pts 73pts	5○ 20○ 49pts 74pts	6○ 19○ 47pts 67pts	8○ 18○ 51pts 54pts	16○ 20○ 49pts 68pts	10○ 17○ 53pts	1○ 3○ 13○ 60pts 98pts	8○ 80pts 71pts	8○ 67pts	2○ 90pts
Date:	01.03 07.12	31.01 23.08	09.03 03.10	07.08 04.12	23.12 12.08	20.10 09.02	13.01 13.08			
Result:	H 1-1 A 0-1	H 1-1 A 1-2	H 1-0 A 1-2	H 2-0 A 0-1	H 0-0 A 0-2	H 1-0 A 3-4	H 1-2 A 1-1			

Recent Meetings

20.10.01	09.02.02	13.08.02	13.01.03
OO 1-0 Attendance: 15,538	OO 4-3 Attendance: 17,553	OO 1-1 Attendance: 16,093	OO 1-2 Attendance: 18,872
Referee: P.Rejer	Referee: M.Clattenburg	Referee: A.Bates	Referee: C.R.Wilkes
O 39 Edinburgh	O 18 Montgomery O 6 Crouch	O 13 Ndlovu O 25 Burton	O 78 O'Neil O 24 Ndlovu
	O 26 Furlong O 45 Prosinecki		O 87 Brown
	O 40 Asaba O 60 Quashie		
	O 90 Furlong		

Prem. Head-to-Head

Facts	O Portsmouth	Sheff Utd O
Games		
Points	0	0
Won	0	0
Drawn	0	0
Goals		
For	0	0
Clean Sheets	0	0
Shots on Target	0	0
Disciplinary		
Fouls	0	0
Yellow Cards	0	0
Red Cards	0	0

Goals by Area

O Portsmouth   O Sheff Utd

0		0
0		0

0   0

Goals by Position

O Portsmouth   O Sheff Utd

■ forward:	0	■ forward:	0
■ midfield:	0	■ midfield:	0
■ defence:	0	■ defence:	0

Goals Scored by Period

	0	0	0	0	0	0
	0	15	30	45	60	75	90
	0	0	0	0	0	0

Average Attendance

All-Time Records

Total Premiership Record	O Portsmouth	Sheff Utd O
Played	114	84
Points	122	94
Won	32	22
Drawn	26	28
Lost	56	34
For	127	96
Against	175	113
Players Used	64	34

All-Time Record vs Portsmouth

Competition	Played	Won	Drawn	Lost	For	Against
League	66	35	9	22	119	92
FA Cup	3	1	0	2	4	4
League Cup	1	1	0	0	1	0
Other	0	0	0	0	0	0
Total	70	37	9	24	124	96

Sheffield United

Stadium History

Sheffield Club and Hallam contested the first football match at Bramall Lane in December 1862. The ground had begun life as a venue for cricket, and the sport continued to be played there until 1973.

The Sheffield United of today were formed in 1889, and it wasn't until the building of the South Stand in 1975 that their stadium became four-sided. Only The Oval shares the distinction of hosting an FA Cup Final, England football international and an England cricket test.

Seating Plan

Arnold Laver Stand

Hallam FM Kop

Bramall Lane

DeSun Stand

Capacity
30,558

family area
away fans
disabled

Stadium Statistics 05/06

Highest attendance
30,558 vs Sheffield Wednesday 03.12.05

Lowest attendance
17,739 vs Coventry City 27.08.05

Average attendance
23,650

How to Get There

Travel Information

Car parking
No official spaces for away fans, though street parking is available.

Train
Bramall Lane is around one mile from Sheffield Midland Station.

Bus
Number 13 from Arundel Gate goes to Bramall Lane.

Area Map

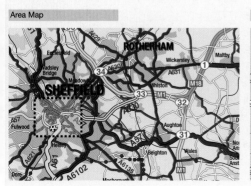

Local Map

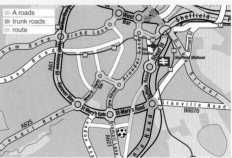

Tottenham Hotspur

Nickname:	Spurs
Manager:	Martin Jol
Chairman:	Daniel Levy
Website:	www.tottenhamhotspur.com

Telephone:	0870 420 5000
Ticket Office:	0870 420 5000
Club Shop:	020 8365 5042

Season Review 05/06

Despite being pipped to Champions League qualification by their great rivals Arsenal on the final day of the season, Spurs could still look back on a campaign in which they made tremendous progress.

Manager Martin Jol was unafraid to put his faith in youth, allowing the likes of Aaron Lennon and Michael Dawson to shine.

Points / Position

won ■ drawn ■ lost H home A away

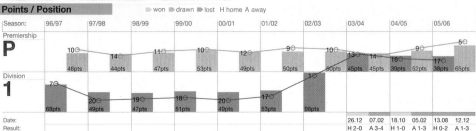

Season:	96/97	97/98	98/99	99/00	00/01	01/02	02/03	03/04	04/05	05/06
Premiership **P**	10 / 46pts	14 / 44pts	11 / 47pts	10 / 53pts	12 / 49pts	9 / 50pts	10 / 50pts	13 — 14 / 45pts 45pts	16 — 17 / 39pts 52pts	9 — 5 / 38pts 65pts
Division **1**	7 / 68pts	20 / 49pts	19 / 47pts	18 / 51pts	20 / 49pts	17 / 53pts	1 / 98pts			

Date:								26.12 07.02 18.10 05.02	13.08 12.12
Result:								H 2-0 A 3-4 H 1-0 A 1-3	H 0-2 A 1-3

Recent Meetings

18.10.04	05.02.05	13.08.05	12.12.05
1-0 Attendance: 20,121	**3-1** Attendance: 36,105	**0-2** Attendance: 20,215	**3-1** Attendance: 36,141
Referee: U.D.Rennie	Referee: S.W.Dunn	Referee: B.Knight	Referee: U.D.Rennie
○ 63 Yakubu	○ 34 Mido ○ 28 Kamara	○ 45 Griffin	○ 57 King ○ 24 Lua Lua
	○ 57 Mido	○ 64 Defoe	○ 85 Mido
	○ 83 Keane		○ 90 Defoe

Prem. Head-to-Head

Facts	○ Portsmouth	Tottenham ○
Games		
Points	6	12
Won	2	4
Drawn	0	0
Goals		
For	8	12
Clean Sheets	2	1
Shots on Target	31	42
Disciplinary		
Fouls	76	80
Yellow Cards	1	4
Red Cards	0	0

Goals by Area

○ Portsmouth   ○ Tottenham

4	3	3	
	1	8	1

Goals by Position

○ Portsmouth   ○ Tottenham

	Portsmouth	Tottenham
■ forward:	5	9
■ midfield:	3	1
■ defence:	0	1
■ own goals:		1

Goals Scored by Period

	0	2	1	1	3	1
	0	15	30	45	60	75	90
	1	0	3	2	1	5

Average Attendance

▶ **20,138**

▶ **36,118**

All-Time Records

Total Premiership Record	○ Portsmouth	Tottenham ○
Played	114	544
Points	122	728
Won	32	195
Drawn	26	143
Lost	56	206
For	127	716
Against	175	732
Players Used	64	139

All-Time Record vs Portsmouth

Competition	Played	Won	Drawn	Lost	For	Against
League	32	11	11	10	53	52
FA Cup	3	3	0	0	10	2
League Cup	3	0	2	1	0	1
Other	0	0	0	0	0	0
Total	**38**	**14**	**13**	**11**	**63**	**55**

Tottenham Hotspur

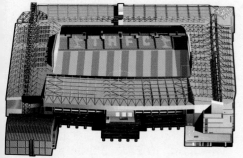

Tottenham moved to White Hart Lane, or the High Road Ground as it was known then, back in 1899. Within five years the ground had a capacity of 32,000, and it had reached 50,000 by 1911. Development of the East Stand was completed in 1934, providing the stadium with enough room to house around 80,000 spectators.

Improved safety regulations, including a switch to all-seater stadia, have seen the capacity dramatically reduced since then, but the stadium is still one to be proud of.

Seating Plan

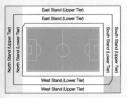

Capacity
36,247

- family area
- away fans
- disabled

Stadium Statistics 05/06

Highest attendance
36,247 vs Everton 15.10.05

Lowest attendance
35,427 vs Fulham 26.09.05

Average attendance
36,073

How to Get There

Travel Information

Car parking
Limited parking available near the ground. Car parks near the ground are pricey. Free parking in residential areas 10 minutes away.

Train
White Hart Lane, Seven Sisters or Northumberland Park.

Tube
Seven Sisters (then long walk).

Bus
259, 279, 149.

Area Map

Local Map

Watford °

Nickname:	The Hornets
Manager:	Adrian Boothroyd
Chairman:	Graham Simpson
Website:	www.watfordfc.co.uk

Telephone:	0870 111 1881
Ticket Office:	0870 111 1881
Club Shop:	01923 496 005

Season Review 05/06

Watford were the surprise package of the Championship, finishing third and going on to gain promotion through the Play-Offs.

Success was built around a belief instilled in his players by ultra-confident young boss Aidy Boothroyd. The likes of Marlon King and Matthew Spring were given a new lease of life, whilst Ashley Young and Jay DeMerit blossomed into stars.

Points / Position

■ won ■ drawn ■ lost H home A away

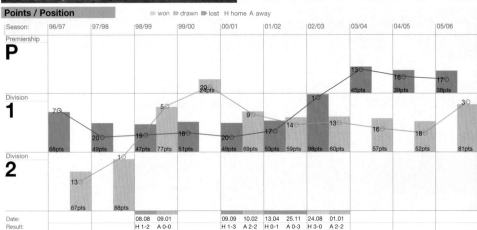

| Date: | | | 08.08 | 09.01 | | 09.09 | 10.02 | 13.04 | 25.11 | 24.08 | 01.01 | | |
| Result: | | | H 1-2 | A 0-0 | | H 1-3 | A 2-2 | H 0-1 | A 0-3 | H 3-0 | A 2-2 | | |

Prem. Head-to-Head

Facts	○ Portsmouth	Watford ○
Games		
Points	0	0
Won	0	0
Drawn	0	0
Goals		
For	0	0
Clean Sheets	0	0
Shots on Target	0	0
Disciplinary		
Fouls	0	0
Yellow Cards	0	0
Red Cards	0	0

Goals by Area
○ Portsmouth   ○ Watford

0	0
0	0
0	0

Goals by Position
○ Portsmouth   ○ Watford

■ forward:	0	■ forward:	0
■ midfield:	0	■ midfield:	0
■ defence:	0	■ defence:	0

Goals Scored by Period

0	0	0	0	0	0	
0	15	30	45	60	75	90
0	0	0	0	0	0	

Average Attendance

All-Time Records

Total Premiership Record	○ Portsmouth	Watford ○
Played	114	38
Points	122	24
Won	32	6
Drawn	26	6
Lost	56	26
For	127	35
Against	175	77
Players Used	64	32

All-Time Record vs Portsmouth

Competition	Played	Won	Drawn	Lost	For	Against
League	42	14	11	17	46	57
FA Cup	0	0	0	0	0	0
League Cup	3	1	1	1	6	4
Other	0	0	0	0	0	0
Total	**45**	**15**	**12**	**18**	**52**	**61**

Watford

Vicarage Road

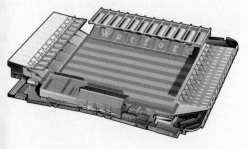

Stadium History

Watford moved to Vicarage Road in 1922, with the ground being officially opened by Colonel Charles Healey. Much has changed since that opening match against Millwall, with only the section of the Main, or East, Stand on the Occupation Road side of the stadium still in existence today.

The Vicarage Road Stand and The Rookery were both constructed during the 1990s, while The Rous Stand was built in 1986. Top-flight Rugby Union outfit Saracens also call the ground their home.

Seating Plan

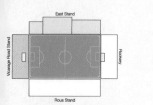

Capacity
22,100

family area
away fans
disabled

Stadium Statistics 05/06

Highest attendance
19,842 vs Coventry City 11.02.06

Lowest attendance
11,722 vs Crewe Alexandra 28.01.06

Average attendance
15,449

How to Get There

Travel Information

Car parking
Due to restrictions around the ground, Church Car Park in the town centre is a good option.

Train
The nearest station is Watford High Street.

Tube
The nearest station is Watford on the Metropolitan line (10–15 minute walk).

Bus
Services run from Watford Junction Bus Station.

Area Map

Local Map

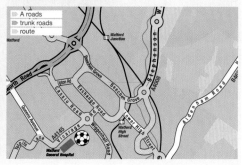

West Ham United

Nickname:	The Hammers
Manager:	Alan Pardew
Chairman:	Terence Brown
Website:	www.whufc.com

Telephone:	020 8548 2748
Ticket Office:	0870 112 2700
Club Shop:	020 8548 2730

Season Review 05/06

West Ham enjoyed a memorable return to the top-flight, finishing ninth and reaching the FA Cup Final. The Hammers came within four minutes of lifting the trophy, but were ultimately undone by some magic from Liverpool's Steven Gerrard.

Manager Alan Pardew won over his many critics with a stylish brand of attacking football firmly in keeping with the traditions of the club.

Points / Position

won drawn lost H home A away

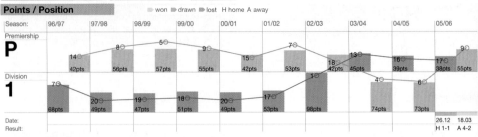

Season:	96/97	97/98	98/99	99/00	00/01	01/02	02/03	03/04	04/05	05/06

Premiership **P**

8○ 14○ / 5○ / 9○ / 15○ / 7○ / 18○ 13○ / 16○ / 17○ 9○
42pts 56pts 57pts 55pts 42pts 53pts 42pts 45pts 39pts 38pts 55pts

Division **1**

7○ / 20○ 19○ 18○ 20○ 17○ 1○ / 4○ / 6○
68pts 49pts 47pts 51pts 49pts 53pts 98pts 74pts 73pts

Date:		26.12	18.03
Result:		H 1-1	A 4-2

Recent Meetings

27.09.92
○○ 0-1 Attendance: 12,158
○ 44 Allen

16.01.93
○○ 2-0 Attendance: 18,127
○ 26 Morley
○ 55 Foster

26.12.05
○○ 1-1 Attendance: 20,168
Referee: A.G.Wiley
○ 17 O'Neil ○ 56 Collins

18.03.06
○○ 2-4 Attendance: 34,837
Referee: A.G.Wiley
○ 69 Sheringham ○ 19 Lua Lua
○ 90 Benayoun ○ 25 Davis
○ 42 Mendes
○ 77 Todorov

Prem. Head-to-Head

Facts	○ Portsmouth	West Ham ○
Games		
Points	4	1
Won	1	0
Drawn	1	1
Goals		
For	5	3
Clean Sheets	0	0
Shots on Target	17	10
Disciplinary		
Fouls	26	24
Yellow Cards	3	2
Red Cards	1	0

Goals by Area
○ Portsmouth ○ West Ham

3 | 0
1 | 3
1 | 0

Goals by Position
○ Portsmouth ○ West Ham

	Portsmouth		West Ham
forward:	2	forward:	1
midfield:	3	midfield:	1
defence:	0	defence:	1

Goals Scored by Period

0	3	1	0	0	1
0	0	0	1	1	1

0 15 30 45 60 75 90

Average Attendance

▶ **20,168**

▶ **34,837**

All-Time Records

Total Premiership Record	○ Portsmouth	West Ham
Played	114	426
Points	122	555
Won	32	148
Drawn	26	111
Lost	56	167
For	127	514
Against	175	590
Players Used	64	142

All-Time Record vs Portsmouth

Competition	Played	Won	Drawn	Lost	For	Against
League	22	10	3	9	33	32
FA Cup	3	1	0	2	4	5
League Cup	0	0	0	0	0	0
Other	0	0	0	0	0	0
Total	25	11	3	11	37	37

West Ham United

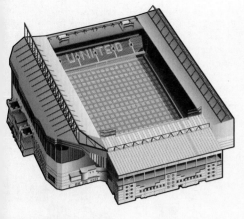

Stadium History

West Ham took up residence at the Boleyn Ground in 1904, beating rivals Millwall 3-0 in the first game played at their new home. The ground has since become renowned for housing good football, and has developed into a modern sporting venue.

In January 1994, the lower tier of the new Bobby Moore Stand was opened. One year later, completion of the Centenary Stand meant that the Boleyn had become an all-seater stadium. Further work has taken place in recent years, thus increasing the capacity.

Seating Plan

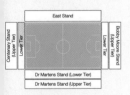

Stadium Statistics 05/06

Capacity
35,647

family area
away fans
disabled

Highest attendance
34,970 vs Tottenham Hotspur 07.05.06

Lowest attendance
29,582 vs Aston Villa 12.09.05

Average attendance
33,742

How to Get There

Travel Information

Car parking
Near the ground is difficult; residents scheme is in operation. Some places can be found over 15 minutes walk away.

Bus
Numbers 5, 15, 58, 104, 115, 147, 330 & 376.

Tube
Upton Park station on the District Line is a short walk away.

Area Map

Local Map

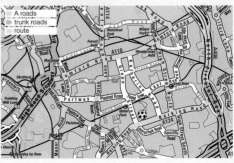

Wigan Athletic

Nickname: The Latics
Manager: Paul Jewell
Chairman: Dave Whelan
Website: www.wiganlatics.co.uk

Telephone: 01942 774 000
Ticket Office: 0870 112 2552
Club Shop: 01942 216 945

Season Review 05/06

Wigan surprised pundits and supporters alike by finishing in the top half of the table. A trip to Cardiff in the Carling Cup Final also served to highlight just how far the club had come in such a short space of time.

The platform for success was built early in the season, with Paul Jewell's men amassing 25 points from their first 11 Premiership matches.

Points / Position

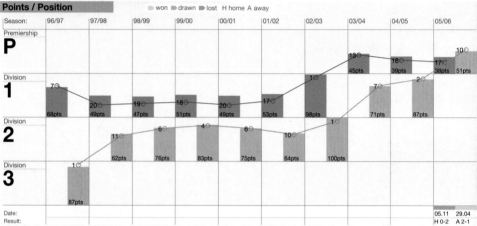

won ■ drawn ■ lost H home A away

Season:	96/97	97/98	98/99	99/00	00/01	01/02	02/03	03/04	04/05	05/06
Premiership P								13 / 45pts	16 / 39pts	17 / 38pts — 10 / 51pts
Division 1	7 / 68pts	20 / 49pts	19 / 47pts	18 / 51pts	20 / 49pts	17 / 53pts	1 / 98pts	7 / 71pts	2 / 87pts	
Division 2		11 / 62pts	6 / 76pts	4 / 83pts	6 / 75pts	10 / 64pts	1 / 100pts			
Division 3	1 / 87pts									

| Date: | | | | | | | | | | 05.11 29.04 |
| Result: | | | | | | | | | | H 0-2 A 2-1 |

Prem. Head-to-Head

Facts	O Portsmouth	Wigan O
Games		
Points	3	3
Won	1	1
Drawn	0	0
Goals		
For	2	3
Clean Sheets	0	1
Shots on Target	13	12
Disciplinary		
Fouls	19	24
Yellow Cards	2	5
Red Cards	0	1

Goals by Area

O Portsmouth   O Wigan

Goals by Position

O Portsmouth   O Wigan

	Portsmouth		Wigan
■ forward:	1	■ forward:	2
■ midfield:	1	■ midfield:	0
■ defence:	0	■ defence:	1

Goals Scored by Period

0	0	0	0	2	0
15	30	45	60	75	90
0	0	1	1	0	1

Average Attendance

▶ **19,102**

▶ **21,126**

All-Time Records

Total Premiership Record	O Portsmouth	Wigan O
Played	114	38
Points	122	51
Won	32	15
Drawn	26	6
Lost	56	17
For	127	45
Against	175	52
Players Used	64	25

All-Time Record vs Portsmouth

Competition	Played	Won	Drawn	Lost	For	Against
League	8	2	2	4	7	7
FA Cup	0	0	0	0	0	0
League Cup	0	0	0	0	0	0
Other	0	0	0	0	0	0
Total	8	2	2	4	7	7

Wigan Athletic

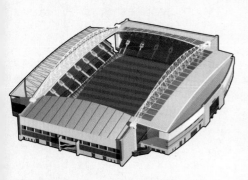

Opened in August 1999, the JJB Stadium is home to both football and rugby league. A 3-0 win against Scunthorpe gave Wigan a great start to life in their new surroundings. Built at an overall cost of £30m, the ground floor of the West Stand even contains a purpose-built Police Station with cells.

Chairman Dave Whelan can be rightly proud of his investment, and would have been delighted to see promotion to the Premiership secured on home soil. Playing top-flight football in 2005/06 resulted in a dramatic improvement in attendances.

Seating Plan

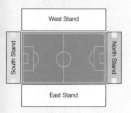

Stadium Statistics 05/06

Capacity
25,023

 family area
 away fans
 disabled

Highest attendance
25,023 vs Liverpool 11.02.06

Lowest attendance
16,641 vs Middlesbrough 18.09.05

Average attendance
20,609

How to Get There

Travel Information

Car parking
There is a huge amount of parking located on and around the Retail Park and Stadium itself. You should have no problems if you arrive in plenty of time.

Train
Wigan Wallgate Station is just ten minutes walk from the JJB Stadium. Follow the signposts.

Bus
There are no particular bus routes as the Bus Station is only a ten minute walk from the Stadium.

Area Map

Local Map

A roads
trunk roads
route

Barclays Premiership 2006-07 | **Premiership history**

[Fixtures subject to change]

Date	Team	Home/Away	05-06	Played	96-97	97-98	98-99	99-00	00-01	01-02	02-03	03-04	04-05	05-06	Goals for	Goals against	Scored first	Best result	Worst
19.08.06	Blackburn	H	2-2	3											3	5	0	2-2	1-2
23.08.06	Man City	A	1-2	3											2	5	2	1-1	0-2
28.08.06	Middlesbrough	A	1-1	3											2	2	2	1-1	1-1
09.09.06	Wigan	H	0-2	1											0	2	0	0-2	0-2
16.09.06	Charlton	A	1-2	3											3	5	1	1-1	1-2
25.09.06	Bolton	H	1-1	3											6	2	1	4-0	1-1
01.10.06	Tottenham	A	1-3	3											5	10	2	1-3	1-3
14.10.06	West Ham	H	1-1	1											1	1	1	1-1	1-1
21.10.06	Chelsea	A	0-2	3											0	8	0	0-3	0-3
28.10.06	Reading	H	N/A	0											0	0	0	N/A	N/A
04.11.06	Man Utd	A	0-3	3											1	8	0	0-3	0-3
11.11.06	Fulham	H	1-0	3											6	4	3	4-3	1-1
18.11.06	Watford	H	N/A	0											0	0	0	N/A	N/A
26.11.06	Newcastle	A	0-2	3											1	6	0	1-1	0-3
29.11.06	Liverpool	A	0-3	3											1	7	0	1-1	0-3
02.12.06	Aston Villa	H	1-1	3											4	4	1	2-1	1-2
09.12.06	Everton	H	0-1	3											1	4	1	1-2	1-2
16.12.06	Arsenal	A	0-4	3											1	8	1	1-1	0-4
23.12.06	Sheff Utd	H	N/A	0											0	0	0	N/A	N/A
26.12.06	West Ham	A	4-2	1											4	2	1	4-2	4-2
30.12.06	Bolton	A	0-1	3											1	2	1	1-0	0-1
01.01.07	Tottenham	H	0-2	3											3	2	2	2-0	0-2
13.01.07	Sheff Utd	A	N/A	0											0	0	0	N/A	N/A
20.01.07	Charlton	H	1-2	3											6	6	3	4-2	1-2
30.01.07	Middlesbrough	H	1-0	3											8	2	2	5-1	5-1
03.02.07	Wigan	A	2-1	1											2	1	0	2-1	2-1
10.02.07	Man City	H	2-1	3											7	6	2	4-2	1-3
24.02.07	Blackburn	A	1-2	3											3	4	2	2-1	1-2
03.03.07	Chelsea	H	0-2	3											0	6	0	0-2	0-2
17.03.07	Reading	A	N/A	0											0	0	0	N/A	N/A
31.03.07	Fulham	A	3-1	3											4	6	2	3-1	1-3
07.04.07	Man Utd	H	1-3	3											4	3	2	2-0	1-3
09.04.07	Watford	A	N/A	0											0	0	0	N/A	N/A
14.04.07	Newcastle	H	0-0	3											2	2	0	1-1	1-1
21.04.07	Aston Villa	A	0-1	3											1	6	0	0-3	0-3
28.04.07	Liverpool	H	1-3	3											3	5	1	1-0	1-3
05.05.07	Everton	A	1-0	3											2	3	1	1-0	1-2
13.05.07	Arsenal	H	1-1	3											2	3	1	1-1	0-1

■ won ■ drawn ■ lost □ not played